Mac Hacks

Chris Seibold

O'REILLY®

Beijing · Cambridge · Farnham · Köln · Sebastopol · Tokyo

Mac Hacks

by Chris Seibold

Printed in the United States of America.

Published by O'Reilly Media, Inc., 1005 Gravenstein Highway North, Sebastopol, CA 95472.

O'Reilly books may be purchased for educational, business, or sales promotional use. Online editions are also available for most titles (*http://my.safaribooksonline.com*). For more information, contact our corporate/institutional sales department: 800-998-9938 or *corporate@oreilly.com*.

Editor: Dawn Mann	**Cover Designer:** Randy Comer
Production Editor: Holly Bauer	**Interior Designers:** Ronald Bilodeau and
Proofreader: Kiel Van Horn	Edie Freedman
Indexer: Angela Howard	**Illustrator:** Rebecca Demarest

March 2013:   First Edition

Revision History for the First Edition:

2013-02-28:   First release

See *http://oreilly.com/catalog/errata.csp?isbn=9781449325589* for release details.

ISBN: 978-1-449-32558-9

[LSI]

Table of Contents

Preface

Ostensibly, you buy a computer to get something done. The something might be as simple as listening to MP3s you've ripped from your CD collection or as challenging as editing a full-length feature film. Apple is happy to sell you products to meet your needs. The trouble is, your needs aren't exactly the same needs as the next guy, and that's where hacking comes in. With a little (or a lot) of effort, you can make your Mac and software perform in the manner you wish them to. Macs that do things exactly the way you want makes the Apple experience that much better.

There are over 50 hacks in this book, and a passel of quick tips and tricks. Some are simple enough—you've probably already pulled them off—while others are a bit more challenging. All, to the right person, can be fun and useful.

So what can you expect? There is a wide range of hacks here. Get your iMac to hover with a VESA mount, swap in an SSD for that tired hard drive, hear a different sound when you start your Mac, and a lot more. Tired of the look of OS X? Discover ways to tweak interface elements. Worried about your Mac's security? You're covered.

How to Use This Book

This is a book about hacking, so deciding how to use this book is completely up to you. You could, if the inclination hits you, use the pages for interesting origami projects. If you want to use the book in a more traditional manner, just start reading—it doesn't matter where. Each hack is as self-contained as possible (and points to other hacks when not) so there isn't any reason not to crack open the book at random and start reading. Chapter 1 contains some hacks that provide background for a lot of the other hacks in the book, so many people will find that a useful place to start. Others might leap to the specific chapter that seems most interesting. A lot of the hacks depend on the command-line interface available via the Terminal program, so Chapter 6 is a good place to start if you haven't used that in a while.

How This Book Is Organized

This book isn't a mere tips-and-tricks compendium that tells you where to click, where to drag, and what commands to type. It takes advantage of OS X's flexibility and new features, recognizes that there are specific tasks you want to accomplish with the operating system and related hardware and software, and offers bite-size pieces of functionality you can put to use in a few minutes. It also shows how you can expand on their usefulness yourself. To give you this kind of help, the book is organized into 11 chapters:

Chapter 1, Before You Hack

> This is the place to start. It covers the steps you need to take to protect your data and prepare your Mac before your start hacking.

Chapter 2, Mountain Lion Hacks

> Mountain Lion is the Mac's latest and greatest operating system, but just because it's the newest version of OS X doesn't mean it's perfect. Make your Mountain Lion experience better by investigating this chapter.

Chapter 3, Customize Your OS X Experience

> Your Mac is *yours*, so why use it exclusively the way Apple intended you to? Discover slick ways to blog, change the startup sound, and make (almost) any app full screen.

Chapter 4, Hacks for a More Informative Mac

> Want to get information delivered right to your desktop? Want constant access to a widget? Stop by this chapter and keep yourself up to date on the world around you.

Chapter 5, Make It Automatic

> Computers are great at doing things without your intervention. This chapter explains how to make your Mac automatically do drudge work for you.

Chapter 6, Fun with Unix

> There's a ton of power hidden on the Unix side of your Mac. In this chapter, you'll learn how to safely tap into this power.

Chapter 7, Lock Down that Mac

> Security isn't just a good idea—it's essential. Learn how to protect your Mac from prying eyes (and sticky fingers) with the useful hacks in this chapter.

Chapter 8, Other OSes

> Got multiple Apple devices? Learn how to manage them from a centralized location. Ever fancy playing a video game made for a Nintendo on your Mac? This is the chapter for you.

Chapter 9, Networking Hacks

Check your WiFi signal with a hidden app and then lock it down (you want a secure network!).

Chapter 10, Multimedia Hacks

Make your music sound better, never miss your favorite show, and discover how to keep your iTunes library on a separate disk. If any of those ideas appeal to you, this is your chapter.

Chapter 11, Hack Some Hardware

Hang that Mac from a VESA mount, get auto recognized by your iPhone, destroy your kitchen with dye! All your daring hardware hacks are in this chapter, so haul your toolbox next to your Mac and get started.

Conventions Used in This Book

This book uses the following typographical conventions:

Italic

Used to indicate new terms, URLs, filenames, file extensions, directories, and folders.

`Constant width`

Used to show code examples, verbatim searches and commands, the contents of files, and the output from commands.

`Constant width bold`

Shows commands or other text that should be typed literally by the user.

`Constant width italic`

Used in examples, tables, and commands to show text that should be replaced with user-supplied values.

Note: Depending on what kind of Mac you have, you may need to do slightly different things when this book tells you to right-click something. If you have a two-button mouse, then simply right-click. If you have a one-button mouse, then press the Command key and click. If you have trackpad, you can two-finger click if you have that feature turned on (set it up in the Trackpad preference pane).

Using Code Examples

This book is here to help you get your job done. In general, you may use the code in this book in your programs and documentation. You don't need to contact us for permission unless you're reproducing a significant portion of the code. For example, writing a program that uses several chunks of code from this book doesn't require permission, but selling or distributing a CD-ROM of examples from O'Reilly books does. Answering a question by citing this book and quoting example code doesn't require permission, but incorporating a significant amount of example code from this book into your product's documentation does.

We appreciate, but do not require, attribution. An attribution usually includes the title, author, publisher, and ISBN, like so: "*Mac Hacks* by Chris Seibold. Copyright 2013 Chris Seibold, 978-1-4493-2558-9."

If you feel your use of code examples falls outside fair use or the permission given above, feel free to contact us at *permissions@oreilly.com*.

Guest Hackers

David Chartier (Hack #13, Hack #14, Hack #26) learned the ways of The Force on an IBM Aptiva running Windows 95. After building, selling, and supporting PCs for nearly a decade, he switched to a Mac midway through college and hasn't looked back. Since then he has written for *Macworld*, *Ars Technica*, O'Reilly, and elsewhere. You can find his home on the web at *http://davidchartier.com*.

Charles Edge (Hack #39) started looking to share his knowledge of the Mac OS X Server operating system in 2004. His first speaking appearance at a large conference was DefCon 2004. Since then, he has spoken at conferences such as MacSysAdmin, Macworld, LinuxWorld, and BlackHat. Charles has written nine books, including *Enterprise Mac Administrator's Guide*, *Enterprise Mac Security*, and *Enterprise iPhone and iPad Administrator's Guide*. For the past 14 years, he has been the Director of Technology for 318, a Mac-first consultancy based in Santa Monica, CA. Charles is also the author of *http://krypted.com*, a site dedicated to heterogeneous networking.

Phil Herlihy (Hack #49 and Hack #52) started out life as a young mad scientist. He was raised by his parents (A CRAY-1 Supercomputer and a PDP-11) in New York C(ircu)ity. He's a self-taught engineer who spends his time relentlessly building, rebuilding, and deconstructing, and only sleeps for about two hours a month. It's rumored that he runs on a quantum-caffeine drive. You can find his work here: *http://braindead lock.net*.

Connor Langford (Hack #37) is a beta tester at Mac Hacks Labs, a Minecraft super enthusiast, and a Webelos scout.

Todd Long (images for Hack #18) is a professional graphic designer and semi-professional backwoodsman residing in Knoxville, TN.

Gordon Meyer (Hack #47) is a Chicago-based writer and speaker who has authored dozens of software manuals, numerous articles for Mac users and technical writers, and *Smart Home Hacks*, a leading book on do-it-yourself home automation techniques.

John "Nemo" Nemerovski (Hack #46) is Reviews Editor for *MyMac*, the leading original-content Macintosh consumer web magazine, for over 15 years.

Nathaniel Seibold (Hack #37) is an assistant at Mac Hacks Labs, a Minecraft enthusiast, and a Webelos scout.

Brett Terpstra (Hack #09 , Hack #23 , Hack #24 , Hack #25) is a coder, an author, a web developer and a Mac lover. He finds joy in crafting regular expressions and making hardware and software do things they weren't supposed to do. (Sometimes it's even beneficial.) Brett shares almost all of his digital hijinks at *http://brettterpstra.com*.

Safari® Books Online

 Safari Books Online (www.safaribooksonline.com) is an on-demand digital library that delivers expert *content* in both book and video form from the world's leading authors in technology and business.

Technology professionals, software developers, web designers, and business and creative professionals use Safari Books Online as their primary resource for research, problem solving, learning, and certification training.

Safari Books Online offers a range of *product mixes* and pricing programs for *organizations*, *government agencies*, and *individuals*. Subscribers have access to thousands of books, training videos, and prepublication manuscripts in one fully searchable database from publishers like O'Reilly Media, Prentice Hall Professional, Addison-Wesley Professional, Microsoft Press, Sams, Que, Peachpit Press, Focal Press, Cisco Press, John Wiley & Sons, Syngress, Morgan Kaufmann, IBM Redbooks, Packt, Adobe Press, FT Press, Apress, Manning, New Riders, McGraw-Hill, Jones & Bartlett, Course Technology, and dozens *more*. For more information about Safari Books Online, please visit us *online*.

How to Contact Us

Please address comments and questions concerning this book to the publisher:

O'Reilly Media, Inc.
1005 Gravenstein Highway North
Sebastopol, CA 95472
800-998-9938 (in the United States or Canada)
707-829-0515 (international or local)
707-829-0104 (fax)

We have a web page for this book, where we list errata, examples, and any additional information. You can access this page at *http://oreil.ly/Mac_Hacks*.

To comment or ask technical questions about this book, send email to *bookques tions@oreilly.com*.

For more information about our books, courses, conferences, and news, see our website at *http://www.oreilly.com*.

Find us on Facebook: *http://facebook.com/oreilly*

Follow us on Twitter: *http://twitter.com/oreillymedia*

Watch us on YouTube: *http://www.youtube.com/oreillymedia*

Acknowledgments

First I'd like to thank everyone who reads this book and tries something they wouldn't have tried otherwise. You're the people who make the book go and you can reach me at *cseibold@me.com*. I'd also like to thank all the guest hackers. I also extend sincere and deeply felt thanks to Dawn Mann, who did an especially inspired job with this book, and I suspect this book will appeal (or be usable) to a wider audience thanks to her tireless efforts. This book is much, much better for going through Dawn than it would be if it had gone through an average editor.

—*Chris Seibold*

1

Before You Hack

Hacking is fun and productive, but it can also introduce an element of danger (perhaps that's part of the fun). You want to minimize that danger, and the best way to minimize the bad stuff that can happen is to back up your data and know what to do when something goes wrong. This is why this chapter is here. You'll discover some basic hacking techniques but, before you try them, you'll learn how to protect your precious data. If something does go wrong, you'll have the tools to fix the problem very quickly. The interesting world of hacking awaits!

HACK 01 Create a Great Backup

Even if you never plan to perform a single hack in this book, you'll still want a reliable backup. This hack explains different methods you can use to back up your Mac so you can be confident that you'll be able to recover quickly when things go wrong.

If you're ever asked what the most important part of a computer is (and that's a question companies sometimes ask employment seekers), you could do much worse than saying, "A good backup." Why not, say, the CPU or graphics card instead? Because a good backup is where all your work, toil, pictures, movies, and other accumulated data is preserved for that inevitable moment when everything stops working. With a good backup, you don't start over, you simply restore. *Without* a good backup, well, good luck getting that loved one to put on a prom outfit 5 years later.

The point is that some things can't be re-created (and even the ones that *can* be re-created might take an obscene amount of time and effort and, likely, still not be as good as the original). So your goal should be to both minimize downtime and minimize lost data—and a good backup helps you achieve both these goals.

What Makes a Good Backup?

The phrase "a good backup" gets tossed around a lot, but it's rarely ever defined. What is a good backup? That depends on what data you don't care about and what data you couldn't stand to lose. For our purposes, "a good backup" is one that saves your precious data and gives you peace of mind. To find the backup method that's right for you, we'll look at several different options for backing up your computer.

Maybe You Don't Need to Back Up

While backing up is a great idea if you store any critical or nonreplicable information on your computer, there's a chance that the amount of data that's stored exclusively on your computer and nowhere else is very small.

For example, if you're a big-time photo sharer, all your pics might be on Flickr. Or you might be a huge fan of iTunes Match, store all your documents in iCloud, and have purchased all your apps via the App Store. If this more or less describes you, you might not even want to hassle with a backup because you're generally using backups all the time. To put a finer point on it, if your Mac were to get wiped out, all your data would still exist in the cloud somewhere. Conversely, if the cloud were to go dark, everything's on your Mac. Your penchant for accessing your data everywhere has saved you the hassle of backing up!

Time Machine

The most user-friendly way to back up your Mac is Time Machine (Figure 1-1), which is built into OS X and is incredibly easy to use. The idea behind Time Machine is simple: you hook a drive up to your Mac and Time Machine copies the drive. Once the drive is copied, Time Machine incrementally copies any changes you make (file by file). If you lose a file or something goes wrong, you can step backwards in time to the good old days when everything was how you wanted it or just retrieve the file that's missing.

Time Machine backups are good enough for most people, but if you're going to be hacking around on your Mac and trying stuff you wouldn't normally try, you'll likely want something a little beefier. Creating a backup you can boot from (which you can't do with Time Machine) is a nice place to start. The next section explains how to create one.

Figure 1-1.
Time Machine's intuitive interface. Use the timeline on the right side of the screen to scroll back in time and retrieve the data you're missing, or restore your Mac to how it was on a specific date.

Quick Hack: More Control over Time Machine

Unless you tell it otherwise, Time Machine backs your Mac up every hour. You might find that to be too often or—if you're working on important stuff —not often enough. Fortunately, with a text editor and a little determination, you can change that interval. Navigate to:

your hard drive/System/Library/LaunchDaemons/com.apple.backupd-auto.plist

Copy that file, and then open it with a text editor. The file isn't long so you won't have any problem finding the line that reads:

```
<integer>3600</integer>
```

3600 is the number of seconds betwixt backups, so increase or decrease that number until the interval seems ideal to you. Replace the original file with the edited version you just created, and Time Machine will back up according to your schedule!

Backing Up with Disk Utility

Your Mac comes with a nice utility for duplicating drives. It's called Disk Utility and you'll find it, as you'd expect, in the Utilities folder (*Applications/Utilities/Disk Utility*).

That takes care of the software you'll need, but you'll also need some media to store your backup on. In a perfect world, you'd have a massive amount of super speedy storage. But since this media is for backup purposes, cost considerations can be more critical than high speed, so whatever you're comfortable with will do. Just make sure the drive/flash stick/ssd/partition you use is the same size or larger than the disk you want to backup.

Attach your backup media to your Mac in the manner required by the media. (I usually just jam the connector blindly into the back of my machine until it fits, but you might want to use more care.) Next launch Disk Utility. Once Disk Utility is up and running, you can get to the business of duplicating your drive. Click the Restore tab and then drag the disk you want to copy from the sidebar into the Source field. You can guess what's next: drag the disk that you want the back up to into the Destination field (Figure 1-2).

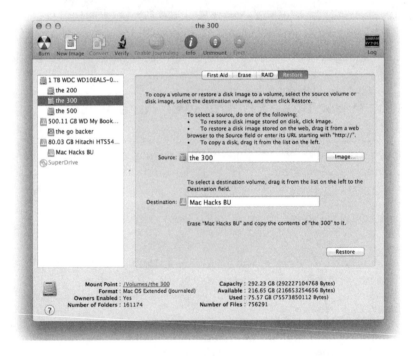

Figure 1-2.
In this case, the partition named "the 300" is being duplicated to the partition Mac Hacks BU. OS X treats separate partitions as different disks even though they can be on the same physical drive. This illustration shows three physical drives and five partitions.

Click Restore and OS X displays a message asking if you're *sure* you want to replace the contents of the targeted drive. You're careful and you've thought this out, so click Erase. Once you do that, you'll be asked for your password.

Type in your password and Disk Utility will go about the business of copying the data to the destination drive. Unlike Time Machine, which copies drives file by file, Disk Utility works by copying drives block by block, which yields an exact copy of the drive and keeps it bootable. (If you use a copy method that copies file by file, the result won't be bootable unless you take some extra steps.) When the process is finished you'll have a new drive with all your old data that you can use to boot your Mac if things go horribly awry. But before you start sloshing cola on your old drive, take a quick trip to System Preferences and choose Startup Disk. If the backup process went smoothly, you'll see an option to use the drive you just cloned as a startup disk. As shown in Figure 1-3, the name of your newest drive has been changed to match the name of the drive you just cloned.

Figure 1-3.
Use the Startup Disk preference pane to make certain that the backup disk is bootable. Note that there are now two drives named "the 300." You can tell them apart by their different icons: the one on the left (the backup) is a USB drive, and the one on the right (the original) is a hard drive.

HACK 02 Create a Bootable Flash Drive

Your installation of OS X has recovery tools built into it. But because those tools are stored on your hard drive, they won't do you any good if the thing wreaking havoc with your Mac *is* the drive. This hack explains how to make a cheap startup disk using a USB stick and a free Apple-supplied program.

In the olden times, back when you had to install new versions of OS X from a DVD, you always had an emergency startup disk. Snow Leopard acting wonky? Cram that DVD into your iMac's superdrive, press Option-O when it starts, and boot from the install disk. It was a slow process but at least it got your Mac going again.

OS X Lion and Mountain Lion are different. Since they don't have physical install disks, the emergency boot option is installed on your drive when you install Lion or Mountain Lion. This is called the recovery partition and it's a tiny slice of the media you use to boot from. This slice holds a bunch of nifty tools for you to use in an emergency (for a more thorough discussion of the emergency boot partition, see Hack #07). The unfortunate thing is that none of those will do you any good if something is wrong with the drive.

What you really need is a way to create a bootable disk. Happily, Apple offers a program to do exactly that, it just isn't all that well known and—truth be told—once you're interested enough to learn about it on your own, it might be too late to solve your problem.

How do you get your own slice of USB-startup-disk heaven? Point your Mac to *the support page for OS X Recovery* (*http://support.apple.com/kb/DL1433*) and click the download link on the upper right side of the page. It's a small file (1.1 MB) so the download will be quick. (If the link listed here doesn't work for you, a web search for OS X Recovery Disk Assistant will find the program).

Recovery Disk Assistant arrives as a *.dmg* file. As you'd expect, double-clicking this file will expand and give you access to the program. You can move it to your Applications folder, but you'll likely want different versions of a recovery disk for all your different Macs, so save the app to each of your Macs.

Pro Tip: Make Separate Recovery Disks for Each of Your Macs

If you have multiple Macs, your inclination might be to make one Recovery USB stick, place it behind glass with a hammer attached by a chain, and use it in the event of an emergency with any of your Macs. That plan *seems* solid, but it might not work.

The general rule is that if you've upgraded your Mac to Lion or Mountain, and created the recovery disk on that machine, it will work on any other Mac you've upgraded in the same manner. So if you've got an iMac and a MacBook Pro that both shipped with Snow Leopard and you've upgraded both of them to Mountain Lion, the recovery disk you created on one machine will work on both of them. But if the iMac has been upgraded to Mountain Lion and the MacBook is still using Lion, the recovery disk *won't* work on both computers. Things get weirder if you have a Mac that came with Lion or Mountain Lion preinstalled. For such machines, only recovery disks made on the same machine you're using them for will work. Want to use a USB recovery stick with your 2012 Retina MacBook Pro? You'd better make sure you made it on that machine.

The easiest solution? Just make one recovery disk for each computer, on each computer. Mark which one is which and hope you never need them.

Grab a blank USB drive that's at least 650 MB in size that has no important data on it (Recovery Disk Assistant erases all the data as it creates the disk). Now is a great time to rename the USB disk to something easily recognizable. (To rename the disk, plug it into your Mac and, when the disk's icon appears onscreen, click the icon and then click its name; then type the new name. This isn't a long-term commitment: once the process is done, you won't see the disk at all, so don't fret over the name.)

So your drive is plugged in, devoid of necessary data, and named something you can spot easily. Great—the hard work is done. Launch Recovery Disk Assistant (Figure 1-4) and let your Mac do the hard work! You'll be asked for your password and then Recovery Disk Assistant will take a few minutes to actually write the disk.

Figure 1-4.
The drive selection screen of Recovery Disk Assistant. Make your choice carefully as the selected disk will be erased.

Once everything is in place, Recovery Disk Assistant will tell you that the process is finished and you'll have a disk you can use to start your Mac when things go wrong. Since the disk is a copy (more or less) of the recovery partition built into your hard drive, it'll give you access to all the same tools you'd have if you booted from the recovery disk (Disk Utility, Terminal, etc.).

There's a downside to this method, however: from now on, when you insert the disk into your Mac's USB slot, nothing shows up onscreen. That's because that disk is dedicated *only* to booting your Mac and helping you recover—you can't use it for anything else. (There is a workaround that will make your Mac display the disk: shut down, plug in the disk, and then hold down the Option key while you start up.) For that reason, you probably want to boldly label the disk with the name of the machine you created it on.

Honestly, the whole process is kind of cumbersome—creating specific disks for specific Macs (but only sometimes)—but in an emergency the disks can be real lifesavers.

HACK 03   Partition that Drive Nondestructively

At some point you'll want partitions on your hard drive, but partitioning a drive usually means erasing the data on it first. This hack reveals how to partition your drives without losing any data.

When you get a new Mac, you're understandably excited and you want to start using that thing right away. You create some data, transfer some pics onto it, and now the Mac is yours. A few weeks later you realize you'd really like to have some partitions on your Mac. The problem is there's no obvious way to partition the hard drive without losing the data you've created.

The most obvious workaround is to back up your disk with Time Machine or clone it, and then boot from some other disk and partition your disk. But that involves a lot of time and hassle. What you want is a method to partition your existing disk *without* a lot of work.

Why Partition?

When you partition a drive in OS X, the operating system will treat that single drive physical drive as multiple drives. The partitions will look like completely separate disks in the Finder and you can treat them as different disks for everyday computing.

Partitioning your drive is useful for a variety of reasons. Partitions can help with organization, troubleshooting, and backup planning. But there's one big caveat: partitions won't help you if the hard drive dies—all the partitions go down with it.

The coolest hacks use tools in unintended ways. This one uses Boot Camp Assistant and a Windows install disk to create a new partition without having to erase your data. Boot Camp Assistant is an application published by Apple that helps you install Windows on your Mac. If you're wondering how installing Windows on a Mac relates to partitioning your drive without losing data, the answer is simple: one of the steps Boot Camp performs is partitioning your drive.

Note: This hack requires a Windows install disk. But it doesn't require a never-used install disk. I used an old Vista install disk, but you can get away with using any disk someone has laying around. You won't be running Windows anyway!

The good news is that Boot Camp Assistant is already on your Mac (you'll find it the Utilities folder), so the only thing you need to hunt down is that Windows install disk. Once you find one, launch Boot Camp and get ready for some ominous warnings. The first screen of Boot Camp Assistant warns you to back up your computer. *Heed this advice!* Your drive is about to be messed with and, without a good backup, you could suffer major data loss. (See Hack #01 for advice on backing up.)

Click Continue and you'll see a few checkboxes offering to get some Windows support files from Apple's servers and install Windows (Figure 1-5). You're not here to install Windows, you just want Boot Camp Assistant to take care of a little drudgery. But if you uncheck all the boxes, then Boot Camp Assistant won't run. If you read the fine print, you'll note that the Install Windows option states that it will add a partition for Windows, which is exactly what you want, so turn off all the checkboxes *except* that one.

Once you click Continue, you'll find the path to happy partitioning. You'll have an option to set partition sizes (Figure 1-6). What partition scheme you use is up to you, but the larger the partition you select the more flexibility you'll have in the future.

Once you've made your decision, insert your Windows install disk and then click Install. Your Mac will restart and attempt to install Windows. But you aren't after Windows, so don't waste time installing Windows; stop the install process by pressing the Eject key while the Mac is rebooting to force it to use its internal drive. Your Mac will go through the normal startup process and when it's done, the new partition will just be sitting there! Back to Disk Utility to format your brand-new partition in any manner you wish (Figure 1-7).

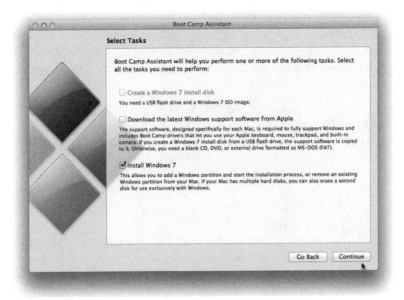

Figure 1-5.
If you ever truly want to install Windows, the process will be different. But for the purposes of partitioning, only check the Install Windows box.

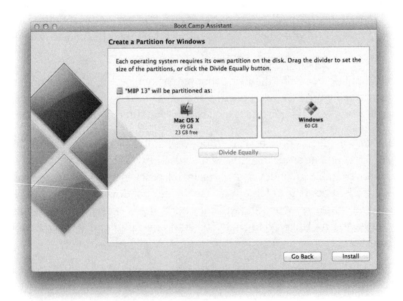

Figure 1-6.
To set partition sizes, either drag the divider between the two partitions or you could opt to use the Divide Equally button. It's your partition—do what you want!

MAC HACKS

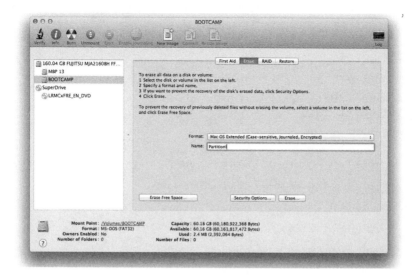

Figure 1-7.
Here Disk Utility is being used to change the partition from MS-DOS FAT to a more Mac-friendly partition. Sure, your Mac can use disks formatted in MS-DOS FAT, but it prefers HJFS+ made specifically with Macs in mind.

Beyond the Hack

It will likely occur to you that tricking Boot Camp Assistant is one way to partition your hard drive, but probably an unnecessary way. After all, if Boot Camp Assistant can nondestructively partition your disk, you can probably do it yourself. You're right—you can do it without Boot Camp Assistant, though you'll need to spend some time with Terminal.

Note: From the department of "It can't be said enough," you really should back up your drive before you try this. Is your data backed up? Good, let's get going!

Fire up Terminal (it's in your Utilities folder) and you'll see a window that looks remarkably like an old-style computer terminal. If you feel a little intimidated by Terminal, check out Chapter 6 before you start; if not, it's time to start typing. Take a deep breath and type:

```
diskutil list
```

Not too hard, right? What that command does is tell your Mac to reveal all the partitions on the drives mounted on your Mac ("mounted" doesn't necessarily mean physically mounted—it just means currently available to your machine; you can have disks plugged in that aren't mounted). The output will vary from machine to machine, but it's generally almost humanly understandable. When I ran `diskutil list` on my iMac in Knoxville, Tennessee, I got an output that looked like this:

```
/dev/disk0
   #:                       TYPE NAME            SIZE        IDENTIFIER
   0:      GUID_partition_scheme              *1.0 TB       disk0
   1:                        EFI              209.7 MB      disk0s1
   2:              Apple_HFS the 200          201.6 GB      disk0s2
   3:      Apple_Boot Recovery HD             650.0 MB      disk0s3
   4:              Apple_HFS the 300          292.2 GB      disk0s4
   5:      Apple_Boot Recovery HD             650.0 MB      disk0s5
   6:              Apple_HFS the 500          504.2 GB      disk0s6
   7:      Apple_Boot Recovery HD             650.0 MB      disk0s7
```

What can we learn from this output? SIZE, as you've guessed is the size of the disk. IDENTIFIER is how the computer tells one disk from another, and TYPE NAME is how you can tell what each disk is. In this particular case, we have a 1.0 TB disk (disk0) that has been divided into seven partitions. The first partition is EFI (disk0s1), which contains some device drivers and other necessary things for your Mac to boot; you won't need to mess with that partition for the purposes of this hack. I created the second partition (disk0s2) for storing movies, so we'll leave that one alone, too. The next one (disk0s3) is a recovery disk generated during the install of Lion or Mountain Lion. We won't be altering that partition in this hack either, so we can skip Apple_Boot Recovery HD.

This brings us to the disk we want to repartition: Apple_HFS the 300 (a.k.a. disk0s4). Before we partition the disk, we should decide what size partitions we want. To figure that out, we need to know how much of the disk's space is already in use (we don't want to lose any data, now do we?). To find that out, at the Terminal prompt, type:

```
df -h
```

The `df` command tells your Mac to list information based on file systems, and the –h flag tells Terminal to list the data in human-readable form. The output will tell you more than you really want to know so, in this case, we'll just pay attention to the disk we're going to partition. Here's the relevant information:

Filesys tem	Size	Used	Avail	Capacity	iused	ifree	%iused	Mounted on
/dev/ disk0s4	272Gi	68Gi	204Gi	25%	17817531	53526975	25%	/Volumes/ the300

Well that is *almost* humanly understandable! If you look closely, you can tell that the disk known as "the 300" is 272 GB in size and that 68 GB have been used, leaving us with 204 GB available. That's certainly enough space to make it worth our while to create a new partition.

Let's see what the limits of our partitions will be using the `diskutil` command:

```
diskutil resizeVolume disk0s4 limits
```

Which tells us:

```
For device disk0s4 the 300:
Current size: 292.2 GB (292227104768 Bytes)
Minimum size: 78.3 GB (78349324288 Bytes)
Maximum size: 292.2 GB (292227104768 Bytes)
```

Those are the limits of what we can do; we're free to choose any value within those limits. In this case we'll use 100 GB for the old disk ("the 300") and 190 for the new disk (which will be named, unimaginatively, "NEWPART"). To get the new partition made, we need to use `diskutil` to tell the program exactly what we want to do. To do all that, type:

```
diskutil resizevolume /dev/disk0s4 100G JHFS+ "NEWPART" 190G
```

That doesn't make a much sense if you just look at it. Here's what each part of that command represents:

- `diskutil` is the program that will be doing the work; it's built into OS X.
- `resizevolume` explains what you want diskutil to do.
- `/dev/disk0s4` tells diskutil which disk you want it to resize.
- `100G` tells diskutil that you want the old partition reduced to 100 GBs.
- `JHFS+` tells diskutil that you want the new partition to be a *Journaled Hierarchical File System Plus*, which is the type of partition your Mac prefers (though you can choose other systems if you like).
- `"NEWPART"` tells diskutil what to name the new partition.
- `190G` tells diskutil you want the disk partition to be 190 GBs.

You'll need to adjust the command to your specific desires. Once you get all that typed into Terminal (careful—spelling and spacing matters), hit Return and `diskutil` will start the process. You won't see the nifty OS X progress bar that you're familiar with;

instead you'll see the Terminal version of a progress bar. (What does a progress bar look like in the Terminal? It looks like [***----], with * representing the completed parts.) The process can take some time (don't close that Terminal window!), but once it's done you'll have all your data *and* a new partition! When it's finished, `diskutil` will print out a list of the disks on your Mac, which includes the new partition:

```
#:  TYPE NAME                 SIZE       IDENTIFIER
0:  GUID_partition_scheme    *1.0 TB     disk0
1:  EFI                       209.7 MB   disk0s1
2:  Apple_HFS the 200         201.6 GB   disk0s2
3:  Apple_Boot Recovery HD    650.0 MB   disk0s3
4:  Apple_HFS the 300         100.0 GB   disk0s4
5:  Apple_Boot Recovery HD    650.0 MB   disk0s9
6:  Apple_HFS NEWPART         192.1 GB   disk0s10
7:  Apple_HFS the 500         504.2 GB   disk0s6
8:  Apple_Boot Recovery HD    650.0 MB   disk0s7
```

You're probably wondering why the partition came out as 192.1 GB instead of 190 GB. The reason is actually kind of interesting: the maximum partition is 292.2 GB but the partitions requested by the Terminal command add up to 290 GB. So instead of wasting that space, `diskutil` adds it on to the larger partition. (What happened to the missing .1 GB? The world may never know.)

HACK 04 Get to Know Your User Account

> Permissions are crucial to the functioning of OS X, and a basic understanding of them will make your hacking forays not only more fruitful but also less fearful.

You likely know that OS X is based on Unix, an operating system invented in Bell Labs that has been around since 1969. In 1969 the idea of a personal computer was pretty far fetched—computers were hugely expensive and computer time was very valuable. Because of that, Unix was designed to be a multiuser system. As such, it needed a method for deciding just what each user can do with the machine. (It would be bad if one student could erase another student's work or, the other extreme, a setup where only one superuser could make any changes at all.) Permissions allow users to change what they need to change while protecting others who use the same machine from accidental data deletion.

When you first set up OS X, you provided a name, OS X suggested a short name which you may or may not have chosen to use, and you were off to the races. "No big deal," you might think, "this is just routine housekeeping when setting up a new machine."

Actually, this step *is* kind of a big deal—the first account you set up in OS X is, by default, an administrator account.

OS offers three main types of accounts: Administrator, Standard, and Managed with Parental Controls. (There are other types listed in the Users & Groups preference pane, but the ones listed above are your best bets for everyday use.) Administrators have a lot of power in OS X—they can make global changes that impact *everyone* who uses that computer—so logging in as an administrator for day-to-day use isn't the best idea; with that much power over the entire system, you can cause serious harm to your account and others'. It's much better to log in as a standard user for day-to-day tasks while reserving the administrator account for those times you need to, well, administrate. Standard users can make changes that impact their own accounts, and Managed users can only do what the administrator specifically allows. The Standard account is the sweet spot because you get to control the stuff you need to control, but you can't mess up anyone else's work or the machine.

The most obvious objection to switching to a standard user account is that you're already using one account and you don't want to re-create everything for your new account. That's a valid objection—but one we can work around.

What You're Really Changing with a Standard Account: The Home Folder Library

A standard user on OS X has plenty of control over their information and preferences. Preferences for each user are stored in each user's Home folder's Library. The Library is what makes your Mac feel like it's yours. You might want to directly tweak the files in your Library, but if you go poking around in your Home folder, you won't see anything that looks like it might be storing your preferences and the like. That's because those things are stored in the Library folder and, starting in OS X Lion, Apple made that folder invisible.

This can be frustrating for longtime Mac users who are used to messing around in that folder. For example, an app is giving you a ton of problems, you might want to jump to the Library folder and delete your preferences for that program, which can sometimes make the app more responsive (the preferences will be regenerated).

Fortunately, Apple gives you a simple way to access your Library folder. In the Finder's menu bar, open the Go menu and then press the Option key. Voilà—a Library option appears in the menu (Figure 1-8)!

Figure 1-8.
Pressing the Option key when viewing the Go menu isn't the only way to find your Library folder, but it's probably the easiest.

Turning Your Administrator Account into a Standard Account

Fire up System Preferences and head to Users & Groups. You'll see a list of users on the left side of the pane with the current user at the very top. Immediately under each user's name is a label that indicates what kind of user they are (Figure 1-9).

If you only have one administrator account, you can't really change your account status because your Mac has to have at least one admin-level user. In that case, the first step is to add another administrator user. Click the lock icon in the pane's lower-left corner and then type in your administrator password in the window that appears. Once the pane is unlocked, you can add a new account. Click the + button above the lock icon and a new window will appear (Figure 1-10).

Fill out the fields and pick a good password (click the key icon if you want Password Assistant to help you pick a secure one); write yourself a meaningful hint and click Create User. You now have *two* administrator accounts. Now you're ready to make your original admin account into a standard account: click your original account in the list on the right side of the preference pane, and then uncheck the box that says "Allow user to administer this computer" (Figure 1-11). That's it—you've turned your overly powerful administrator account into a safe-to-use-daily standard account! (Well, after you restart your machine, anyway.) In Figure 1-11, a former administrator account has become a standard account.

Figure 1-9.
You can do a lot more with this pane than just add users. Click the Login Items tab if you want programs to start automatically when you log in.

You might be experiencing some regret at this point. What about all the power you gave up? How will you get things done when you need to be an administrator to accomplish something? Will you have to log out and log back in? Don't fret: everything will be almost exactly the same. You'll still have all the same powers, you'll just have to occasionally enter the admin username and password you just created instead of the password associated with your now-standard account—a small price to pay for increased security.

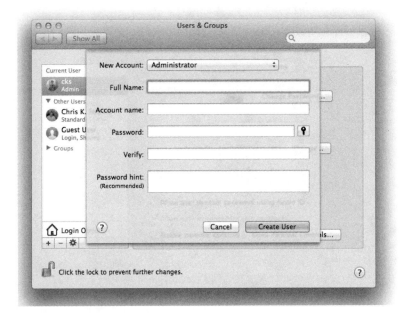

Figure 1-10.
Adding a new Administrator to your Mac. This one won't be for day-to-day use; instead, you'll use it on those special occasions when you want to boss your computer around for a bit.

Figure 1-11.
Behold your new standard user account. Finally, everyone can sleep soundly at night.

Enabling the Root User

Now you know the safe way to do things when it comes to user accounts, but that method might not be to your liking. You might be one of those folks who wants to control *everything*—you're so certain of your abilities that you don't want to stumble along using a standard account to safeguard other users' data or the integrity of your machine. If you're one of those people, the root account may be for you.

Warning: Enabling a root account is a bad idea—a really *bad idea. Don't do it.* You *can accomplish anything you want to by just being an administrator user or authenticating when you're trying to do something potentially damaging. But if you still insist on being lord of the realm, this section explains what to do.*

You've been warned, but if you want to go ahead and enable the root account anyway, the process is simple. Open the Users & Groups preference pane, click the lock icon and enter your admin credentials, and then click Login Options. In the pane's list of settings, click the Join button. Doing so will display a pane where you can enter a server for your Mac to look at. You don't need to worry about which server to choose. Just click the Open Directory Utility button and marvel at the Directory Utility window (Figure 1-12).

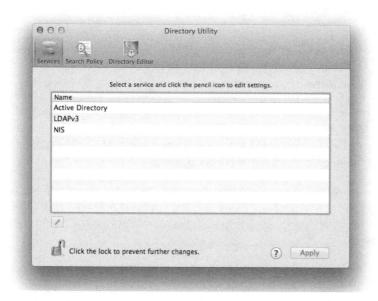

Figure 1-12.
Active Directory, LDAPv3, NIS—is this some sort of repository for bad acronyms? Nope. Even though this window might not make any sense at all in light of what you're trying to do, this is exactly where you want to be.

You are about to become the supreme overlord of your Mac. First, unlock the pane by clicking the lock icon and authenticating. Next, head to the top of your screen, click Edit, and then select Enable Root User, You'll see some fields you can use to create a password for the newly enabled root user. Enter the password and bang—you've got a root user for your Mac!

To log in as the root user, log out or switch users. You'll see an option on the Login screen named Others. Choose this option and then type in **root** for the login name and the password you created for that account.

Once you're logged in as the root user, you can do anything you want. You can look at any file on your machine (even other people's) delete any directory, delete any file, or completely ruin the system on a whim. Logging in as root isn't *necessarily* dangerous if you're very careful with what you do while you're logged in, but a moment's lapse of attention and you can do serious damage.

Note: If you don't administer the Mac you use, you might be worried that the administrator could log in as root and see all your personal files. That's certainly possible. The way to prevent that is to move your home directory to a portable media you can physically control (see Hack #35) or encrypt the data using FileVault 2 (Hack #34).

HACK 05 Home Folder to Go

Most (but not all) of the information that makes your Mac seem uniquely yours resides in your Home folder. Discover how to take this folder with you everywhere you go so that any Mac feels (almost) like home.

Take the case of the mysterious Mac Guy A. He had a problem: he was constantly using different Macs. He might use one of 20 different Macs in his school's computer lab, give a lecture using yet another Mac or, even worse, he might find himself in front of his girlfriend's laptop for an extended period of time.

"No big deal," you argue, "he can use iCloud. Store his documents there and he can access them everywhere." A seemingly sure solution—until the network gets iffy (like it is at more than one place he visits) or he runs up against his data limit (iCloud storage isn't unlimited).

So the problem remains. He doesn't want to haul his Mac Pro around in a heavy-duty backpack (plus think how long the extension cord would have to be!), he can't use his iPad for all his computing needs, and carrying both the iPad *and* a laptop seems overly burdensome. He does have one thing going for him: he's around a lot Macs, a lot of the time. If he could just make all those Macs his, he would be in computing nirvana!

The good news is that you can make any Mac you meet yours. The bad news? You'll need some portable storage—something with more space than your current Home folder but that's easy to carry around. This could be an SSD drive, a high-speed flash drive connected to your keychain, etc. Whatever you're comfortable carrying that is of sufficient size will fit the bill.

How Much Storage Do You Need?

To decide how big of a chip or drive you need to take your preferences anywhere you go, first find out how big your Home folder is. In a Finder window, select Go→Computer (or press Shift-Command-C); then, select your startup drive and double-click the Users folder (Figure 1-13).

Inside the Users folder, click your specific user folder. Then see how much space the Home folder currently demands by selecting File→Get Info (or pressing Command-I). The size of your user folder appears right near the top of the Get Info window. Base your purchase decision on this number. If the amount of data seems overly large, you can selectively leave out folders like Photos, Music, and Movies (the usual culprits).

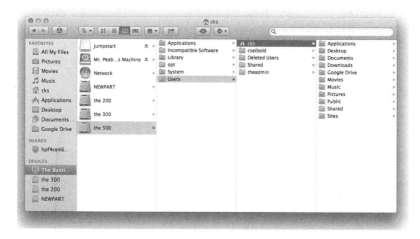

Figure 1-13.
Discovering the Home folder using the column view layout in the Finder.

What Your Home Folder Means to You

Your Home folder houses everything that you like and have customized about your Mac: your music, your photos, and the veritable morass of preferences that tell your applications just how you like them to behave.

Of course, not *everything* travels with your Home folder. Your Application folder houses the applications you use and they won't go for the ride unless you manually copy them to a folder on the memory stick you're using. You've got two choices: either make sure the applications you want to use are on the Macs you'll be using, or take your unusual applications with you.

Turns out there's an Application folder right in your Home folder. Usually this is reserved for apps that are installed for a single user, but there's no reason you can't copy the apps you want to travel with to this folder. It won't work for every app, but most apps don't mind travelling like this.

Portable Apps

Not every application is a good traveler. While most OS X applications enjoy drag-and-drop functionality, some very important applications do not. Mail and Safari are two examples; they store preference files in your System Library, so even if you copy Mail to your portable Home folder, you won't be able to fire up Mail and use it as though you were on your main machine. But all is not lost: a bevy of portable versions of popular Mac apps are available from Sourceforge. See *this list of OS X portable applications* (*http://www.freesmug.org/portableapps*) to get started.

Setting Up Your Portable Drive

The first obstacle to deal with is the fact that your drive/chip/whatever you're using probably didn't come formatted with Macs in mind. Your Mac prefers a Mac OS Extended Journaled format. So fire up Disk Utility (Applications→Utilities→Disk Utility), select the device in the lefthand column (Figure 1-14), and then click Erase and let Disk Utility do the hard work. When it's done, you'll have a blank drive ready to hold your Home folder.

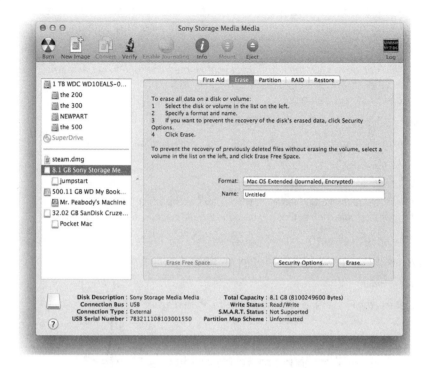

Figure 1-14.
Changing the factory settings to an OS X–preferred format.

Transferring your user account

Using Macs is easy, right? So slapping your Home folder on another drive is as simple as a dragging and dropping it, right? Well it is—with one caveat: turns out that a Mac needs to know where to look for your Home folder in order to use it, and telling a Mac where to look for your Home folder isn't a trivial task. First, you have a decision to make: do you want the portable media to house your current Home folder and rely solely on said media for all your Home-folder storage needs, or do you want your media to contain a *copy* of your Home folder? There's no right answer here: if you're going to spend a lot more time at your home computer consider using a copy; if your time is equally spent between machines, consider using the portable media as your stand-alone Home folder. The difference isn't huge, but it also isn't negligible. Depending on the steps you take, you can create a Home folder you use all the time (on your main machine and all the other Macs you use) or one that you'll use *only* when you're on a Mac that's not yours.

Whether you've decided to go with a new Home folder or just go portable media all the time, the process is the same. First, locate the Home folder you want to use on the go and copy it to the media you are going to use. This will duplicate the data from the chosen folder to your destination (you'll be asked to authenticate during the process). Don't worry, copying data is nondestructive, so you won't lose any data doing this.

Note: If you decide to copy the contents of your Home folder one folder at a time, you'll miss the Library folder because it's invisible. To temporarily make invisibles visible, open Terminal and type:

```
defaults write com.apple.finder AppleShowAllFiles TRUE
```

And then press Return. This command tells the Finder to show the hidden files. Next, type:

```
killall Finder
```

This command restarts the Finder. Now you can see the Library folder and copy it over to your portable media. Once you're done, head back to Terminal and type:

```
defaults write com.apple.finder AppleShowAllFiles FALSE
```

This re-hides the Library folder and other invisibles. Finally, type:

```
killall Finder
```

This restarts the Finder and makes everything normal again.

Quick Tip: Where Is that Users Folder?

The Users folder is located at the root of your computer's directory, which is a geeky way of saying that the Users folder can be found by selecting Go→Computer from the Finder's menu bar (or pressing Shift-Command-C). Inside the Users folder are folders for each account on your machine. Your active Home folder—also called your User folder—looks like a house; all the rest look like folders (Figure 1-15).

Once you have the Home folder copied to your chosen destination, you've got to tell the Mac you're using as your main machine where to look for the Home folder. Yeah, your computer is smart, but it isn't psychic (though Google might be).

The deliciously easy procedure to tell your Mac where your new Home folder resides? Head over to the Accounts preference pane (System Preferences→Users & Groups), click on the lock to make changes and then authenticate. Once authenticated you'll need to explore the Advanced options, which Apple has cleverly hidden from view. To get to them, in the lefthand column, right-click the account you want to change, and an Advanced Options item will magically appear (Figure 1-16).

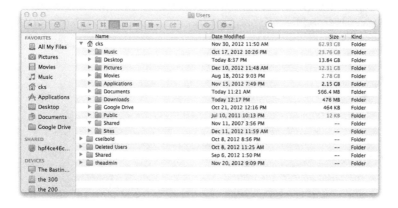

Figure 1-15.
The contents of the Users folder. Note that the current Home folder (also called the User folder) has a little house icon. The contents of that folder are what we are going mobile with—it's what makes your Mac seem like *your* Mac.

Figure 1-16.
Accessing the Advanced Options of the Users & Groups pane.

Once you've accessed the Advanced Options pane, you'll see a scary warning message. Don't worry, what we're doing won't hurt anything. Look for the Choose button next to the "Home directory" field. Simply click that button and navigate to where your new Home folder resides (Figure 1-17).

Figure 1-17.
Now OS X knows to look on your media for your Home folder.

As mentioned earlier, Macs aren't psychic. So you'll have to run through this process on each Mac you're planning to use.

Two Home folders or a Home folder to go?

So you want your Home folder to go but you don't *always* want to rely on your portable drive for your Home folder. In other words, you want your Home folder on your keychain when you're away but when you're in your dorm or apartment you want your Mac to rely on the internal hard drive. That configuration makes a lot of sense—why not use the built-in hard drive when you're using your home computer?

Of course, if the latest files aren't at your fingertips, that defeats the purpose of having a portable Home folder (convenience). For example, if you modified a Final Cut Pro movie while you were working on a Mac using your portable drive as the Home folder, when you want to work on the same presentation at home, you won't want to manually dig through your USB drive to find the latest version.

What you need is a way to keep the Home folder on your portable media synced up with the Home folder on your main Mac. There are many ways to get this done, either using a command line and something like rsync or a third-party application. There's no single "right" method for keeping the folders synced, but one of the easiest is using Automator.

Keeping everything synced

You could start from scratch and create your very own Automator workflow (see Hack #23 for instructions), but why reinvent the wheel when someone else has done most of the legwork? On your home Mac, point your browser to *the Sync Folders download page* (*http://automatorworld.com/archives/sync-folders*) to grab a copy of it. Sync Folders is a very handy Automator action written by Ben Long that can take the contents of two folders and make sure the folders exactly mirror each other while ensuring the newest version of each file overwrites the older files. Once you've downloaded the Sync Folders action, double-click the file and a window will pop up asking if you want to install the "Sync Folders" action. Of course you do, so click Install.

Sync Folders then needs to know what you want synced (in this case, the two versions of your Home folder), and that we want the folder synced both ways with the newest version of each file in both folders. The first thing to do is drag your Mac's Home folder from a Finder window (just grab it in the sidebar) into Automator's workflow pane (the upper-right pane). Then do the same with the Home folder you've created on your portable storage. Make sure the pop-up menu next to Pass On is set to Both Folders, and you're ready to try it out. Click the Play button and witness the results of the workflow.

You probably don't want to fire up Automator *every* time you want to sync your portable Home folder and the Home folder on your main machine. No problem: one of the great things about Automator is that it lets you save a workflow as an application so you can just launch the application instead of mucking about with Automator. To save Sync Folders as an application, choose File→Save As (you may have to press the Option key to make this menu item appear), name the workflow something meaningful, and choose Application in the File Format menu (Figure 1-18); then click Save. Once the file is saved you can sync the two folders anytime simply by launching your new application.

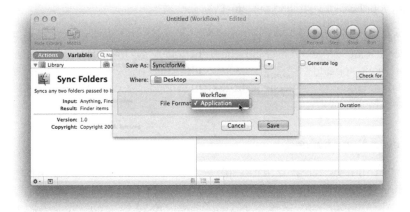

Figure 1-18.
Depending on how you want to use it, you can save an Automator action as a workflow or as an application.

Using Your Home Folder on the Go

Using your newly portable Home folder is simply a matter of reversing the steps for creating your new Home folder. Simply create a new account on the target machine with the same name as the account on your portable media and you're ready to go. Once you've created that account, head to the Users & Groups preference pane's Advanced Options and point OS X to the portable media–based Home folder.

HACK 06 **Fun with PLIST**

> PLIST files are strewn all over your Mac, but chances are you never see them. That's too bad, because PLIST files offer one of the most direct ways to hack your machine. Spend a few moments with this hack to discover techniques for mastering PLIST files.

PLIST is short for "property list," and these files are the main method OS X (and some other operating systems) use to organize data so that it's accessible by programs; they're also structured enough that you can generate your own PLIST files if need be. That very brief explanation doesn't really tell you much, but the *full* explanation of what PLIST files actually do is a little dense. (If you're really interested in the functionality of PLIST files, check out *its manual entry (http://developer.apple.com/documentation/Darwin/Reference/ManPages/man5/plist.5.html)* or type `man plist` into Terminal.)

PLIST Files for Hackers

When you are bending your machine to your will, the most frequent PLIST files you'll be mucking with are the ones that store the default values of parameters for various programs. These can range from default colors to default behaviors. These files are typically found in the Library→Preferences folder of your Home directory (to view them, in the Finder, use the Go menu, press and hold the Option key, and choose the Library folder that appears; then open the Preferences folder). Tweaking these files can yield unexpected behaviors that are mostly harmless. If you screw one up, you can always just drag the PLIST file to the trash, and your Mac will generate a new one. The downside of doing so is that you'll lose your preferences for that program, so the better way (as with all hacks) is to back up the file so you'll have a ready-made replacement.

There's more than one way to access PLIST files. The quickest is Terminal, via the `default` command. An example will help.

Some programs can be made to display a Debug menu (most can't), and Disk Utility is one of these. Turns out that the Debug menu in Disk Utility is actually very useful in Mountain Lion because it includes an option to show all the partitions on your Mac's drives. Why is this useful? Lion and Mountain Lion rely on a hidden partition not normally shown in Disk Utility, and it's a partition you could accidentally delete. Knowing whether the partition is there offers some peace of mind. Time to add the Debug menu so you can check for the partition:

1. Quit Disk Utility if it's running.
2. Fire up Terminal (Applications→Utilities→Terminal).
3. At the $ prompt, type this:

        defaults write com.apple.DiskUtility DUDebugMenuEnabled 1

4. Launch Disk Utility.

Like magic, Disk Utility has a brand new Debug menu (see Figure 1-19). To see all your partitions, choose "Show every partition." If you see Recovery Disk in the list on the left side of the Disk Utility window, you know you've still got the extra partition used by Lion and Mountain Lion.

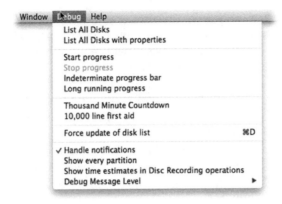

Figure 1-19.
Disk Utility's Debug menu. You might not have seen it before, but it can be very useful.

Using Terminal is great when you know specifically what you want to change, but not so useful if you just want to know what you *can* change. To find that out, you need the property list file itself. As mentioned earlier in this section, you'll usually find the PLIST files you want to hack in the Library folder of your Home directory.

To open PLIST files, you need a property list editor. If you don't *have* a property list editor lying about (and you probably don't), you'll want to get one. In older versions of OS X (Snow Leopard and earlier), a property list editor was bundled with Developer Tools as a standalone application. In later versions of OS X (Lion and newer) you can use Xcode, which is free to download from the Mac App Store. (You don't have to use Xcode—there are a lot of other programs you can use to edit PLIST files—but it's hard to beat Xcode's price.) Once you've got a PLIST editor you can live with, find the Disk Utility PLIST file we played with earlier (*~/Library/Preferences/com.apple.DiskUtility.plist*) and open it up (Figure 1-20).

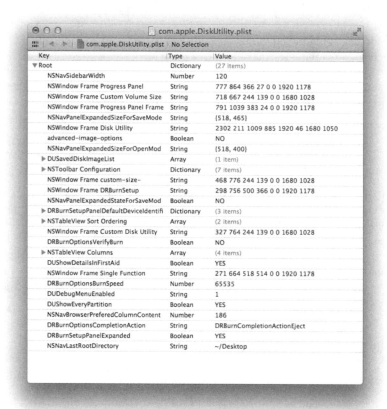

Figure 1-20.
Using Xcode to poke around Disk Utility's PLIST file. You can make a ton of reversible choices here, so don't be afraid to play! Your options might look different than the ones pictured here; that's to be expected, because the PLIST options change as you deviate from the standard configuration.

Note: If you're wondering what ~ (tilde) is doing in the commands for Terminal, you're not alone. It's a shortcut that means Home. So instead of typing Hard Drive/ Library/Users/cks (for example), you can simply type ~ and the Terminal will know what you mean.

You can change any of the lines you see when the file is opened. Most of the them won't mean much to you, but some have obvious functionality. For example, by fiddling with DRBurnOptionsVerifyBurn (toggling YES and NO) you can stop OS X from verifying a disk after you burn it. (This is also a great example of why the PLISTs are different from Mac to Mac: if you've never burned a disk, this option won't be on in your PLIST because your Mac has never been faced with that decision.)

So now you know how to tweak PLIST files with the command-line and a program. Most people would say that's enough, but if you're messing with these files a lot, you might want to use something more familiar. It turns out you can also touch up PLIST files with a text editor, but it will take just a wee bit of work.

PLIST files are stored in binary format, so you'll have to convert them to something a text editor can read. The easiest way to do so? Terminal. Since we've abused Disk Utility's PLIST file enough for now, try poking around with Safari's PLIST file instead (*~/Library/Preferences/com.apple.Safari.plist*). Since it's smart to work with a copy, right-click the file and choose Duplicate from the contextual menu. Then launch Terminal and convert the file with the command line by typing:

```
plutil -convert xml1 ~/Library/Preferences/com.apple.Safari\ copy.plist
```

Here, the plutil command invokes the property list utility, -convert xml1 (that's the letters X, M, and L followed by the number 1) tells plutil to convert the property list to XML, and the rest is just the path to the file. Once the command has run, navigate to the converted file with Finder, right-click it and choose Open With→Other, and then pick TextEdit. The formerly unreadable PLIST is now easily understandable (see Figure 1-21).

Figure 1-21.
The same PLIST file side by side. The one on the left is the converted version (so it's comprehensible). The one on the right is the unconverted version, which looks like it was created by an explosion at a keyboard factory.

You can now edit the PLIST file however you like with TextEdit. When you're done, you'll have to convert the file *back* to binary format:

```
plutil -convert binary ~/Library/Preferences/com.apple.Safari\ copy.plist
```

Then simply rename the file to remove the word "copy" from its name, and Safari will happily use your handcrafted PLIST until you tire of it.

There's much more to learn about PLIST files, but these tidbits should get you comfortable enough to start PLIST-hacking adventures and let you know what's going on when these types of files get abused throughout the rest of this book.

When you've been tweaking your Mac and something goes wrong, the natural thing is to imagine your actions just destroyed OS X. That's probably not the case—your Mac was probably going to let you down no matter what you did (hardware failures usually aren't the user's fault), so don't feel guilty. No matter the cause, the important thing to know is what to do next—and that's when this hack comes in handy.

OS X is a robust operating system, but while problems are rare, they do show up from time to time. Since these issues always seem to present themselves at the worst possible moment, it helps if you know the best ways to troubleshoot them, and that's a great reason to keep this book around!

There are a lot of things that can go wrong with your Mac: hardware problems, software glitches, and configuration issues can happen at any moment. Most of the problems you'll encounter can be easily addressed or diagnosed by following the steps in this hack. If the information here doesn't resolve things, it could be a unique issue, in which case a trip to the Apple Store or a call to Apple is in order.

Tip: A complete list of Apple's technical support numbers (http://www.apple.com/ support/contact/phone_contacts.html) is available. In the U.S., dial 1-800-275-2273.

Misbehaving Applications

One of the most common problems on a Mac is an application that isn't behaving as expected. This problem comes in many forms: an application that unexpectedly quits repeatedly, simply stops responding, or just doesn't perform the way it normally does. This section suggests ways to resolve all these issues and more.

An application stops responding

Occasionally, an application will simply stop reacting to anything. Your mouse or trackpad will still work, other programs will be fine, but if you try to use the troublesome program, all you'll get is a spinning beach ball cursor (instead of the mouse pointer) and you'll have no way to input anything.

Don't panic—there's an easy fix. Simply right-click or Control-click the stalled application's icon in the Dock to bring up its Dock menu (Figure 1-22). If you see "Application Not Responding" in faint text at the top of the menu, you'll also see a Force Quit option. Select Force Quit and OS X will kill the program.

Figure 1-22.
When an application isn't playing nicely, Force Quit is your best option.

You may also need another one way to kill applications, because occasionally a program can become unresponsive without OS X realizing it. For these times, launch the Force Quit Applications dialog box either by heading to the Apple menu and selecting Force Quit or using the key combo Option-Command-Esc. You can also try holding down Shift as you click the Apple menu, and then select Force Quit *application name* to kill the front-most application.

There's some good news when it comes to force quitting applications in Lion and Mountain Lion. In previous versions of OS X, any changes you made between the last time you saved a document and the moment the application started misbehaving were gone forever. But these newer versions of OS X include Auto Save, which automatically saves your work as you go. So if you're forced to quit an application, OS X preserves the work you've done since the last time you saved.

Warning: For the time being "Save early, save often" is still good advice, since OS X's Auto Save feature only works with applications specifically built with Auto Save in mind. That means that work you do in apps designed for Lion and Mountain Lion will be saved, but applications that haven't been updated for those versions of OS X won't automatically save your work.

The Finder stops responding

The Finder is just another program, so it can get hung up, too. If that happens, either head to the Apple menu and choose Force Quit or use the key combination Option-Command-Esc. If nothing happens, try clicking the Dock or some other application first, and *then* use the Apple menu or Option-Command-Esc to invoke the Force Quit dialog box.

Note: When you select an application in the Force Quit dialog box, the dialog box's button reads "Force Quit." However, if you select the Finder, the button reads "Relaunch" instead. Why the change in nomenclature? Unlike every other application, the Finder will be restarted immediately after it's forced to quit.

Force quitting greedy processes

If you suspect something is eating up too much processor time or too many system resources (because your Mac is running really slowly, say, or the fans are running at full speed for no obvious reason), Force Quit won't help you figure out which application is hogging all the resources. Instead, open Activity Monitor (Applications→Utilities→Activity Monitor), click its CPU tab, and then check the % CPU column for any processes that are using a lot of CPU resources for more than a few seconds. (Safari and its helper applications occasionally do this, particularly with runaway Flash or JavaScript code.) When you identify a suspect, single-click the renegade process's name and then click Activity Monitor's big red Quit Process button (you can't miss it—it's shaped like a stop sign).

Warning: Be careful which applications you quit in this way. There are some programs that your Mac runs in the background, and many of these are important in helping your computer operate normally. Here's a rule of thumb: if you don't recognize the name of the program as an application that you launched, don't kill it. Instead, do a Google search on its name (for good measure, include the terms "Mac OS X" and "cpu," too). Chances are good you'll find a solution for whatever is causing that process to use up so much CPU time.

Startup Problems

A misbehaving application is bad enough, but a Mac that won't start properly is truly disconcerting. The good news is that most such problems are usually repairable. The general method of attack in this case is to get your Mac to a state where you can run Disk Utility and repair the drive. However, there are some situations where you can't even get to that point. This section discusses your options.

Your Mac beeps at you instead of starting

If your Mac just beeps when you try to start it up, it's trying to tell you something: one beep means there's no memory (RAM) installed, and three beeps means your RAM doesn't pass integrity check. (This goes for Intel Macs only; Power PC Macs have slightly different beeps, but they can't run Lion or Mountain Lion.) The problem could be a bad RAM module, so you'll need to open up your Mac and replace the module.

Try installing some memory that you're certain is fully functional to see if that resolves the problem. If you don't have any spare memory lying around, try removing each RAM module and replacing them one by one until you've isolated the bad module.

> Tip: If you don't know how to replace memory in your Mac, check the user guide that came with it. Or if your Mac is still under warranty, just bring it into an Apple Store for service.

Your hard drive is making noises

If you suspect you've got a physical hard drive problem, you need to check things out quickly before they get much, much worse. If you hear a strange noise coming from your machine, that's an obvious sign of a hard drive problem; but they can also be indicated by the computer stalling for several seconds at a time (or making a clicking sound when stalling).

Just as with a car, when a bad sound is emanating from your hard drive, it's usually a bad thing. If you've ever listened to the National Public Radio show *Car Talk*, you know that one of the highlights is when callers try to imitate the sounds their cars are making. If you're inclined to try identifying the sound by ear, head over to *http://data cent.com/hard_drive_sounds.php* and take a listen to the sounds of dying drives, sorted by manufacturer.

> Warning: If your hard drive is failing, you're likely to lose more data every moment it's running. If you don't have current backups, your best bet is to replace the drive immediately, and either seek a data-recovery professional or, if you don't have the money for that, install the damaged drive in an external drive enclosure and use the GNU ddrescue utility (www.gnu.org/software/ddrescue (http://www.gnu.org/software/ddrescue)) to recover the data on the damaged drive.

If you aren't hearing any unusual sounds but still suspect your hard drive is causing your problems, head to Disk Utility (Applications→Utilities→Disk Utility) and check the S.M.A.R.T. status of the drive.

Using a computer means loving acronyms, and this time the acronym is clever, if a little forced: S.M.A.R.T. stands for Self-Monitoring Analysis and Reporting Technology. The idea behind S.M.A.R.T. is that many hard disk failures are predictable, and computer users, if given a heads-up that their hard drive is on the verge of failing, will be able to recover data *before* the failure actually happens. You can discover your drive's S.M.A.R.T status by opening Disk Utility and selecting the disk you're worried about in the list on the left. In the lower-right part of the Disk Utility window, you'll see the S.M.A.R.T Status (Figure 1-23): either Verified (everything is fine) or "About to Fail." If you get the "About to Fail" notice, don't waste any time: if your Mac is under warranty, take it into an Apple Store; otherwise, back up your data as soon as possible (see Hack #01) and start pricing out the cost of a new drive.

> *Note: S.M.A.R.T. status isn't available for every drive. External drives that support S.M.A.R.T. don't have a way to report that over USB or FireWire, so if you don't see the status of a particular drive, don't panic.*

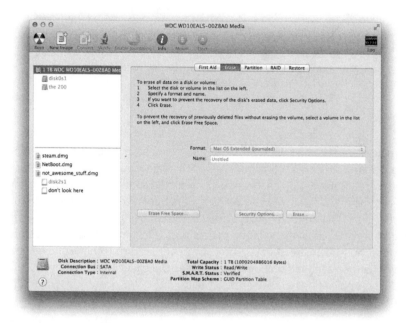

Figure 1-23.
This drive is fine.

> *Warning: S.M.A.R.T. isn't perfect (that's no surprise—nothing is). You can have a problematic drive that S.M.A.R.T. won't recognize. So if you're having consistent problems and S.M.A.R.T. keeps telling you everything is fine, don't discount the drive as the source of the problems after you've exhausted other fixes.*

Startup troubleshooting

Thankfully, the hardware failures just described are relatively rare. Much more common are software failures. Corrupt files, wonky login items, and even font problems can cause a startup failure. These issues are generally repairable, hopefully without data loss. Unfortunately, when you have one of these problems, the cause isn't immediately obvious. When faced with a Mac that won't boot, there are a few things you can try to get your computer back to a usable state:

Restart your Mac

A lot happens when OS X starts up: it checks your Mac's hardware, prepares the system software, and more. During the startup process, there are ample opportunities for something to go wrong, especially right after you install an update to OS X or even an application. If your Mac won't complete the startup sequence, don't panic; simply restart the machine by holding down the power button until you hear a chime; chances are everything will be fine.

> Warning: If you see a flashing question mark when you try to start your Mac, it means that your machine can't find its startup disk. In that case, skip down this list to "Restart in Recovery Mode."

Safe Boot

If a simple restart doesn't do the trick, it means you have problems that persist across restarts, so the next step is a Safe Boot. In Safe Mode, all your Mac's startup items are disabled, font caches are cleared, and some other possibly problematic items are avoided. More important, Safe Boot gives you a chance to run Disk Utility, uninstall any software that may be misbehaving, or back up your data before whatever is causing the problem gets worse. To get your Mac to boot into Safe Mode, hold down the Shift key after you hear the startup chime and release the key when you see the spinning wheel appear. Once your Mac has booted, run Disk Utility (Applications→Utilities→Disk Utility).

> Note: When you're booting in Safe Mode, the Login window automatically appears even if you usually use Automatic Login on your Mac. Don't be alarmed by the change—it's a sign that Safe Mode is working as expected.

Restart in Recovery Mode

Before Lion and Mountain Lion, one remedy to try when your Mac went bad was to boot from the DVD you either got with your Mac or purchased when you upgraded to Snow Leopard. But since you don't use any physical media—DVD or otherwise—when you install Lion or Mountain Lion, this trick won't work anymore. Fortunately, Apple realizes that, when problems occur, you might need to boot your Mac from a different source than usual, so OS X now includes Recovery Mode.

Note: You need to be connected to the Internet to use Recovery Mode to re-install Lion or Mountain Lion. The reinstall option will download every byte of the OS X installer, so you might want to try other fixes before going through with the entire process.

Recovery Mode allows you to boot from a virtual partition called Recovery HD. When you boot into Recovery Mode, you'll find yourself running a special system that lets you restore your Mac from a Time Machine backup, reinstall OS X, use Safari to look for solutions to your problem online, or run Disk Utility. (Don't be afraid to launch Safari even if you're not connected to the Internet; there's a static web page with basic instructions that automatically opens when you launch Safari.)

Note: You can only run one application at a time in Recovery Mode, so if you're running Disk Utility, say, you can't also launch Safari. Being aware of this limitation can save you some frustration and endless restarts.

In addition to Recovery Mode's obvious choices, you can also run Firmware Password Utility, Network Utility, and Terminal by visiting the Utilities drop-down menu at the top of the screen. With all of these options, most users will find the choices presented in the OS X Utilities window sufficient to fix their Mac woes.

Here's how to boot your Mac in Recovery Mode (the process should be familiar if you've booted Macs from alternative disks before): hold down the Option key while starting your Mac. You'll be presented with a screen that shows all the viable startup partitions available. Choose Recovery HD and you'll be well on your way to diagnosing (and hopefully fixing) whatever problem is currently plaguing your Mac.

This section emphasized tools that come with Lion and Mountain Lion because, well, if you've installed either version of OS X, you have access to these tools. But you should be aware that these tools aren't the only ones available when things go wrong. There are several disk-repair programs available (many of which are more powerful than Disk Utility) from third parties, such as *DiskWarrior* (*http://www.alsoft.com/diskwarrior*) and *TechTool Pro* (*http://www.micromat.com/techtoolpro*).

Reset your PRAM

This maneuver gets its own section only because it's one of the oldest troubleshooting techniques in Mac history.

PRAM (parameter random access memory) is where your Mac stores many of its hardware settings. Resetting the PRAM almost never resolves a startup issue, but it's something Apple support usually asks you to do when troubleshooting a problem (and it does, in some rare cases, help). To reset the PRAM, turn on your Mac, *immediately* press and hold Option-Command-P-R, and continue to hold those keys until your Mac restarts and your hear the startup chime a total of three times. After you do this, you may have to reconfigure some of the system settings (like date, time, and possibly keyboard/mouse settings if you've customized them).

2

Mountain Lion Hacks

Mountain Lion is OS X version 10.8. If you count the public beta version, that's ten iterations of OS X—and it *still* isn't perfect! That shouldn't be surprising; there are millions of people who use OS X and each one of them is going to want it to behave slightly differently. Apple provides preferences that let you personalize a lot of settings, but sometimes you need to go beyond what Apple provides to get Mountain Lion running the way you want it. This chapter teaches you how to get things just so.

HACK 08 Copy the Mountain Lion Installer to a Flash Drive

Making a portable copy of the Mountain Lion installer means you'll never need to spend time downloading it again. And there are many other benefits of having a bootable copy of the Mountain Lion installer on hand, as this hack explains.

Note: This hack describes copying the Mountain Lion installer to a flash drive, but this technique also works for the Lion installer, and you can use any storage media you wish. If you're using an older version of OS X than Lion, chances are your Mac came bundled with an emergency boot disk—the install DVD that shipped with your Mac (it's round, silver, and labeled "OS X Install").

The most obvious reason for having a copy of the installer on a flash drive is that it saves you from downloading 4 GBs of data for every Mac you want to install Mountain Lion on. Which means this is a must-have hack for people with multiple Macs, but not an important hack for those with just one Mac, right? Not so fast. It turns out that having a copy of the installer on a flash drive is a great idea even if you only have a single Mac.

Just what are the benefits of keeping a spare copy of Mountain Lion installer laying around if you don't intend to install Mountain Lion again? For one thing, just because you don't *intend* to install Mountain Lion again doesn't mean you won't end up reinstalling Mountain Lion. Things go wrong and when they do you'll be very glad that you've invested the time and cost to create a backup installer.

You might dismiss the idea of a standalone installer if you're familiar with OS X's emergency procedures. When things go bad on your Mac, you can start up your machine in Recovery Mode using a hidden partition called the Recovery partition, which gives you access to some emergency tools (Disk Utility, support documents, etc.) and lets you download Mountain Lion again. The idea is slick but if the failure point is the startup drive itself, then the Recovery partition won't be available. In addition, there's a chance that the Recovery partition might not even exist on your machine: if you've cloned your disk, that partition might not have made the trip with the rest of your data. In that case, you'll definitely be glad you took the time to make a copy of the Mountain Lion installer.

Finally, consider the time aspect of a system crash. The average Internet download speed in the U.S. is 5.8 Mbps (worldwide, it's 2.3 Mbps). The Mountain Lion installer is just over 4 GB, so if you're using an average American connection, you're looking at over one and a half hours just to download the installer. Factor in that your Mac isn't going to crash when you've got plenty of time (it's some weird rule of computers— they only break during a time crunch) and that it only takes 30 minutes to pull off this hack versus several hours to redownload Mountain Lion and this becomes the must-do hack of this book.

> ## Quick Hack: Make a Flash Recovery Partition
>
> Maybe you're happy with the recovery tools Apple supplies but you're still worried that if your Mac's hard drive fails, the Recovery partition will be unavailable—a legitimate fear. The obvious solution is to copy the Recovery partition to a disk. You could do that with the Terminal, but Apple makes it even easier. The *Recovery Disk Assistant program* (*http://support.apple.com/kb/DL1433*) makes the process of creating said disk painless. For more detailed instructions, see Hack #02.

The first step in creating a backup of the installer is to download Mountain Lion. If you've already downloaded and installed Mountain Lion, you're not out of luck—you can download Mountain Lion again via the App Store, *just make sure you don't install Mountain Lion once the download is complete*. If you do, the installer will disappear and you'll have to repeat the download process.

Once you have Mountain Lion downloaded, you'll probably be tempted to just copy the installer onto the target flash drive. Doing that would save you from spending time downloading the installer again, but what we are after is a *bootable* installer. Why bootable? Well, your data is likely protected if you use Time Machine or another similar backup option (see Hack #01), but when things go south you need something you can boot from because you can't start your computer using Time Machine. So here's how to create a bootable installer.

First, locate the Mountain Lion installer (which is aptly named Install OS X Mountain Lion). Some users will be tempted to find it using LaunchPad. LaunchPad is a great way to *launch* applications, but for the purposes of this hack, you'll want to find the actual location of the installer. The default location is in the Applications folder, but if you've modified your Mac you might find the file elsewhere. For most Macs the path will look like this: *[startup drive]/Applications/Install OS X Mountain Lion*. If that doesn't match your Mac, no big deal—Spotlight can find the file for you. Once you've found the file, right-click it, select Show Package Contents from the pop-up menu (Figure 2-1), and you're on your way.

Figure 2-1.
The Application icons you see in OS X are actually packages that hold a wide variety of program resources. Selecting Show Package Contents allows you to see what makes up the application.

Once you've selected Show Package Contents, you'll discover a folder you've probably never seen before that's unimaginatively named "Contents." Opening this folder reveals a dizzying number of files and folders. You're after the one called *InstallESD.dmg* and you'll find it in the Shared Support folder.

Now it's time for Disk Utility to lend a hand. Launch Disk Utility (*Applications→Utilities→Disk Utility*), and then drag *InstallESD.dmg* onto the left side of Disk Utility window (Figure 2-2). When you let go of your mouse, Disk Utility adds *InstallESD.dmg* to its source list.

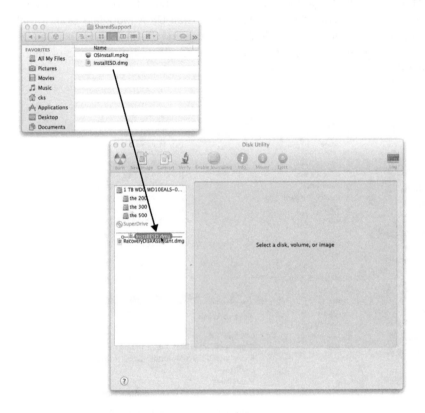

Figure 2-2.
Disk Utility is picky about where you can drag the file's icon file—aim for the lower half of the window's left pane. (This process doesn't actually move the file—*InstallESD.dmg* stays in the Shared Support folder—it just adds it as a source for Disk Utility to use.)

Now you can insert the media you want to restore the file to (if you've already inserted the destination flash drive, that won't cause any problems).

Note: The Mountain Lion installer is just over 4 GB so you'll want a flash drive that's at least 5 GB. 5 GB isn't a common size, though, so you'll likely have to settle for an 8 GB flash drive (you can find them for less than $10 if you shop around). And don't try to repurpose a flash drive you already own that contains valuable data—this process will erase the data on the drive.

Once the drive is mounted and ready, in the Disk Utility window, click the Restore tab. Then drag the destination disk to, you guessed it, the Destination field. (In Figure 2-3, the disk is named "jumpstart".) Next, drag *InstallESD.dmg* to the Source field. When everything is just right, Disk Utility will look a lot like Figure 2-3.

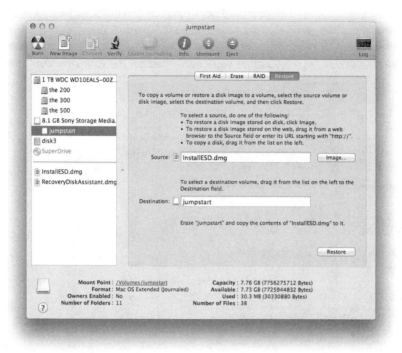

Figure 2-3.
Be careful with what you select as the destination, because the data on the destination disk will be overwritten.

Once everything is in place, it's time to let your computer works its magic. Click Restore, click Erase (you'll lose any data that's already on the flash disk), and authenticate with an admin level password.

Once your computer is happy that you are who you say you are, it'll bow to your will and start restoring *InstallESD.dmg* to the flash drive. How long the task takes depends on your Mac. On a 2009 24" iMac, it took about 20 minutes. Disk Utility will tell you what it's doing while it's doing it, and estimate the time the task will take. Feel free to turn your attention elsewhere—the remainder of the process is a hands-free experience.

What's the last step? Seeing if all your hard work paid off! The quick and easy way to check whether everything went as planned is to head to System Preferences→Startup Disk. When you see your newly made drive as an option there (Figure 2-4), you know everything has worked! Now let's hope you never need to use your new bootable installer!

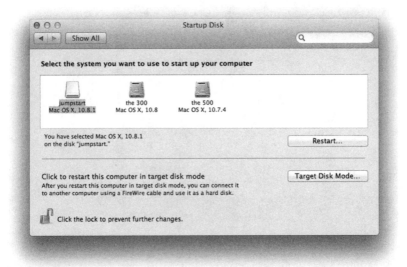

Figure 2-4.
Your new disk is ready to power your Mac on restart. If you look inside it, you'll find the installer and system files you expect.

HACK 09 Resurrect Web Sharing in Mountain Lion

Mountain Lion got rid of one very useful feature: Web Sharing. However, the underlying technology is still there, so you can add that functionality back to Mountain Lion.

You may want to use Web Sharing if you're interested in doing things like hosting a web page (Hack #15). In Mountain Lion, there's no longer a Web Sharing option in System Preferences interface (it's still available in Mountain Lion Server, though), and Apache is disabled by default. (Apache is a full-fledged web server that's part of OS

X). Now that there's no button to click enable Web Sharing, turning it on requires a few more steps.

Note: This hack explains how to bring your Apache web server back to life after a Mountain Lion upgrade. If you want an easy way to run multiple local web-development environments (such as different versions of PHP) and aren't already using Mountain Lion's built-in Apache server, you might want to look into MAMP (http://mamp.info/en/index.html) instead.

First, you need to start Apache. Open a Terminal window and type:

```
sudo apachectl start
```

You'll need to authenticate (that's the **sudo** part: it stands for "super user do" and tells your Mac that you have the power), and you'll probably wonder if you'll have to do this *every* time you log out or shut down. Don't worry—I'll show you how to automate the authentication process in a minute.

If you had a previous setup under an older version of OS X, once you start Apache, you'll probably quickly notice that your virtual hosts aren't working. So let's get them working.

You're going to have to make some changes to the configuration file, and it's best to do that with a text editor. OS X has a few different text editors built in; for this exercise let's use nano in the Terminal. Open the file by typing:

```
sudo nano /private/etc/apache2/httpd.conf
```

Nano will open the file for you in a Terminal-type fashion (Figure 2-5).

Next, uncomment line 477 (very close to the end of the file) by deleting the # at the beginning of the line. When you're done, the line should look like this:

```
Include /private/etc/apache2/extra/httpd-vhosts.conf
```

If you want to use PHP, you need to enable the included PHP 5.3.13. Uncomment line 117, too, so that it reads like so:

```
LoadModule php5_module libexec/apache2/libphp5.so
```

Once you've made those one or two edits, hit Control-O to save the file. Then restart the Apache server by opening a Terminal window and typing:

```
sudo apachectl restart
```

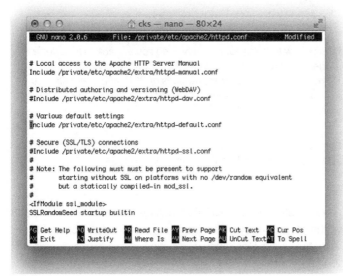

Figure 2-5.
Editing the *httpd.conf* file in the nano editor.

Automating Apache

To make Apache run all the time, you need a way to launch it in the background with root (administrator) permissions. There's more than one way to pull this off. The short script below does it with a launchd daemon. (Launchd is what starts and stops daemons, and daemons are processes that run in the background without your intervention. There's also a way to do it with a single command, but the launchd method is more informative.)

Create a file called *com.brettterpstra.apache.plist* (you can change the `brettterp` `stra` part to whatever you like, but keep the *.plist* filetype) in *~/Library/LaunchDaemons* (create this folder if it's not already there). By default, this folder is owned by the root user and the group "wheel" with permissions 644 and contains the following:

```
<?xml version="1.0" encoding="UTF-8"?>
<!DOCTYPE plist PUBLIC "-//Apple//DTD PLIST 1.0//EN" "http://www.apple.com/
DTDs/PropertyList-1.0.dtd">
<plist version="1.0">
<dict>
    <key>Label</key>
    <string>com.brettterpstra.apache</string>
    <key>ProgramArguments</key>
    <array>
        <string>/usr/sbin/apachectl</string>
```

```
        <string>start</string>
    </array>
    <key>RunAtLoad</key>
    <true/>
  </dict>
</plist>
```

This file has to be owned by root so it can run automatically without authentication. To change the file's owner to root, open a Terminal window, navigate to the directory the file is in, and then type:

```
chown root com.brettterpstra.apache.plist
```

This method of changing the file's owner works and it is pretty cool, but if you are upgraded to Mountain Lion from a previous version of OS X, you might be able to use an even easier method. If you're upgraded there should still be a launchd daemon in your System Library folder that you can simply enable. To do that, open a Terminal window and type:

```
sudo defaults write /System/Library/LaunchDaemons/org.apache.httpd Disabled
-bool false
```

Now apachectl launches by default when your system starts up, without any intervention from you.

—Brett Terpstra

HACK 10 Make Notification Center Less Annoying

A lot of people love Notification Center but many find it too intrusive. This hack teaches you how to fine-tune or even shut down Notification Center.

A Shortcut for Notification Center

One of the big improvements in Mountain Lion was Notification Center. The concept is alluring: all your important updates on the right side of the desktop. But it's odd that Apple didn't include any easy way to get at this new feature that's so integral to Mountain Lion—unless you have a trackpad, that is (in that case, a two-finger swipe from the far left of the pad displays Notification Center).

But even the trackpad method is maddening for two reasons: it leaves out those people who prefer using a mouse (don't the mice-using masses deserve some consideration?), and you have to take your hands off the keyboard to invoke it, which slows you down.

Time to rectify Apple's oversight by adding a keyboard shortcut for Notification Center! Head to System Preferences, open the Keyboard preference pane, and then click

Keyboard Shortcuts. You'll be faced with a longish list of areas where you can change the keyboard shortcuts. You *could* click through the whole list to find what you're looking for, but thanks to your brilliant decision to buy this book, you can skip the "Guess where Apple hid it" game and just click Mission Control in the lefthand column. Once you do, you'll see a blank space in the righthand column where a Notification Center keyboard shortcut would live if only one existed (Figure 2-6). (If you look closely, you'll see that says "none" where a keyboard shortcut for Notification Center would go.)

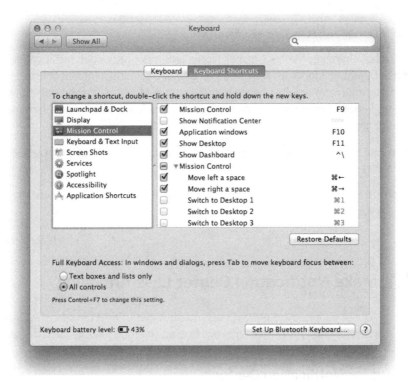

Figure 2-6.
The first unchecked box is where a keyboard shortcut for Notification Center would live—if there were one. You can also change any other keyboard shortcuts while you're here.

Time to add that shortcut! Click the checkbox and an input box will appear so you can type in your preferred shortcut. Sounds easy, right? Maybe not: OS X has lots of shortcuts, and if you choose one that's already taken, you'll get a warning that the shortcut is already in use (Figure 2-7).

Figure 2-7.
You'll have to come up with something unique if you don't want Mountain Lion to be confused.

So what's a good, unique toggle for Notification Center? The best keyboard shortcuts are the ones that somehow remind you of what the shortcut actually does. For example, the keyboard shortcut to cut text is Command-X, and an X kind of looks like a cut or scissors. So what's a good option for Notification Center? Option-? isn't taken and, since you're opening Notification Center because you're wondering what's new, it makes some sense. That's just one possibility, though—any memorable key combo that isn't used already is fine. And if you really want a shortcut that's already taken, you can simply remove the conflict. For example, want to use F12? Uncheck the box next to Show Dashboard and then enter F12 as the shortcut for Show Notification Center!

Make Notification Center Less Intrusive

Now that you've given it a dedicated shortcut, you'll use Notification Center more— and you might end up wanting it to bother you less. How much Notification Center bothers you is fully customizable. You can head to its preference pane (System Preferences→Notification) and remove every app from Notification Center by dragging them to the Not In Notification Center section of the list, as shown in Figure 2-8.

Figure 2-8.
Every single application has been removed from Notification Center so this Mac will be a much less bothersome place.

After removing all the apps from Notification Center, you might think that you're free of it; but if you look to the top right of your screen, you'll note that its weird icon is still stuck there. Even though you've removed apps from the Notification Center, you'll still get an intrusive banner when you get a FaceTime request or an alert for Reminders. Removing an app from Notification Center just removes the app's history. If you want to get rid of banners and alerts altogether, you've got more work to do. Head back to the Notifications preference pane and set each app's alert style to None.

Warning: You might be tempted to uncheck the "Badge app icon" and "Play sound when receiving notifications" settings, too. But if you do that for Mail (to cite one example), you'll no longer see the number of unread messages displayed on the Mail icon in the dock.

You've removed every app and you've turned off every banner and alert. Are you finally rid of notification Center? You can't remove *every* app from the Notification Center: the App Store is too persistent (see Figure 2-9).

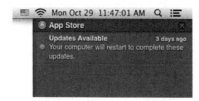

Figure 2-9.
Removing the App Store isn't even an option in the Notifications preference pane. Notification Center just won't die!

Even though you've removed every app and turned off every banner, Notification Center still notifies you. It's maddening. Fortunately, you can shut off *all* notifications by Option-clicking the Notification Center icon. If you've already moved everything out of Notification Center, the Notification Center icon will turn gray. If an app was left in Notification Center or if an app has added itself to Notification Center, you'll get a nifty sliding switch labeled "Show Alerts and Banners" that you can slide to off, as shown in Figure 2-10.

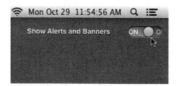

Figure 2-10.
Toggling this slider to Off finally removes all the notifications from Notification Center.

That's a neat trick and you will cease to be notified (but only for a while—as soon as OS X thinks it has something important to tell you, it'll turn Notification Center back on!), but the grayed-out Notification Center icon will still be in the upper-right corner of your screen reminding you it's doing nothing. Do you have to put up with the now useless Notification Center icon cluttering your menu bar? Nope! Keep reading to get rid of it for good.

Truly Killing Notification Center

There are a lot of ways to kill Notification Center from the somewhat obvious but unwise (delete the Notification Center app entirely) to the kludgy (moving the application to somewhere that OS X can't find it) to modifying the app's PLIST file. All of those options work, but the easiest and most elegant way to turn off Notification Center was discovered by an OS X Daily user. Just enter one line in Terminal and Notification Center will disappear, taking its annoying icon with it. The command:

```
launchctl unload -w /System/Library/LaunchAgents/
    com.apple.notificationcenterui.plist
```

If you're a lawyer, it's best not to ask a question in court if you don't know the answer. The same goes for entering commands in Terminal: if you don't have a good idea what a line of code is going to do, you're probably better off not running it. With that in mind, here's a closer look at this command:

- `launchctl` controls launchd (another command-line tool), which (in turn) controls what gets launched—in other words, which programs OS X starts running automatically.

- `unload` tells launchctl not to load the specified file.

- `-w` changes the program from on by default to off so you don't have to type this command every time you start your Mac.

- `/System/Library/LaunchAgents/com.apple.notificationcenterui.plist` is the path to the file that launchctl is going to modify.

Once you're comfortable, type the command into Terminal and hit Return. Now look at the upper-right corner of your screen and you'll see only the Spotlight icon. Notification Center is gone and the icon went with it! You can finally live a Notification Center–free life. When you want Notification Center back, simply run the same command, but change `unload` to `load`. It's that easy!

Hacking the Hack

Perhaps killing Notification Center for all time is a little extreme for you. Maybe you would just like Notification Center to act more like a standard application: running when you want to use it, not running when you don't want to be bothered. Happily, you can get Notification Center to behave in that exact manner. After you've killed Notification Center as described earlier in this hack, go to *Computer→Mac HD→System/Library→CoreServices* and find the Notification Center app. Double-click its icon and Notification Center will spring to life. If you're going to be doing this a lot, you probably won't want to dig all the way to the Core Services folder to turn Notification Center on, so make an alias of the app by Option-clicking its icon in the CoreServices folder and selecting Make Alias. Then move this new alias somewhere easy to get to (you'll need to authenticate) and you'll be able to launch Notification Center with a double-click any time you wish.

Shutting down Notification Center is a bit more problematic. Since Apple never intended you to use Notification Center like a regular app, it doesn't have a quit button. You can't even use the Finder's Force Quit option. But that doesn't mean a trip to the Terminal is necessary (though entering `killall Notification Center` in the Terminal will work)—you can quit Notification Center with Activity Monitor. Just fire up the utility, select Notification Center in the list, and then hit the Quit Process button in the upper left (Figure 2-11).

Figure 2-11.
Quitting programs with Activity Monitor isn't the easiest way to do it, but if the application lacks a quit option, it's one way to stop the app from running.

HACK 11 Quick Hacks for Mountain Lion

Every iteration of OS X introduces some annoyances, and Mountain Lion is no different. This hack explains how to fix the little things that bug you about Mountain Lion.

Make Those Keys Repeat

When you're poking through your Mac's preference panes, you'll stumble on the Keyboard pane, which includes sliders for Key Repeat and Delay Until Repeat. You will, naturally, assume these sliders control the behavior of keys, specifically how fast the keys repeat if you continue holding them.

Turns out that assumption is only partially correct. These sliders do control how fast the keys repeat and so forth, but only for a *few* keys, such as the delete key when your cursor is in a text box. But what if you drop a barbell on your toe and want to type FFFFFFFFFFFFFFFFF by pushing and holding the F key in an angry manner? Try it and you get F. Yep, that's it—one F, hardly enough to tell the world about the pain you're currently feeling. Want to type an assertive "no" as in NNNNNNOOOOOO!!!? Try it and you'll get the pop-up options shown in Figure 2-12.

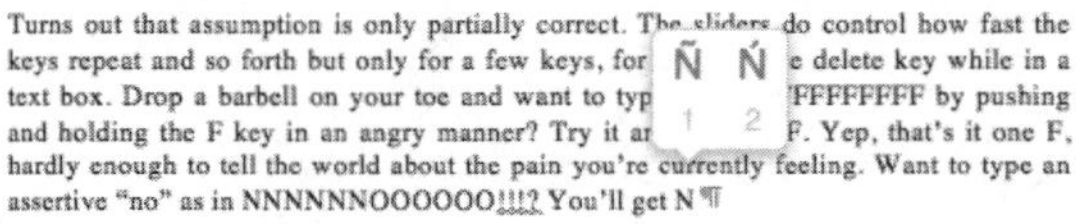

Turns out that assumption is only partially correct. The sliders do control how fast the keys repeat and so forth but only for a few keys, for Ñ Ń e delete key while in a text box. Drop a barbell on your toe and want to typ FFFFFFFF by pushing and holding the F key in an angry manner? Try it ar 1 2 F. Yep, that's it one F, hardly enough to tell the world about the pain you're currently feeling. Want to type an assertive "no" as in NNNNNNOOOOOO!!!? You'll get N ¶

Figure 2-12.
The accented Ns are cool and useful but not what most people expect. Getting your Mac to perform as you expect is a key reason to hack it!

That's right—as part of the system-wide Autocorrect feature first seen in Lion, you can't use repeating out of the box. Time for you to be the boss. Type the following command into Terminal to get your repeating keys back:

```
defaults write -g ApplePressAndHoldEnabled -bool false
```

Then restart your Mac and you'll be able to hold any key and watch the letter repeat. As you can probably guess, you can turn the nonrepeating keys behavior back on by entering that command again, but replace the word `false` with `true`.

Turn Off Autocorrect

Sure, nonrepeating keys are annoying, but not as vexing as Autocorrect is to most folks. In trying to make OS X more iOS-ish, Apple added an autocorrect feature that automatically replaces words with what OS X feels is the correct choice. This isn't always (or even usually) the case.

To get rid of this unwanted behavior, head to the Language & Text preference pane, click the Text button, and then uncheck "Correct spelling automatically" as shown in Figure 2-13.

Reveal Your Library Folder

Starting with OS X Lion, the Library folder for your user account disappeared. It still existed, you just couldn't see it anymore. This is kind of a shame because there are a lot of times that dedicated Mac users want to poke around in the Library folder. Fortunately, it's easy to get to: open the Finder's Go menu and then hold the Option key, and the Library folder shows up as an option. (The world owes Dawn Mann a big thank you for discovering that trick.)

But with that method, you have to remember to press the Option key each time you want to access that folder. What you may want is a way to *permanently* show the Library folder. No problem! Fire up Terminal and type:

```
chflags nohidden ~/library/
```

Hit Return and your Library is revealed (Figure 2-14)!

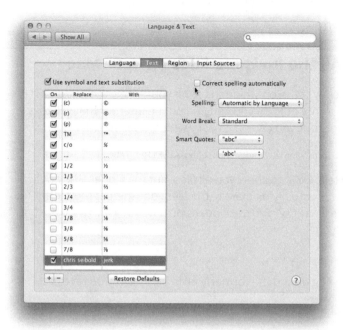

Figure 2-13.
Turning off the annoying Autocorrect. Since you're here, you can also add text substitutions by clicking the + in the pane's lower left and then typing in your substitution.

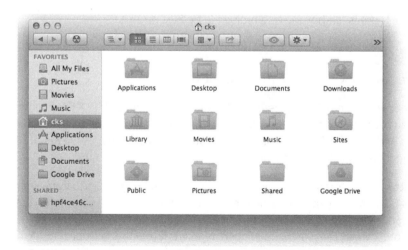

Figure 2-14.
The glorious return of your Library folder. Now you can easily delete corrupt preferences and such.

Want to hide your Library folder again? Undo the previous command with this:

```
chflags hidden ~/library/
```

See All the Invisible Files on Your Mac

The Library folder isn't the only hidden file on your Mac—there are tons of them. There are plenty of apps you can find on the Internet that will toggle this setting for you, but you can do it easily with the Terminal by typing:

```
defaults write com.apple.Finder AppleShowAllFiles True
```

That command tells OS X to show you all files, but the Finder (the application responsible for actually displaying the files) doesn't get the memo. To actually make the files appear in the Finder, you have to restart it. To do that, in the Terminal Type:

```
killall Finder
```

This restarts the Finder and the formerly invisible files will be revealed.

To hide them again (if you decide they add too much clutter), launch Terminal and type:

```
defaults write com.apple.Finder AppleShowAllFile False
```

Followed by (you guessed it):

```
killall Finder
```

That's all there is to showing and hiding *all* the files in OS X.

Get Save As Back the Way You Expect It

In Lion, the Save As command was replaced by Duplicate in standard OS X File menus. Save As had been around forever, and some programs (like Word) relied on their own File menus and kept the Save As option. It was all so confusing that Apple restored Save As functionality in Mountain Lion.

Unfortunately, the restored Save As feature isn't the Save As you're used to from older versions of OS X. You invoke it with a different keyboard shortcut than you used in the old days (Shift-Command-S now invokes the Duplicate command instead) or by pressing Option when the File menu is open. If you're fine with the Duplicate functionality or jumping through the extra hoop required to invoke Save As, then you can stop reading. But if you, like millions of others, want your classic Save As functionality back, time to head to the Keyboard preference pane.

Once there, click the Keyboard Shortcuts button and prepare to get your Save As back! Select Application Shortcuts in the left column and then choose All Applications in the right column. This is where Apple lets you create custom keyboard shortcuts that work in *all* your apps.

You can't use the old keyboard shortcut for Save As (Shift-Command-S) because that shortcut is being used by Duplicate. To free up that shortcut for Save As, you first need to give Duplicate a different shortcut. To do that, click the + button and then type **Duplicate** (spelling counts) into the Menu Title field. Finally, type your preferred shortcut into the Keyboard Shortcut field (Figure 2-15) and then click Add.

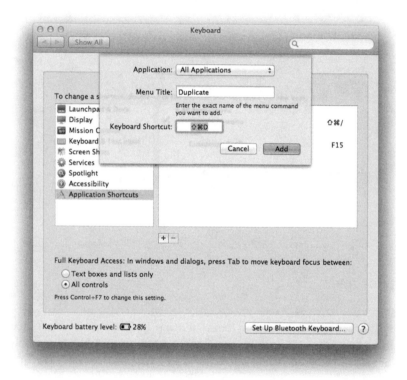

Figure 2-15.
Replacing the keyboard shortcut for Duplicate. If you're ambitious, you can come up with any number of useful keyboard shortcuts for your Mac using this technique.

Since Duplicate is no longer using Shift-Command-S, that combination is free for us to use as the Save As shortcut, just like the old days! To assign that shortcut to Save As, simply click the + button, type **Save As...** (*with* the ellipsis) into the Menu Title box and then set the keyboard shortcut to Shift-Command-S. Finally, click the Add button and you're done! Figure 2-16 shows the command looking right at home in its usual place.

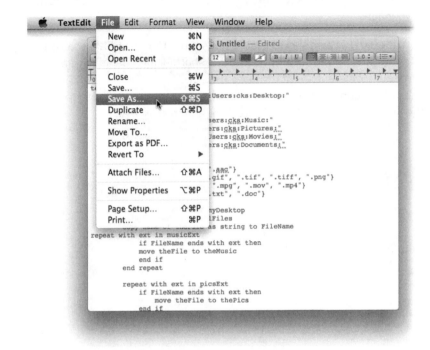

Figure 2-16.
The return of Save As—in its proper place and with the keyboard shortcut we expect!

Turn Off Resume

Resume doesn't bother everyone—just those of us who occasionally turn off our computers. The idea behind Resume is that all the apps that you were using reopen when you restart your Mac. Seems like a great idea—when you reboot, your computer will automatically be restored to right where you left off. What's not to like about that?

The problem is that OS X is really good at multitasking, so a lot of people rarely bother to quit the apps they're using; they just switch to the next app they need. That means that when they shut down their Macs, the next time they hit the power button, they'll have to wait. Why? Because OS X has to launch all fifty apps they were using when they shut the Mac down. But they don't want to *use* all fifty apps right then—they just want to jump on their web browser and get their morning news.

You can stop your Mac from opening all the apps you had open when you quit using your Mac by heading to System Preferences and selecting General. Once there, check the box next to "Close windows when quitting an application." Once you do that,

Resume will be turned off globally and your Mac will start with a clean slate—it won't launch every app you had open when you shut it down!

If you still want to use Resume's saved state feature on an individual basis (sometimes the feature is cool), hold the Option key when you quit an application and you'll see that Quit [application name] will be replaced with "Quit and Keep Windows." (Shift-Command-Q). Select that option, as in Figure 2-17, and when you launch that app anew, the windows will be exactly as they were when you last used the app!

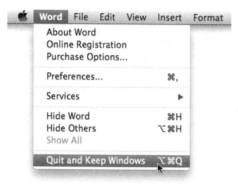

Figure 2-17.
All the benefits of Resume, none of the annoyances. Though remembering to hold the Option key does take some getting used to.

HACK 12 A Clean Install of Mountain Lion

Many Mac folks prefer to install their new version of OS X onto a freshly formatted blank drive. Learn how to pull off a clean install with Mountain Lion.

In the olden days of OS X, when it was called "Mac OS X," you installed new versions from physical media (DVDs and CDs). It seems archaic now but that was how it was until broadband became ubiquitous. There's nothing to miss about the old days of shiny disks that would spin forever while updating your Mac, right? Turns out the DVD that the latest version of OS X lacks *did* have one advantage that people really seem to miss: the clean install.

A clean install is exactly what it sounds like: a fresh install of Mountain Lion that installs only Mountain Lion and nothing else. Why would this be beneficial? Some folks want to start with a new, untouched system and build from there, transferring only the necessary files from their old machines. Others strongly feel that you get better performance and a more reliable system if OS X is newly installed instead of just upgraded.

Whatever your reason for wanting a clean install, this hack will help you get it done. But before you jump on in and start the process, you'll want to take some precautions. Creating a clean install is a *destructive* process, and data is guaranteed to be destroyed. So if you want to save that data, the first thing you need to do is make sure you have a really nice backup. You can clone your drive, using Time Machine or some other scheme, but if you ever want to see your data again, you need to duplicate it somewhere. (See Hack #01 for the how-to.)

This a good time to make sure your backup has all the files you want to save already duplicated. Many programs (including Time Machine) allow you to exclude files and folders from the backup to save space. If you want those files back, you need to make sure they're included in your backup. This isn't a case of "Oh gee, something might happen in the future"; it's "You're about to erase your drive—the future is now." So double check to make sure *everything* you want backed up *is* backed up.

Performing the Clean Install

Once your backup is all set, you're ready to get down to business. The Mountain Lion clean install is wonderfully simple in theory (erase drive, install Mountain Lion), but slightly horrifying in reality (erase gigabytes of data). The process is also a little frustrating in implementation. What was once as easy as popping in a disk and waiting a few minutes (or hours) has become a time sink full of hoops to jump through—if you only have one Mac, that is.

Clean Install with Two Macs

If you have *multiple* Macs lying about, the process is simple:

1. Obtain Mountain Lion Installer.
2. Boot Mac from secondary drive or start Mac in Target Disk Mode (attach Macs with FireWire or Thunderbolt cable and then hold T while starting the Mac you want to install OS X on).
3. Erase disk of Mac that you intend to install OS X on.
4. Install fresh copy of Mountain Lion.

Clean Install with One Mac

That 4-step process is also the *basic* plan if you only have one Mac and one startup disk; you just have to perform a few additional steps before performing the steps listed above (and you'll use the startup disk in place of the secondary Mac). To get started, download a copy of the Mountain Lion installer from the App Store, and then create a bootable copy of the installer as explained in Hack #02.

The next step depends on what version of OS X you are currently running. If your Mac is running Lion or Mountain Lion, restart your Mac while holding down the Option key; this boots you into Recovery Mode. Choose the bootable installer drive you made earlier to boot your Mac. Once your Mac is running, select Disk Utility from the startup screen and then click the Continue button. Once you're in Disk Utility, choose the Erase option and select the disk you want to erase. Choose either Mac OS Extended (Journaled) or Mac OS Extended (Journaled, encrypted) as the format, name the disk and then, optionally, select Security options. Finally, click Erase, and when your Mac asks if you're *sure*, click Erase again. That's it—the hard drive data is gone!

Note: You don't have to use a bootable installer if you don't have one. That's just a timesaving step. You can choose to reinstall OS X using only the recovery partition, but prepare to invest some time—the download for the new software is over 4 GBs.

If you have a Mac running Snow Leopard, you don't have Recovery Mode, so you'll need to devise some other way to boot your Mac. If you have the disks that shipped with your Mac, you can use those to boot your Mac and erase the hard drive. If that isn't an option, download, copy, and install Mountain Lion. Then follow the instructions given for a Mac with Mountain Lion already installed.

Once your targeted drive is erased you can quit Disk Utility and select Install OS X. The installer will install Mountain Lion onto a blank slate and you'll have that clean install/freshly formatted disk experience you've been craving. Once that's done, you can restore from the backup you created earlier or start the journey into Mac Land anew.

3

Customize Your OS X Experience

Your experience when you're using your Mac is what makes the experience worthwhile. But if you're constantly being bombarded by stuff like Flash-based video ads for autopsy TV shows (ugh), your experience is hampered. If you can blog more effectively, your experience is enhanced. Why not take a few minutes and make your experience the most it can be while sitting in front of your Mac? After all, a more comfortable you is probably a happier, more productive version of you.

HACK 13   Tame Your Browsers

> Get more out of your day-to-day browsing by controlling Flash, re-enabling RSS, and accessing your bookmarks from anywhere.

Since there are tons of extensions available for the three big browsers—Safari, Chrome, and Firefox—we could write an entire book *just* about extensions and probably still not make a dent. Instead, I'd rather focus on adding some things the browser makers left out, as well as tweaking some of the little things that can make a big difference in your browsing workflow, starting with Flash.

The Road to Flash-less Happiness

Chances are, Safari has crashed on you more than once and your MacBook has gotten hot enough to cook dinner on it. I'll bet good money that if you check your crash logs, Flash would often be the culprit.

Adobe's multimedia player has become the bane of the Web's existence, and Apple knows it: Apple banned Flash from the iPhone and iPad. In addition, Adobe recently gave up on developing Flash for the entire mobile industry. If you're ready to give up Flash on your Mac, there are a couple of simple steps you can try.

Disable Flash

Your first step to Flash freedom is a Safari plug-in called ClickToFlash. This is a nice middle ground between leaving Flash enabled in Safari all the time (as it is by default) and uninstalling Flash completely (more on that in a minute). Once you install Click-ToFlash, when you use Safari to visit a page with a Flash-based ad, video, game, or interactive presentation, that item will be hidden and replaced with a graphic that simply says "Flash." The actual Flash plug-in won't be loaded and the multimedia ad (or whatever) won't run until you deliberately click the Flash banner (hence the plug-in's name).

You can get the plug-in from *Marc Hoyois' GitHub page (http://hoyois.github.com/ safariextensions/clicktoplugin)*. Install it like most other plug-ins: click to download it, click the "Show downloads" button to the right of Safari's address bar, double-click the ClickToFlash download, and you should be good to go. Once you install it, the plug-in's preferences appear in Safari (Figure 3-1).

Figure 3-1.
ClickToFlash's preferences show up as a web page. This not only lets you fine-tune the plug-in to your liking, it also verifies that it was installed correctly.

Uninstall Flash

A lot of people like ClickToFlash because it helps you avoid some of Flash's worst troubles—frequent crashes, overheated MacBooks, and batteries that drain in just an hour or two. But if you're like me and you long for a day when Flash is simply no longer part of the Web, you may want to take the next step and completely uninstall Flash.

One downside to ClickToFlash is that, even if you have it installed, Safari still tells websites that you have Flash installed. That lets many websites fall back on the "if it ain't broke, don't fix it" approach, which means they'll try to serve up the same old Flash-based content (instead of HTML5, which mobile devices need and the web increasingly prefers) even though you're only using Flash on a case-by-case basis. An increasing number of websites offer non-Flash media for devices that truly don't have it, like the iPhone and iPad. But plenty still take a Flash-first approach, and too many are still Flash-only.

If you *really* want to be rid of Flash in Safari, your best option is to just uninstall it. There will still be a way to use Flash (more on that in a minute) if you truly need it for, say, a work-related website or a video site that refuses to modernize.

To uninstall Flash, visit *Adobe's Uninstall Flash Player page* (*http://helpx.adobe.com/flash-player/kb/uninstall-flash-player-mac-os.html*), which has download links for a couple different uninstallers, based on the version of OS X that you have. Follow the instructions on that page.

Toward the end of the uninstall process, you'll need to delete some Flash files from both your main OS X Library folder, as well as your home user Library folder (*~/Library*). As you probably know, Apple decided to hide the home user Library folder starting in OS X Lion. To get there, switch to the Finder, open the Go menu, and then press the Option key. A Library option will appear in the middle of the menu; click it to get to your home user Library folder and delete the files in Adobe's instructions.

> *Note: In OS X, the tilde (~) is a shorthand for your Home directory. So, for example, instead of typing* Computer/Users/CKS/Home/Library, *you can just type* ~/Library.

Once you're finished, head to *Adobe help* (*http://kb2.adobe.com/cps/155/tn_15507.html*) to confirm that Flash is gone.

Trick sites into not needing Flash

Earlier I mentioned that an increasing number of sites now serve you non-Flash content when they know you don't have it installed. Most of the time, they're great at doing this on mobile devices, but some sites drop the ball on Macs. To make a long story short, when some sites see your browser agent is that of a desktop or notebook computer, they just assume that you have Flash and don't bother to offer anything else.

You probably won't run into this very often, but if you encounter one of these stubborn sites, you don't have to reinstall Flash to view the content you're after. You can just enable Safari's Develop menu: Go to Safari→Preferences, click the Advanced tab, and then turn on "Show develop menu in menu bar" checkbox. When you do that, the Develop menu appears between the Bookmarks and Windows menus.

Along with various tools developers can use to test their websites, the Develop menu includes a User Agent option that lets Safari masquerade as Firefox, Chrome, Internet Explorer, or even Opera. For our purposes, the most important options in the User Agent submenu start with "Safari iOS." When you select one of these options, you can make web servers think that you're using the iOS version of Safari. I recommend choosing the iPad option because most sites serve a desktop-friendly version—including multimedia—to iPads, but a much more compact site to iPhones and iPods that usually doesn't work as well on a Mac.

Now, when you happen to stumble onto a site that complains Safari doesn't have Flash, simply head to Develop→User Agent→"Safari iOS *version #* – iPad." The page will reload and, in most cases, display the media you came to see. Fortunately, flipping that User Agent switch is temporary; it only works for that window or tab, and only for this visit. Your other tabs will still report like and behave like the desktop version of Safari, so you won't have to keep running to the Develop menu to toggle the User Agent back and forth.

Open Safari Pages in Chrome

OK, maybe you don't need Flash for 99% of the things you do on a daily, monthly, and yearly even basis. But maybe you really *do* need Flash for that one website that won't modernize and doesn't serve non-Flash content or tools. I've seen this happen with niche web stores and even massive sites. For example, even though Facebook plays videos just fine on iPad (videos that users upload or share from YouTube), it won't serve non-Flash versions of these same videos to desktop browsers *even if* you change your User Agent. My entire house of non-Flash cards has come tumbling down...or has it?

It never hurts to keep a second browser around for testing or simply for a rainy day, and these cases where Flash is an absolute necessity certainly qualify as rainy days. I haven't run into them myself in my years of having Flash uninstalled, but I know people have, so here's a two-step solution to let you view those rare Flash-requiring videos without having Flash installed for Safari and the rest of your Mac.

If you don't have it already, the first step is to install *Google Chrome* (*http://www.chrome.com*). It's a great browser from Google that just happens to also pack its own copy of Flash. After that, if you don't have Flash installed for Safari but you need to view a site that includes Flash, you can simply copy and paste it's URL over to Chrome.

But who wants to do all that manual copying and pasting? Not *Mac Hacks* readers, I'm sure. Plenty of other people feel the same way and have already figured out better ways of sending the current Safari page over to Chrome for their Flash needs. One of them is T.J. Luoma at TUAW, and he wrote *an AppleScript* (*http://aol.it/efjQO6*) that you can use in any number of ways.

The AppleScript is simple: it takes the current Safari window or tab, opens Chrome (if it's not running), and then opens that page in a new Chrome tab. You can plug this script into a utility like FastScripts or any Mac productivity utility like Alfred, Launch-Bar, or Quicksilver. Whether you give it a keyboard shortcut or just search for it on those rare occasions you need it, T.J.'s AppleScript should make it easier to live the (mostly) Flash-less dream.

All Your Bookmarks Everywhere

Every browser these days offers a way to sync your bookmarks with most (or all) of your other devices. Apple has iCloud for your Mac and iOS devices, Firefox has its native sync for traditional computers and its Android version, and Google Chrome syncs with other computers as long as you're signed into your Google account. But what if you use multiple browsers and want your bookmarks to leave their own ecosystems and come along for the ride? That's where Xmarks can come in.

Xmarks (*http://www.xmarks.com*) is a plug-in and service that syncs your bookmarks and even your open tabs across multiple browsers and devices. On Macs, the free version of Xmarks supports Safari, Chrome, and Firefox; on PCs, it supports those same browsers and tosses Internet Explorer in for good measure. If you also want to get to your bookmarks on your mobile devices and sync your open tabs—including iPhone, Android, Dolphin HD browser for Android, and even BlackBerry—Xmarks can do that for just $12 per year.

Help Safari Get its RSS Groove Back

In 2012, Apple released Safari 6 with Mountain Lion. The browser gained some great new features, but it also lost one that left many users high and dry: support for RSS. (Apple actually yanked RSS support from OS X Mountain Lion entirely, including Mail.) So when you click RSS links in Safari 6, the program won't even show a feed preview anymore, let alone offer reading or bookmarking tools; it just kicks you over to your RSS client, assuming you've installed one. But plenty of sites don't display RSS subscription links of any kind because most browsers, including earlier versions of Safari, notified you in some way that a feed is available.

To make Safari 6 display an RSS button when RSS content is available, you can try Daniel Jalkut's *Subscribe to Feed extension* (*http://bit.ly/OH2pGA*). This is one of those single-purpose extensions that can be a big help. It installs a button in Safari's toolbar with the typical "pie slice" RSS icon. You can tell whether a site has a feed because this button stays grayed out when you're on a feed-free site, and turns a darker gray when you're on sites with feeds. When you find a site that has a feed but no feed link, and assuming you have an RSS feed reader installed like Reeder or NetNewsWire, clicking the Subscribe to Feed button will automatically find the site's feed and open your RSS app so you can do as you please with the feed.

Safari Reading List

The last Safari trick I have time for involves Safari Reader. Sure, it's a good way to strip all the fluff out of a website to read the content you're really there for. It's also a decent on-the-spot alternative to popular "read later" services like Instapaper and Pocket. But if you print out articles and other web pages for archiving or old-school sharing around the office, Safari Reader is a great way to get picture-perfect, cruft-less prints.

To print from Safari Reader view, simply trigger it on a webpage (View→Show Reader). Reader view slides in front and center, and if you mouse over it, a set of controls appears at the bottom of the window. Click the printer icon to display the typical print dialog box with a preview of what you're about to print. Adjust the settings to your liking, and then click Print.

If you compare that view to what you will typically get on most web pages by hitting Command-P *without* getting Safari Reader involved, I think you'll be pleasantly surprised. Apple's standard print dialog box does an OK job of stripping out web page cruft on some pages, but it seems like they put more of that ability into Reader, since cutting out cruft is its entire reason for its existence. It's a great way to print just what you need from a web page.

—David Chartier

HACK 14   Blog with Your Mac

> Blogging is simply a task like any other that's performed with tools, and the Mac offers some of the best tools around. This hack helps you set up a blog and recommends some tips and tricks for making blogging effortless.

Blogging is great. You find something you know, write about it, and with any luck, get to meet and learn from other people all over the world who are into the same things you are. Social media is similar, but with blogging you can own the experience—it's your site, your presentation, your rules. Not everyone will be the next Dooce, Penny Arcade, or Daring Fireball. But with any luck it'll be fun, and with a little more luck and some hard work, it could turn into a real thing—perhaps one that even makes (a little) money.

Before you start turning down sponsorship opportunities, though, you have to take the first step, which is to *start a blog*. But how do you do that? What do you write about? How long or short should your posts be? What service should you use? What should your first post be about? I'm glad you asked.

Step 1: Why Are You Here?

Before you start focusing on the trees, the best thing to do before you start a blog is to step back and think about the forest. *Why* do you want to start a blog, and what do you want to write about? Food? Technology? Politics? You might need to sit down to hear this, but there are probably one or two...thousand blogs out there already that have those topics covered. Dig a little deeper—what *about* food, technology, or politics will get your inner writer out of bed in the morning?

Think about a couple topics you care about and what makes your connection to—and experience with—them unique. Are you a high school cook who's neck deep in the health and culture fight over the food we feed our kids? Are you an IT admin who has watched your bosses beat down doors to alter policies and allow Apple products into the company? Are you in the middle of a career in politics and can't stand the way American media outlets bungle coverage of current events? *Now we're getting somewhere!*

Spend some time thinking about how you, your ideas, and your experiences can make your blog more useful than a garden variety Wikipedia article so it stands out from the crowd.

Step 2: Get Set Up

Now that you have an idea of what you want to say, it's time to start gathering tools. Of course, the first thing you'll need is the actual blog itself, and there are way too many options to cover in this hack, so I'm just going to cover a couple of possibilities.

Of the myriad options available, Tumblr and WordPress are my favorites, so I'll focus on those. Here's my elevator pitch so you can choose which one to try (or you can do both; they're free to sign up for and use in a basic form): I love Tumblr because it strips away all the fat, it's just flexible enough in the right ways, and it's surprisingly stylish. WordPress is great because it's incredibly powerful and has a bit of that "everything to everyone" aspect like Microsoft Office and Adobe Photoshop, but without quite as much pain and nights lying awake crying.

If you choose Tumblr, here are the basic steps:

1. Go to *the Tumblr home page* (*http://tumblr.com*) and click Sign Up.

2. Enter your email, create a password, and pick a username (you can change it later).

3. Respond to the various prompts, type in the captcha, and pick a few topics you like to help find some popular users to follow.

4. When you get to the Dashboard, sit back and enjoy a sense of accomplishment.

Now it's WordPress's turn:

1. Go to *the WordPress home page* (*http://wordpress.com*) and click Get Started.

2. Enter your email address, password, username, and a blog address (like *super-blog.wordpress.com*), and then click Create Blog.

3. Check your email and click the Activate Blog button in the verification email WordPress sent so you can get into your new blog.

4. Once you click that verification link, sit back and enjoy a sense of accomplishment.

Note that neither of these processes required you to come up with a title for your new blog. Both sites kinda handle that for you as you get started, and you can then change it later once you find your voice. Smart, ay?

Step 3: Start Blogging

OK, you have a blog. Now what? Gosh, you're just asking all the right questions. But this is the part where I need to ask you a few questions, because there are a lot of factors here that depend on you and your circumstances.

Like many things in life, you get out of blogging what you put in. Even if you decided on the nichiest niche topics in Step 1, there's undoubtedly an audience waiting for you. But how much time, realistically, can you afford to put into your blog? Does your day job or the classes you're taking afford some flexibility to fire off a couple posts every day, or can you only squeeze in a little time once in a blue moon after the kids are in bed? Do you want to write pithy posts that are easy to create like BuzzFeed and Daring Fireball's Linked List, or do you not get out of bed for anything less than 1,000 hand-crafted, slaved-over words?

What you write, how you write, and how much you write is entirely up to you. If your audience likes it, they'll turn into repeat customers and, perhaps with a little prodding (remember: a *little*), invite their friends to swing by.

But to give people a reason to swing by in the first place, a good idea for your first post is to state your name and what you hope to accomplish. There is certainly a place for posts that are 1,000+ words, but keep this one short and sweet—no more than 2–4 paragraphs. Toss in a sentence or three about your experience with or sheer interest in the topics you want to write about to help people learn about you and your angle. "I love technology" doesn't really turn heads these days; millions of people love technology. "I work in a hospital and I'm insanely interested in the different ways mobile devices are changing the lives of handicapped people" is getting somewhere.

Step 4: Make Blogging Easier

One of the most important ways to remove friction from any task, especially blogging, is to have the right tools. The full range of blogging tools is beyond the scope of this hack, but I can at least point you in the right direction.

Get a bookmarklet

Both Tumblr and WordPress let you create new posts via their websites, but they also offer *bookmarklets* that make blogging even easier. Bookmarklets are similar to the other links you place in your browser's bookmarks bar for quick access, but instead of taking you to a website, a bookmarklet is a tool that lets you *do* something. In the case of Tumblr and WordPress, their bookmarklets open a new window containing a post editor—it's perfect for that moment of inspiration or for writing about something you found on the Web.

> Note: Make sure your browser's bookmarks bar is displayed before you install a bookmarklet. If you don't see a bookmarks bar below your browser's address bar, check the View menu for an option like "Show bookmarks bar."

To get Tumblr's bookmarklet:

1. At *Tumblr* (*http://tumblr.com*), click the settings icon (it looks like a gear).
2. At the *bottom* of the settings page (*not* on the left side), click Apps. (The link in the left toolbar is for something else.)
3. Drag the big "Share on Tumblr" button to your browser's bookmarks bar. (If you don't see a bookmarks bar below the address bar, check your browser's View menu for an option like "Show bookmarks bar.")

Voilà—you're ready for some on-the-go blogging. Now, when you find an article, a Flickr photo, a YouTube video, or virtually anything you want to share or write about, just click the "Share on Tumblr" button in your bookmarks bar, and a small Tumblr post window will open to let you get down to business. Since Tumblr lets you create different types of posts based on the content you want to highlight—a photo or gallery post, a quote post, a link post, and so on—the posting interface might change slightly to offer you (and eventually your readers) the best experience. If you select some text on the page before clicking the "Share on Tumblr" button, it will be included in the post as a quote with a proper source. When you're finished adding your thoughts to the post, click the "Create post" button and you're done. Pretty easy, huh?

To get WordPress's bookmarklet:

1. At *WordPress* (*http://wordpress.com*), click the My Blog tab.
2. Under the name of your blog, click the Dashboard link.
3. On the left side of your dashboard, click Tools.
4. Drag the Press This button to your bookmarks bar. A new Press This button appears on your bookmarks bar, with the text of the button's name selected so you can change it to something more meaningful (*WordPress*, perhaps).

Now you're all set up to blog with WordPress as you surf the Web. If you find a page you'd like to blog about or you just have some thoughts to get out of your head, click the bookmarklet to open a new window with most of WordPress's bare necessities, including a place to enter your post's title and to assign it categories and tags.

Now you're ready to blog on a moment's notice, or just jot down some ideas and save a draft until you can flesh it out later. But if you want to *really* step up your game, it's time to check out MarsEdit.

Get the full Mac blogging experience with MarsEdit

Now, blogging in a browser is fun and all, but you're a Mac user, so you deserve a Mac experience. To get it, I recommend MarsEdit (Figure 3-2), a reputable, well-designed, and feature-full Mac blogging client that supports Tumblr and WordPress, as well as a variety of other blogging sites. It's probably the best money you can spend towards blogging. You can download a *free trial* (*http://www.red-sweater.com/marsedit*), and if you like it, it'll set you back $40 to buy it.

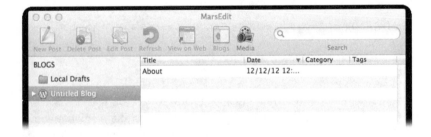

Figure 3-2.
MarsEdit may not look like much, but it's got lots of powerful features.

MarsEdit brings some great stuff to blogging on the Mac, from deeper support for OS X features like the Services menu, a learning dictionary, and keyboard shortcuts that let you write faster, to Flickr integration and the simple luxury of saving drafts of your posts locally and working offline. While I could probably write a whole chapter in this book on stuff you can do with MarsEdit, I'll just get you started.

Turns out, MarsEdit has its own bookmarklet that works quite a bit like the Tumblr and WordPress bookmarklets you just learned about. Launch MarsEdit, and then click MarsEdit→Install Browser Bookmarklet. MarsEdit launches your default browser, where you simply drag the "Send to MarsEdit" link to your bookmarks bar. You now have quick, one-click access to writing about the current web page in a full-featured, Mac-native blogging client. Even better, if you select any text on the page, it'll be included as a quote, complete with a properly cited source, in the MarsEdit post window that opens.

As I mentioned earlier, one of MarsEdit's many handy tricks is its ability to make your Flickr account a source for adding photos to your posts. To do that, launch MarsEdit, click the Media button in the toolbar, and then the Flickr tab. On that tab, you can endow MarsEdit with your Flickr account's superpowers to make it dead simple to add your photos to your blog posts. Whenever you need one, just click the Media button in a new post window, go to your Flickr account, and drag the photo over. It's a great way to make use of your photographic prowess on your blog.

Finder: The Mac Blogger's Secret Weapon

OS X offers a great way to get your photos and videos from iPhoto or Aperture, and even music from iTunes, into your blog posts no matter what browser, service, or app you're using. It's actually a pretty simple, understated convenience of OS X's Finder.

If you're writing a post in Tumblr or WordPress and click whatever button lets you add a photo, video, or audio track to your post, look carefully at the "choose a file" dialog box that opens in your browser. In the left sidebar, scroll down to the very bottom where you should see a Media section with three subsections: Music, Photos, Movies. Click those subsections and you'll see entries in the main area of the dialog box that give you access to your iPhoto, Aperture, and iTunes libraries, complete with a small search box (Figure 3-3).

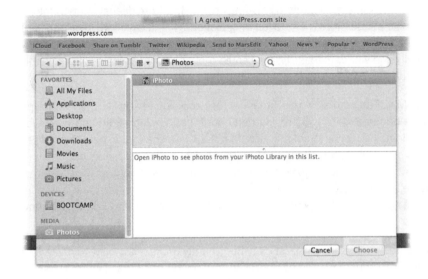

Figure 3-3.
This window is your ticket to easily finding any media on your machine so you can include it in a blog post.

You can browse through your iPhoto events and albums, Aperture projects, and iTunes playlists to find the media you want to upload. (Just be sure that you're uploading media you created yourself or for which you obtained express permission from the creator.) If you've added your Flickr or Facebook accounts to iPhoto or Aperture, you can even access those collections from this dialog box.

However and whatever you decide to blog, the important thing is to find a workflow and service that fits you. When you remove friction from the process, the only things left to worry about are your words, pictures, and so on—which is exactly how it should be.

—David Chartier

HACK 15   Host a Web Page on Your Mac (and Get at Your Files Anytime)

The biggest trick to hosting a web page on your Mac isn't the software or the content—it's being able to tell people how to *get* to the webpage. Take away that hassle with this supremely useful hack.

Twitter, Facebook, and other social media sites are great, but sometimes you want to go over their character limit or burst out of their confines. There are situations where you want to be the boss, where you want total control. On those days, you want to publish your own web page! For times like those, you need a static IP address.

Imagine, for example, you have a friend with a quirky sense of humor. Further, imagine you draw a weird cartoon on a nightly basis that you want to share with him. You *could* clog up your Twitter feed by posting a link to the imgur location of the 'toon, but some of your other followers might not appreciate your masterpiece. Or you could simply email it to him, but that seems like a lot of effort for one guy. Why not just have him check a page you host on your Mac? He'll get cracked up and no one will be the wiser.

Let's get started.

Do You Have the Bandwidth?

First, check you Internet connection. This hack relies on your Mac sending information out and, for most home Internet connections, the upstream bandwidth is a lot less than the downstream bandwidth. Which means that, while your Mac might not have any trouble streaming three online HD movies at once, uploading a web page might be a little too much for your Mac to handle. Head to *Speakeasy* (*http://www.speakeasy.net/speedtest*) to test your upload speed (Figure 3-4).

Figure 3-4.
Expect a large inequality between upload and download speed. Why the difference? Consumers don't often judge ISPs by their upload speeds.

In this test case, the upload speed was 1.95 Mbps. The question now becomes, is that enough to satisfy the uploading needs of this hack? It is if you make a small web page and have a moderate number of visitors. In this example, the extremely simple web page (covered later in this hack) clocks in at 43 Kb. So in the best-case scenario, the host Mac could conceivably serve 46 (1.95 Mbps/43 Kb ≈ 46) pages per second. (Actually, that estimate is too high because it leaves no bandwidth left over for browsing, but it also tells us that serving up the occasional page shouldn't be a problem.)

> *Warning: Check with your ISP to make sure hosting a web page from your Mac is allowed under their terms of service. They'd probably never notice if you kept everything small-time, but better safe than sorry, right?*

Make a Web Page

You can only host a web page on your Mac if you have something to host. So let's make something! In this hack, we'll use *KompoZer* (*http://www.kompozer.net*), a good, free WYSIWYG HTML editor, but feel free to use whatever you're comfortable with.

Here's the code for our super-simple web page (shown in Figure 3-5):

```
<html>
<head>
<meta content="text/html; charset=ISO-8859-1"
http-equiv="content-type">
<title>Toon of the moment</title>
</head>
<body>
Toon of the day:<br>
<img style="width: 278px; height: 370px;" alt="Vol's Christmas Present"
src="file:///Users/cks/Desktop/Untitled-3.gif"><br>
</body>
</html>
```

When you're serving web pages from your Mac at least one of them has to be called *index.html*. Since this example only uses one page, guess what that page is going to be named? (See Figure 3-6 for the answer.)

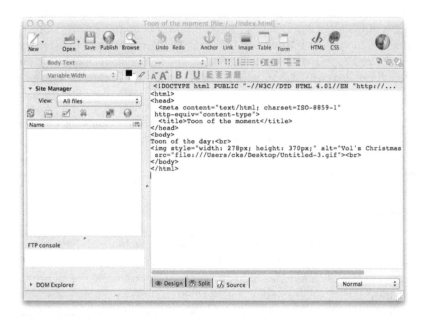

Figure 3-5.
The code for this basic web page in KompoZer.

Figure 3-6.
Saving the web page with the proper name (*index.html*) and in the proper location (your Sites folder). These are choices that matter, so be careful!

You're almost done, all you have to do now is tell your Mac to share your web page. In older versions of OS X (Lion and earlier) you can simply head to System Preferences→Sharing and then check the box next to Web Sharing; your Mac will then tell you where users on your local network can reach your site. In Mountain Lion, things are trickier. How tricky, you ask? Tricky enough to get their own hack! See Hack #09 for details.

Once you enable personal web sharing, you're done. Anyone on your local network can navigate to your computer and see the site you made. This is useful for an office or home network, but we want more from this hack—we want folks across town or across the country to see the web page!

Fake a Static IP

The reason that outsiders can't see your web page is because there isn't any way to tell them how to get to it. In the wider world, this isn't a problem because of *domain name servers* and *static IP addresses*. Domain name servers translate the name of a website into the proper IP address. For example, when you type www.google.com into your browser, a domain name server changes that address into computer-friendly numbers that match up with the range of IP addresses that Google has reserved. Unfortunately, you probably don't have a static IP (but if you do, you're finished with this hack!).

As you probably know, *IP* stands for Internet Protocol. An IP address identifies where your computer can be found over the Internet. Most ISPs (Internet Service Providers) use *dynamic* IPs, meaning that your computer's address can change from time to time. This setup is fine when you're using your computer to browse the Web, but not very useful when you (or others) want to find your particular machine somewhere on the Internet.

You can, of course, get a static IP address for your favorite Mac. Some ISPs will give you a static IP if you just ask, but more often the ISPs see static IPs as things of value and want to charge a fee for giving you one. The fees vary widely (I found rates anywhere from $5 to $35 a month) and if you use a laptop in multiple locations, a single static IP address will only work at one location.

What's required is a method to approximate the functionality of a static IP address without actually *having* a static IP address. One solution would be to give your computer a name, store said name in a centralized location, and then have your computer relay its current IP address to the centralized location. That way, when you or someone else went looking for your computer, they could look for its name (rather than its IP address) and then be forwarded the current IP address of your machine. As luck would have it, that's exactly the way No-IP works—and the best part is that it's a completely free service.

The first step is, predictably, a quick trip to *No-IP* (*http://www.no-ip.com*). Download the client for OS X. While you're at the site, sign up for an account, too—you won't be getting very far in this hack without one. The signup process is pretty standard and it's a small price to pay for the increased functionality coming your way.

Next, install No-IP. The installation process is standard except that the No-IP installer installs a *daemon* (a program that automatically starts and runs in the background). The daemon—which is required if you wish to run No-IP as a background process—is not activated just by installing (you have to turn it on manually), so don't worry that installing No-IP is adding another background process; it won't run in the background until you instruct the No-IP client to do so.

Check your email and, in the email No-IP sent you, click the activation link. Then, head to your Applications folder and fire up No-IP DUC. After you authenticate, you'll see the external IP address of your Mac (Figure 3-7). This is the number the outside world can use to find you.

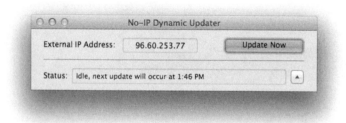

Figure 3-7.
No-IP has discovered your external address! You've completed the first step toward getting your web page to the rest of the world.

That's great, but it doesn't really help you too much unless you want to send that IP address out to all your friends whenever it changes. That's too much work. You want No-IP to do its thing automatically; for that to happen, you need to enable the daemon.

To start the daemon, we need to take care of a few things. First No-IP needs to know who you are. In No-IP, choose No-IP DUC→Preferences. You may be asked to enter your email address and password; if so, enter them. If not, in the Preferences dialog box, click the Change button next to Email/Username and then log in with your username and password. Then click the Settings tab and check the box next to "Automatically Start at Login." Finally, go to the Daemon tab and click the box next to "Launch Daemon at System Startup" (Figure 3-8). You'll be asked for your user password. The process is safe, so go ahead and enter your magic string of authorization.

Figure 3-8.
The last step of setting up No-IP DUC to run in the background and automatically! People can reach this Mac's website at *machacks.no-ip.org*. Go ahead and try it!

At this point, all the hard work is done: you've created a web page, gotten a dynamic IP address updater, and have a name for your web page. If your Mac is plugged directly into the Internet, you're all set. If you go through a router, you have some work left to do. You need to open port 80; exactly how to do that varies depending on your router. Chances are you can visit your router's configuration page and get it done with a minimal amount of effort.

Oh, you want to actually *share* the web page you made? Just tell people to go to www.thenameyouchoseearlier.org. They'll see your page just like you're some big-time corporation!

Extending the Hack

This hack focused on creating a web page on your Mac, but you don't have to use No-IP just to share web pages. You can put a variety of files in your Sites folder and then use No-IP to access them while on the move. For example, say you want to listen to your 14,001 favorite songs, but that's one song too many for your iPod touch! If you tossed that song in your Sites folder, you could play it over the Internet by typing the name of your website into a browser and appending /nameofsong.mp3 on the end. For example, if your website is www.dawnofmanslegos.no-ip.org and you added *the-mefromtron.mp3* to your Site folder, to hear the song on the go, you would head to www.dawnofmanslegos.no-ip.org/themefromtron.mp3.

HACK 16 Change the Startup Sound

> Push the power button, get the noise! That's the way it's been on Macs forever—but it doesn't have to be that way any longer. This hack shows you how to automatically silence the chime and play a different sound.

If you were one those people who was into Macs before they were cool, someone who sincerely believed that OS 9 was the superior operating system of the day, you've been using Macs long enough to get tired of the startup sound. Or maybe you don't dislike the sound, but you have a legitimate reason to want it gone: you want to start your Mac up without waking your roommate, say, or you might be making one of those soufflés that fall with the merest of sonic vibrations.

Whatever your reason, you can get rid of the startup sound. But just silencing the chime isn't very hard or interesting, so what if we amped up the interest level by silencing the chime *and* adding a new sound? The silencing part is easy, but the process of getting your Mac to play a different startup sound is a bit more kludgy.

First, let's get rid of the sound altogether. To pull this off, you'll need the following tools:

- A finger or stick
- The ability to remember to push a button

That doesn't seem like a lot to ask, does it? But it turns out it actually is. Because with this method, you mute the startup chime by remembering to push the mute button on the keyboard (using your finger or that stick) *every single time* you shut down or restart your Mac. Forget to push the mute button when you're shutting down and the sound will play as your Mac starts up.

"That's not much of a hack," you might be saying, "That's barely even a tip!" You want something that takes care of muting the chime automatically! Don't give up—we're going to get this worked out and make the process either super easy or fairly complex.

Turns out there's an application that gives you the ability to control the startup sound. Download the *Psst app* (*http://www.satsumac.com/psst.php*), which controls the startup sound's volume so you don't have to. Sadly, it doesn't work on *every* Mac—there's a list of supported models on *Satsumac* (*http://satsumac.com*)—but it seems to work for most setups.

Once you download Psst, expand the *.dmg* file and then drag the app's icon to the Applications folder. Then fire up Psst. Once you do, you'll see a Start Psst button; click it and then adjust the slider to control the volume of the startup chime. To disable Psst, simply launch the program again and click Stop Psst (Figure 3-9). It really is that simple.

Figure 3-9.
Psst is a minimalist app that does only one thing: lets you control how loud the startup chime is on your Mac. That may not seem like a big deal...until you have to start your Mac in a library or other quiet place.

That takes care of killing the start chime, but this hack also promised to explain how to add a new sound when your Mac starts. First the bad news: to *really* change your Mac's startup sound, you're going to have to do some serious work.

People debate where the startup sound actually resides; some aver it's hidden somewhere on your hard drive, while others say it's in the logic board's ROM. To test the hard drive theory, your humble author opened a Mac Pro and removed the hard drives; when the Mac Pro was restarted, the startup chime still sounded. Conclusion: the sound isn't on the hard drive, which means it's hard to replace. You could, one supposes, dump the ROM, edit it, and then burn it back to the chip or perform some other incredibly complex process not worth messing with.

Fortunately, you can make your Mac use a different startup sound with just Automator and Login Items. (There are probably a million other ways to do this, but this method has been tested and works. The one caveat is that this method doesn't result in the new sound playing at the exact same point in the startup cycle that the standard chime does; instead, it plays once your desktop appears onscreen.) But before we get started with that, head to iTunes and create a new playlist with a name you can remember (Startup Sound, perhaps). Then choose the sound file you want your Mac to play and add it to that playlist.

Now we'll use Automator to create a super simple application to play that sound (or song). Launch Automator, click the Application icon, and then click Choose. Next, in the Library column on the left side of the window, choose Music. When you do that, you'll get a whole pile of options in the middle column; there, choose Get Specified iTunes Items and drag it into the pane on the right side of the Automator window. You'll see a cool representation of the Get Specified iTunes items you just chose. Click Add and, in the menu that drops down, select the playlist you created earlier (Figure 3-10).

Figure 3-10.
Adding the playlist we created earlier. This will serve as your new startup sound.

Back in the Automator window's center column, choose Play iTunes Playlist and drag it underneath Get Specified iTunes Items in the righthand pane (Figure 3-11). That's about all there is to it. Click the Run button in the window's upper-right corner to test out your creation. You might see a warning that the application won't receive input when run inside Automator, but you can ignore it. Automator will then run the application you created—you'll see green checkmarks appear in the log pane and hear your chosen file play!

Turns out all the hard work is done. All we have to do now is save the creation as an app, and then add that to the Login Items for your user account. In Automator, choose File→Save and give your creation a name. After making sure you're saving it as an *app* (choose Application in the File Format pop-up menu), hit Save.

Figure 3-11.
Automator will run your application through its paces. The green checkmarks mean everything is going as expected. If you look closely in the Log section, you can even see how long each step took.

Now to finish off this hack, open System Preferences and choose Users & Groups. You can't do much without authenticating, so click the little lock in the window's lower-left corner and type your password. Now that you have the power, click the user account you want to spice up with the new sound, and then click the Login Items tab. In the Login Items pane, click the + button and navigate to the application you just created. Double-click the app and it'll get added as a startup item. (If you want iTunes to stay hidden, check the box in the Hide column; otherwise you'll be greeted by the full iTunes window.)

That's it—you're done! Now the process of shutting down and starting up your Mac goes like this: when you shut down or log out, the volume is muted (or changed to whatever you set with Psst). When you start your machine again, the volume is turned back to the level you set it at before you shut down, and your new sound plays after your desktop shows up—all with no intervention from you!

Using Terminal Commands: A Better Way?

Downloading Psst and whipping up an application to change the startup sound gets the job done, but it seems a little convoluted and the sound plays pretty late in the startup experience. Could the Terminal offer us a superior result and experience? Anyone who has tried the hack will tell you with confidence that the answer is "yes." So let's get started.

We'll be using the Terminal for the rest of this hack so if that gives you the willies, check out Chapter 6 before you begin.

Feeling comfortable? Great! Open Terminal and type:

```
sudo nano /system/library/muteon.sh
```

Here's what that code means:

- `sudo` is short for "superuser do." Basically, this tells your Mac that you're the boss and it has to listen.
- `nano` starts up Nano, a built-in Terminal program for text editing.
- `/system/library/` tells Nano where to write the file. You don't have to save the file there, but it's an easy location to use.
- `muteon.sh` is the file you'll create with Nano. The `.sh` means it runs in Bash, the shell for OS X.

Now that you know nothing bad will happen, hit Return to run the command. You'll likely be asked for your password; type it in and hit Return. When you do, something odd will happen: Terminal will switch to the Nano environment (Figure 3-12).

You're using Nano! Now type:

```
#!/bin/bash
osascript -e 'set volume with output muted'
```

What does all that mean?:

- `#!` is called a shebang, and it tells the interpreter to run this file.
- `/bin/bash` is just the path to the interpreter.
- `osascript` tells the interpreter to use AppleScript.
- The `-e` flag lets everyone know the next thing you type is either a statement or a program file. In this case, it's the statement `'set volume with output muted'`, which tells AppleScript to mute your machine's volume.

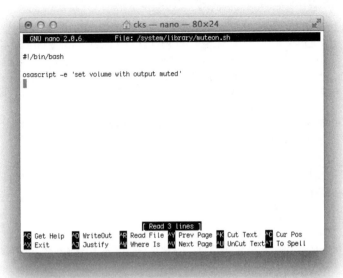

Figure 3-12.
The Terminal's Nano text editor. You're still using Terminal, but the window looks a little different because Nano is designed to make text editing in Terminal a little easier.

Press Ctrl-O and then the Return key to save what you just typed. (Nano writes all this to a file that you can see, if you desire, by heading to *Computer/Startup Disk/System/Library* as shown in Figure 3-13.) Then Exit Nano by hitting Ctrl-X.

That takes care of turning the volume off so the startup chime won't sound, but we also want the volume *back on* after the computer boots. That means another script, but since you are familiar with the first one, this one will be easy to follow because it's really similar. In Terminal, type:

```
sudo nano /system/library/muteoff.sh
```

In the Nano window that appears, type:

```
#!/bin/bash
osascript -e 'set volume without output muted'
```

Then press Ctrl-O followed by Return to save, and then Ctrl-X to exit Nano.

The necessary scripts are now in place, but we have to make them executable. In Terminal, type:

```
sudo chmod u+x /system/library/muteon.sh
```

It's useful to know exactly what's going with this command:

- As you know, `sudo` grants you superuser privileges.

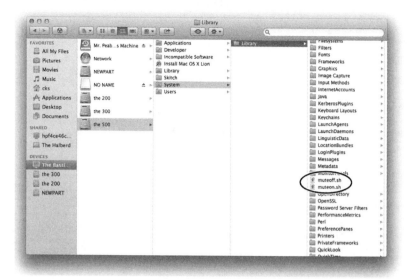

Figure 3-13.
You created this file with Terminal but that doesn't make it magic—it's a file just like any other. If you want to poke at it with a GUI text editor, you're free to do so.

- chmod is short for "change mode"—in this case, we're changing the file to an executable.

- u tells chmod to add you as a user, and x tells chmod to make the file executable.

- /system/library/muteon.sh is the path to the file you want to change.

Now that that is taken care of, you'll need to do the same thing to the *muteoff* file by typing:

```
sudo chmod u+x /system/library/muteoff.sh
```

We've got the necessary files in place, but the system doesn't know about the files. We need to let the system know to look for them so that your Mac knows you've provided instructions for it to follow. To do that, OS X lets you use login and logout *hooks*—ways to get your Mac to play a script (like the two you just created) when you log in or out. Chances are that you haven't messed with adding hooks before, but if you're wondering what you did that very blurry night you watched the *Lord of the Rings* trilogy and took a drink every time anyone walked somewhere, it's easy to check whether you have any hooks already installed. In Terminal, type:

```
sudo defaults read com.apple.loginwindow LoginHook
```

Similarly for the logout hook:

```
sudo defaults read com.apple.loginwindow LoginoutHook
```

If you don't find any hooks (you'll see a message that ends with "does not exist"), you're free to add your own. Even if you *do* find hooks, you can still overwrite them if you are so inclined. To do so, type the following in Terminal:

```
sudo defaults write com.apple.loginwindow LogoutHook /system/library/
muteon.sh
```

And one to turn the sound on again:

```
sudo defaults write com.apple.loginwindow LoginHook /system/library/
muteonff.sh
```

That's it: your Mac turns on without the chime! Wait—something's missing. We also wanted your Mac to play a different sound when it started. No problem. Using the stuff we learned earlier, we'll set up a script to do that:

```
sudo nano /system/library/playsoundfirst.sh
```

As before, Nano will fire up. In Nano, type:

```
#!/bin/bash
afplay your file's name goes here
```

Like the scripts we wrote earlier, this text will invoke a command. In this case, afplay will play the file of your choosing. You can either drag the file you want afplay to play into the Nano window (as shown in Figure 3-14) or type the path to the file. You're free to choose *.mp3*, *.aiff*, and plenty of other file types; just pick something you want to hear. Then save with Ctrl-O followed by Return, and exit Nano with Ctrl-X.

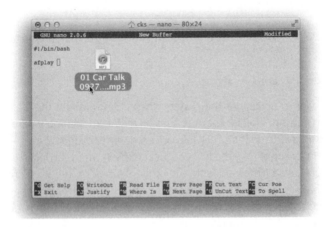

Figure 3-14.
Don't choose a long-playing file for your startup sound. For example, choosing Car Talk (as shown here) is a guaranteed mistake.

Warning: Pick the file you want to hear very carefully because your Mac will be unresponsive while the file is playing. This isn't a big deal if you pick a system sound, but if you pick an hour-long podcast, you'll regret your choice!

Now we need to make this file executable by typing:

```
sudo chmod u+x /system/library/playsoundfirst.sh
```

As before, we have to use a hook to tell the command when to run:

```
sudo defaults write com.apple.loginwindow LoginHook /system/library/play
soundfirst.sh
```

That's it—you're completely done. No more startup chime *and* you get a new sound that either plays as soon as you type in your password (on a multiuser machine) or before the desktop shows up (on a Mac with automatic login enabled).

HACK 17 Full Screen for (Almost) Any App

> Everyone wants full-screen apps, but not every app offers that feature. This hack explains how to add this enhancement to a lot of apps and fill your screen with almost any app!

When OS X Lion first came out, Full Screen mode was a big selling point. With laptop screens starting at 11 inches on a MacBook Air, every pixel counts when you're trying to be productive. But the usefulness of Full Screen mode goes beyond laptops and comparatively tiny screens—full-screen apps also block out a lot of distractions that might otherwise impede your productivity.

Unfortunately, adding full-screen capability is up to developers, not Apple, so not every app features it. But for Cocoa-based apps, it turns out you don't have to wait for the developer to add this functionality; you can add it yourself thanks to a free utility called Maximizer.

Before you can have glorious full-screen apps, you need to get the tools that let your Mac pull this off. First, you'll need SIMBL (SIMple Bundle Loader—hey, the computer world needs more acronyms, right?) and—you guessed it—a copy of Maximizer. Head to *the SIMBL download page (http://www.culater.net/software/simbl/simbl.php)* to get a copy of it (download the version for Snow Leopard and Leopard—it still works). For Maximizer, head to *chpwn's page (http://chpwn.com/apps/maximizer.html)* and click the huge Download link.

When you look at your Downloads folder, you should see a file named *Maximizer.bun dle* and a *SIMBL-0.9.9* folder. If you do, you've got all the tools you need—we just need to get them to the right places. It's a good idea to install SIMBL first, so we'll start there. SIMBL comes with a package that installs it, so a simple double-click on the installer file (*SIMBL-0.9.9.pkg*) will get the job done (be prepared to authenticate).

Note: One of the SIMBL installer's screens gives you a choice that's not truly a choice. The second screen (Figure 3-15) gives you an option with seemingly no option; since you have no choice, just click Continue.

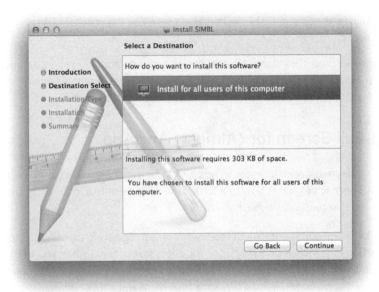

Figure 3-15.
The weird not-a-real-choice screen of SIMBL. You could, with some package opening and manual dexterity, install SIMBL for a single user, but it really isn't worth the effort.

Quick Hack: SIMBL Isn't Just for Maximizer

SIMBL can do a lot more than just enable Maximizer. SIMBL can run a variety of plug-ins, and since you've installed it, you might as well check out *the list of useful plug-ins* (*http://code.google.com/p/simbl/wiki/SIMBLPlugins*). You'll find useful plug-ins that help you control the behavior of windows in OS X (Sizewell), a plug-in to manage iPhoto keywords (iPhoto Keyword Manager), and plenty of other cool tools for OS X.

With SIMBL installed, it's time to install Maximizer. This involves moving the *Maximiz er.bundle* file you downloaded earlier to the proper folder on your Mac. The path for the folder is *Computer/your hard drive/Library/Application Support/SIMBL/*

Plugins. You can either dig for that starting at the root of your Mac; use Terminal to copy the file from your Downloads folder to that destination (Hack #29); or, since you know right where you need to go, you can use the "Go to Folder" command (Shift-Command-G) in the Finder's Go menu (Figure 3-16).

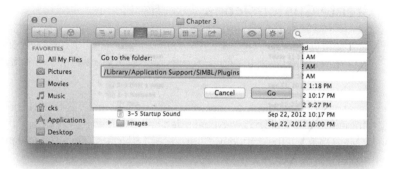

Figure 3-16.
Using the "Go to Folder" command since the destination is precisely known. This isn't a good way to browse, but when you know where you need to go, this command is really slick.

Once you're in the Plugins folder, just drag the *Maximizer.bundle* into that folder. Restart any programs you want to get the full-screen treatment and, *bam*—if they're Cocoa-based apps, they'll have full-screen arrows (Figure 3-17)!

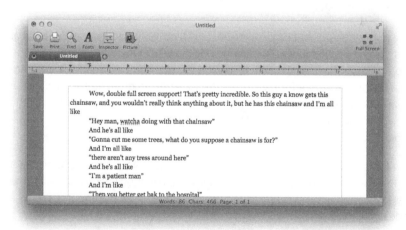

Figure 3-17.
Bean had full-screen support before full screen was cool. In this image, you can see Bean's native full-screen button (the four-way arrow icon) and the full-screen arrows added by Maximizer.

HACK 18 Create Custom Icons

It's a safe wager that there are some annoying or flat-out terrible icons on your Mac. Replace the crud by making new icons with this creative hack.

Icons are a central part of the GUI experience: without pleasant pictures to click, how would you get things done? Apple has web pages dedicated to helping you design the perfect icon for Mac OS X, but the company's first piece of advice is, "For great-looking icons, have a professional graphic designer create them."

That's solid advice, but the hassle factor and the cost is too much for any true hacker to bear. You also have to wonder how seriously people take the rest of Apple's advice, like these two paragraphs:

Use universal imagery that people will easily recognize. Avoid focusing on a secondary aspect of an element. For example, for a mail icon, a rural mailbox would be less recognizable than a postage stamp...Strive for simplicity. Try to use a single object that captures the icon's action or represents the control. Start with a basic shape.

This advice is more useful, but do people actually follow it? Take a look at the icons of two popular programs: Safari and Photoshop (Figure 3-18). Obviously, the Safari icon adheres to Apple's guidelines: its shape is just a circular compass, and the program could be described as a tool for navigating the Internet. Photoshop's icon is also a basic shape (a square), but it's hard to imagine how someone firing up a Mac for the first time would guess that a blue square with "Ps" on it represents an image-editing program.

The lesson from all this? Forget Apple's guidelines unless you're trying to create a mass-market application (and if your mass-market application is popular, forget the guidelines anyway). Because you're designing icons for your own computer, feel free to use or design whatever icons you want to see.

Figure 3-18.
These icons are the same size, but they don't convey the same amount of information.

Changing Icons the Easy Way: Cut and Paste

The easiest but least satisfying way to change a problematic icon in OS X is to simply find an icon that you like better and paste it over the icon you want to change. For example, suppose you find the Time Machine icon annoying—which you might: that odd blue hue with the inane backwards clock deal coupled with the fact that it looks more like a modded Apple remote than anything else make this a likely candidate for replacement. Once you've decided on the victim, er, icon you want to replace, the next step is to find something to replace it with. If there's already a better icon on your computer, great; if not, there are several online sources for a vast number of icons that will be revealed with a quick Google search.

Once you find a suitable replacement, the process is straightforward. If you're using a picture file (completely allowable!), open the picture in Preview and then choose Edit→Select All (Command-A). Follow this with the Edit→Copy command (Command-C). You've successfully copied the image onto the clipboard, so all that's left to do is paste the image where it needs to go. To do just that, head to the Finder and select the file or program with the hated icon; then select File→Get Info (Command-I). In the Info window, click the tiny image in the upper-left corner (circled in Figure 3-19) and then choose Edit→Paste (Command-V) and the icon will be changed! (You may need to authenticate before your Mac changes the icon.)

Figure 3-19.
The image on the left has been copied and is ready to paste into the Info window on the right. All that's left to do is click the circled icon and then hit Command-V (paste).

That's not the only way to change an icon. What if you want to replace an app's standard icon with the icon for another app? For example, imagine you're at work and you've downloaded a super fun game with a festive icon. You might want to change that icon to something suitably boring and business-y (the Microsoft Graph icon is a great one for this). To get started, open both apps' Info windows (Command-I), as shown in Figure 3-20.

Figure 3-20.
The target and the source. Never again will someone think I'm playing with Microsoft Graph when I could be playing Angry Birds!

All that's left to do now is a quick copy and paste. Click the source app's mini icon in the Info window's upper-left corner to select it (it will be surrounded with a soft blue hue). Then select File→Copy (Command-C).

Repeat the process within the target app's Info window, but change the copy command to Paste (Command-V). (You may have to authenticate, too.) You're done—the new icon has replaced the old one! See Figure 3-21 for an example.

Figure 3-21.
The switch is complete. No one will ever suspect I actually occasionally work!

Undoing the Hack

This hack actually scares some folks because what happens when you start to loathe that replacement icon—are you stuck with it forever? When you use either of the above methods, the process is nondestructive. You can get the old icon back any time by opening the app or file's Info window (Command-I), and then selecting the tiny icon in the upper-left corner (circled in Figure 3-19) and choosing Edit→Cut (Command-X).

Designing Your Own Icons

As alluded to earlier, Apple has plenty of advice when it comes to designing icons. One of the keys? Get a professional to do it for you. The bad news is that professional graphic designers charge a ton of money (they're pros; what do you expect?). The good news is that everyone who owns a Mac and a copy of Photoshop thinks they're a professional-level graphic designer, so you can get plenty of free help. Really, don't be afraid to ask. But if you're friendless, you can use the following advice to make your very own icon.

Generating the image

When creating or choosing an image to iconify, there are a few things to keep in mind. The first is image size: icons can be as large as 1024×1024 pixels (you wouldn't to use an icon that big on your Mac, but large icons look nice in the App Store). That's more pixels than a 50-inch high-def TV displays, more pixels than the original iMac's screen displayed. It's a cool *million* pixels, all for your icon, so you'll want to start out with an image at least that big and preferably bigger.

The second consideration is the file type. In this hack, we'll use Photoshop Elements and the command-line program iconutil. Iconutil only accepts files of the icns and iconset file types, which can get confusing, but don't worry about that for now. When you save your icon file in Photoshop Elements, save it as a TIFF file. Later in this hack, you'll learn how to convert it to an icsn file and, if necessary, an iconset file.

Now that the limits are specified, it is time to generate the image. This example uses Photoshop Elements, but you can pull this off with any image editor. Begin by creating a new image. I want to see all the ugly, so I went for 1024×1024. If you have the option, set the background to Transparent.

At this point, you're likely to be presented with a blank canvas to work with. Apple recommends simple shapes, and simple shapes are far easier to create than complex ones, so create something simplistic. In this hack, I'm starting with just a solid circle generated with the Ellipse tool shown in Figure 3-22.

You could stop here. The icon is ugly and unrepresentative, and it could be the worst Mac OS X icon ever. But it's more fun to try to make it look somewhat OS X-ish. After all, if you're making the worst icon ever, this won't do; people will say you didn't even try. On the other hand, if you attempt to make it look OS X-ish, people will think, "Man, that's sad. I can tell they put effort into it." The latter scenario is hilarious, and hilarity is worth the extra effort.

To OS X-ify the icon, we need to perform a few more steps in Elements. OS X icons are supposed to look as though a light source is directly above them, so a flat circle just isn't going to cut it. Time to light the top half of the circle. First, create a new layer. You'll note that the moving, dashed line is still present (Photoshop types call this "marching ants"). Since the light needs to come from the top and shine down, limiting the selection to half of the circle is useful. Choose the Rectangular Marquee tool and select the bottom 5/8 of the circle while holding the Option key (holding the Option key tells Photoshop to *exclude* the selected area from the overall selection). If everything went right, the top portion of the circle is now selected. It would be better if the icon could display a hint of three dimensions, so refining the selection with the Elliptical

Figure 3-22.
Ah, a big circle. The beginning of the world's ugliest icon.

Marquee tool is a good next step. Again, hold the Option key to exclude the portion of the image you are selecting. Your result should look like Figure 3-23.

Figure 3-23.
The top portion is ready for enhancement.

There are an infinite number of ways to proceed at this point, but invoking the power of the Gradient tool seems to be the favorite of Photoshop types. Set the foreground color to white and set the Gradient tool to create a "Foreground to Transparent" gradient, as shown in Figure 3-24. Then apply a linear gradient.

Figure 3-24.
The perfect gradient settings. (Well, probably not.)

Drag across the circle to apply the Gradient, ensuring that the white portion starts at the top, and the transparent portion ends at the end of the selection. This puts the gradient you just applied right at the top of the circle, but that isn't very OS X-ish. So hit Command-T to invoke the Free Transform tool, and then move the gradient down from the top edge of the circle a comfortable distance. Continuing with the Free Transform tool, squish the bottom edges in a bit to follow the outline of the circle more closely. Hit Return to make the changes stick. The result should look like Figure 3-25.

That's it for the top, but careful inspection of OS X icons reveals that the bottom of them *also* includes a light source. (There must be really good lighting in Apple's icon-design offices.) To get the bottom looking lit up, though not as lit up as the top, a little more work is required. At this point, you need a method of selecting most of the rest of the circle without selecting the part you already enhanced. I used the Elliptical Marquee tool followed by the Polygonal Lasso tool to refine the selection, but there are plenty more elegant ways to pull this selection off. Once the area is selected, create a new layer (Shift-Command-N) and then switch to the Gradient tool. Again, use the "Foreground to Transparent" setting, but this time, to give a more rounded appearance, change to the Radial Gradient option (instead of Linear). Apply the gradient, and you should have something that looks like Figure 3-26.

Figure 3-25.
Adjusting the gradient you added.

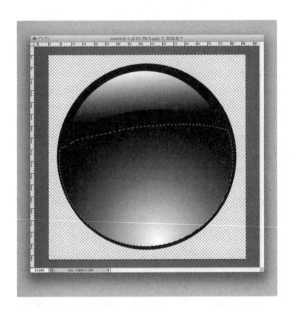

Figure 3-26.
Wow, this is really starting to become the ugly icon I had hoped for.

If you're happy with the shape and look of the gradient you just added, you can move to the next step. If you want to fine-tune it a bit, hit Command-T to bring up the Free Transform tool and tweak things as necessary.

At this point, the icon is just a solid circle with some gradients on it—not the most exciting blob in the world. In addition to its unexciting nature, it isn't quite ugly enough. I'm going to fix that by adding a big red X in the middle. In this example, I've used the Text tool set to a 900-point sans serif font. The results are approaching the ugly ideal I set out to capture (see Figure 3-27).

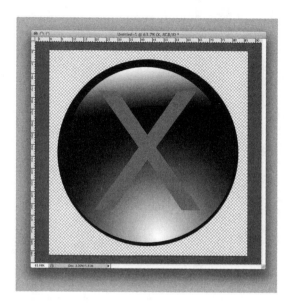

Figure 3-27.
Full on ugly!

The good news is that the process of creating an image to use as an icon is almost complete. All that's left are a few small tweaks. First, in Elements' Layers panel, reorder the layers so the layer with text is *beneath* the layers with the gradients, as shown in Figure 3-28.

Now for some final adjustments: change the gradient layers' Opacity settings to 80%, and hit all the layers with a Gaussian Blur of 10. The last thing OS X icons usually feature is a drop shadow. In Photoshop Elements, there's a Drop Shadow table associated with the layer style option. Choose the background layer (the one with the big black circle) and then add the "High" drop shadow. Good news: you've created the world's ugliest OS X icon! Well, mine is probably much worse than yours, so compare your result to Figure 3-29.

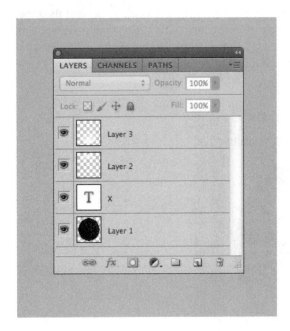

Figure 3-28.
Reordering the layers.

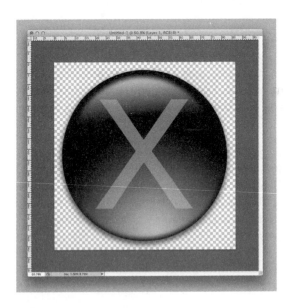

Figure 3-29.
I win the ugly icon contest!

With the image complete and your eyes spurting blood from taking in that much ugly, it's time to turn this image into a proper icon. To get started, resize the image to 1024×1024 (the maximum size for an OS X icon) and then save the file in Photoshop's native PSD format.

Composing the icon

After you've created your image, all that's left to do is to turn the image into an icon. First thing you'll need to do is save your image as a TIFF file that's 1024×1024 pixels. Then you have to turn that TIFF file into an icns file. You'll need to use the Terminal to pull this off. Open Terminal and type:

```
tiff2icons pathtofile/filename.tiff
```

Once you hit Return, tiff2icons (a command-line program) will turn your TIFF into an icns file (the file type OS X wants for its icons), generating a 32×32-pixel icon as well as an icon that is the original size (1024×1024). If you're just making icons to replace icons you don't like on your Mac, you can quit at this point. But if you're cranking out a high-level Mac application or if you're doing this for a friend, you'll want to go the extra mile and crank out an *icon set* (a group of files with all the icons sizes OS X likes built right in), too. Terminal to the rescue once again! Type:

```
iconutil pathtofile/filename.icns -c iconset
```

This is another really simple command. It tells iconutil to take the file you created with tiff2icons and convert it (that's the -c part of the command) to an iconset. When you hit Return, iconutil turns your icns file into an entire icon set suitable for regular Macs *and* those with Retina displays!

Quick Hack: You're Already Done!

Once the image you want to use is saved, you're ready to use it as an icon replacement if you so desire. To pull this off, right-click (or Command-click) the *.psd* file you just created and choose Copy from the contextual menu. Then fire up Preview (found in the Applications folder) and choose "New From Clipboard" (Command-N) in Preview's File menu. Now hit Command-C to copy the image. Next, right-click the file whose icon you want to replace, and choose Get Info. Paste your new icon right over the old one as described earlier in this hack. If you're wondering why you have to make a trip to Preview—why couldn't you just cut and paste directly?—the reason is that directly cutting and pasting between the image file and the icon you want to replace results in an icon without the transparency. You worked hard to get the transparency right and a quick detour through Preview will ensure that the icon behaves as you expect.

You've got your icons to go! The easiest way to change a program's icon to the new *.icns* file is to open the program's Resources folder and replace its *.icns* file with the new *.icns* file you created. (A program's Resource folder is inside its *.app* folder. For example, Safari's resource folder is located at *~/Applications/Safari.app/Contents/Resources*. If you want to see it the GUI way, Control-click the Safari icon in the Finder and choose Show Package Contents.) Give the new file the same name as the existing *.icns* file and drop it in the folder. For instance, if you were to replace Safari's *compass.icns* file with one you created, the result would look like Figure 3-30. Just imagine how many Docks can be ruined with your new creation!

Figure 3-30.
Wow—from beautiful to rueful in just a few easy steps.

MAC HACKS

4

Hacks for a More Informative Mac

Using your Mac is a two-way street: you create things and send them to the larger world and, in turn, you can see what's going on just about anywhere and digest it in front of your computer. What if you want to get the information that's important to you in a more passive manner? You could use something like News Notifications (which costs 99 cents in the App Store) and have Notification Center notify you of stories, but perhaps that seems disruptive. What if you want to see information that doesn't demand your attention and appears on your desktop unencumbered by Finder windows and desktop items? You can have all that with just a little bit of effort that pays off over time as you use your computer. This chapter explains how.

HACK 19 Quit the Finder

> The Finder is just another program, so why run it if you're not using it? If you're using the Dock, Spotlight, or a third-party launcher as your primary method of navigating to and launching files, the Finder isn't doing you much good. Don't be frustrated by the lack of control over the Finder—add an option to quit.

The Finder in OS X is likely both the most-used program and the most loathed. The Finder seems perpetually stuck halfway between behaving like the Finder in Mac OS and behaving like a web browser. Fortunately, there are many options to use instead of the Finder. Users who like raw speed can rely on Quicksilver (*http://qsapp.com*). Those in love with Spotlight are more than happy to launch all their applications via everyone's favorite magnifying glass. And those inclined to use Terminal don't ever have to use the Finder; they have complete control.

If you're one of the people who use an alternative to Finder, you're probably wondering why your Mac is burdened with the overhead of the Finder program (yes, the Finder is just a program) if you don't use it on a regular basis. A good question, and the simplest answer is "because the Finder is a hassle to turn off." Sure, you could always kill the Finder via Terminal, but if you're not already using Terminal, that can be big hassle, too. It would be better and easier if the Finder had a quit option in its File menu. So let's add one.

To add a quit option to the Finder menu, you need to edit the Finder's PLIST (property list) file. (There's lots more about PLIST files in Hack #06.) The one you're looking for lives here: */Users/username/Library/Preferences/com.apple.finder.plist*. That's the file named *com.apple.finder.plist* in the Preferences folder found in the home Library folder (see Figure 4-1). Be sure to back up the file by making a copy of it before you proceed.

Note: If you have trouble finding the Library folder (in Lion and Mountain Lion, it's hidden by default), see Hack #04.

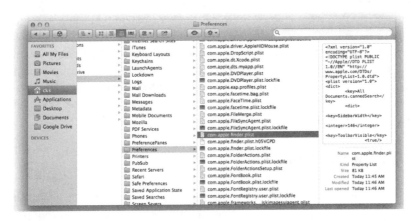

Figure 4-1.
Getting to the Finder's PLIST file takes some digging.

With the file located and backed up, you can safely work on it while it's in your Preferences folder. Open the *com.apple.finder.plist* file using a property list editor, an application specifically designed to edit PLIST files. If you've installed Xcode (which is free from the App Store) that will likely be your default PLIST editor. If you're not happy with Xcode (it's is a little bit of overkill for this hack), a quick search on *Version Tracker* (*http://www.versiontracker.com*) will yield a variety of options.

After you've opened the file in your preferred property list editor, look for the line that reads QuitMenuItem. Change NO to YES, and you're on your way to quitting the Finder (see Figure 4-2). After you make that change, save the PLIST file.

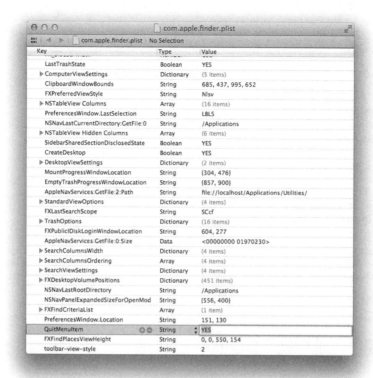

Key	Type	Value
LastTrashState	Boolean	YES
▶ ComputerViewSettings	Dictionary	(5 items)
ClipboardWindowBounds	String	685, 437, 995, 652
FXPreferredViewStyle	String	Nlsv
▶ NSTableView Columns	Array	(16 items)
PreferencesWindow.LastSelection	String	LBLS
NSNavLastCurrentDirectory:GetFile:0	String	/Applications
▶ NSTableView Hidden Columns	Array	(6 items)
SidebarSharedSectionDisclosedState	Boolean	YES
CreateDesktop	Boolean	YES
▶ DesktopViewSettings	Dictionary	(2 items)
MountProgressWindowLocation	String	{304, 476}
EmptyTrashProgressWindowLocation	String	{857, 900}
AppleNavServices:GetFile:2:Path	String	file://localhost/Applications/Utilities/
▶ StandardViewOptions	Dictionary	(4 items)
FXLastSearchScope	String	SCcf
▶ TrashOptions	Dictionary	(16 items)
FXPublicIDiskLoginWindowLocation	String	604, 277
AppleNavServices:GetFile:0:Size	Data	<00000000 01970230>
▶ SearchColumnsWidth	Dictionary	(4 items)
▶ SearchColumnsOrdering	Array	(4 items)
▶ SearchViewSettings	Dictionary	(4 items)
▶ FXDesktopVolumePositions	Dictionary	(451 items)
NSNavLastRootDirectory	String	/Applications
NSNavPanelExpandedSizeForOpenMod	String	{556, 400}
▶ FXFindCriteriaList	Array	(1 item)
PreferencesWindow.Location	String	151, 130
QuitMenuItem	String	YES
FXFindPlacesViewHeight	String	0, 0, 550, 154
toolbar-view-style	String	2

Figure 4-2.
You'll have a Quit option once you save this file.

Note: If you don't see the `QuitMenuItem` option, don't be alarmed. Simply perform the following Quick Hack instead, which uses Terminal rather than a property list editor.

Quick Hack: More than One Way to Write a PLIST File

The Finder's PLIST file is interesting to look at and includes fun stuff to play with, but digging through folders and scanning for PLIST files isn't strictly necessary. You can accomplish the same task using the Terminal. Simply launch Terminal and type this command:

```
defaults write com.apple.finder QuitMenuItem YES
```

Then hit the Return key.

That's it; you're done. To see the change, you'll need to log out of your account and log back in or, in the Terminal, type:

```
Killall Finder
```

Then, open the Finder menu, and notice the Quit option shown in Figure 4-3.

Figure 4-3.
Wow, a new choice in the Finder menu!

After you select the newly added Quit option, you'll see the usual menu bar at the top of the screen and the Dock at the bottom, but the area once reserved for Finder windows and the desktop (Figure 4-4) will be completely blank except for a desktop background (Figure 4-5). That isn't a surprise: the desktop is *controlled* by the Finder, and each icon you see on the desktop is, in reality, another window your Mac is forced to render. So even if you don't quit the Finder, keep that desktop clean!

When performing this hack, many people get suddenly scared because all their files and drive icons disappear from the desktop without warning. Don't worry: nothing has been deleted. You just can't *see* them because the Finder is no longer running. Think of it as an instant desktop cleanup for those of us who have too many files lying around.

There are going to be times when you need the Finder. Spotlight is great for finding files if you know what you're looking for, but if you just want to randomly wander through your file hierarchy, Spotlight isn't going to do the trick. To get the Finder up and running again, just click the Finder icon in the Dock, and the Finder will spring to life ready to serve until you quit it again.

Figure 4-4.
That is one ugly, cluttered desktop. Maybe if I quit the Finder...

Figure 4-5.
A pristine desktop means you're Finder free.

Undoing the Hack

If you decide that you can't live without an always-on Finder, you can easily return the Finder back to the original state. You can retrace the earlier steps of finding the proper

PLIST and then changing YES to NO. Or, as before, you can use the Terminal instead of a property list editor. Simply type this:

```
defaults write com.apple.finder QuitMenuItem NO
```

As soon as you hit Return, the PLIST file is changed, the Quit option won't disappear from the Finder's menu until you log out or restart.

HACK 20 Move a Widget to the Desktop

> Tired of switching to Dashboard just to get the latest stock prices or check the weather? Move that much-loved widget to the desktop.

Dashboard, once a huge selling point for OS X, is becoming more irrelevant with every iteration of OS X. But sometimes a widget is what you need: not too much power and not too little. Take, for example, the Stock widget. This nifty widget, which first shipped with Tiger, beautifully and informatively displays the current price of your financial holdings. With money on the line, stock prices are something that people like to check with obsessive frequency. Sure, watching shares of the company you own skyrocket and plummet can be nerve-racking, but it's information you want to know.

The most obvious thing to do is constantly hit the Dashboard shortcut key (quick aside: you can assign a different shortcut key by going to System Preferences→Mission Control) or repetitively launch Spaces. However, constantly invoking Dashboard can get a little mundane. What we need is a method to move the widget from the Dashboard to the desktop. You can either search the Web for a program that does that for you, or you can save time and money (plus feel a little hackerish) by doing it yourself.

The first thing to do is to wander over to System Preferences→Mission Control and uncheck the box next to "Show Dashboard as a space" (Figure 4-6).

Once that task is complete, it's time to use Terminal. Launch it and then enter the following innocuous line:

```
defaults write com.apple.Dashboard devmode YES
```

Next, hit Return. At this point, you're probably wondering why nothing seems to have changed. The truth is that plenty has changed, just nothing you can see. You've entered Dashboard's Developer mode—a convenient way to test and tweak widgets without invoking Dashboard.

There's one more thing you need to do before you can get that wonderful widget onto your desktop: you need to kill the Dock. The most obvious way to do this is to log out and log back in, but that has the disadvantage of killing any *other* applications that are running. Since you used the Terminal to enable developer mode, why not use it to terminate the Dock, too? Here's the simple one-line instruction:

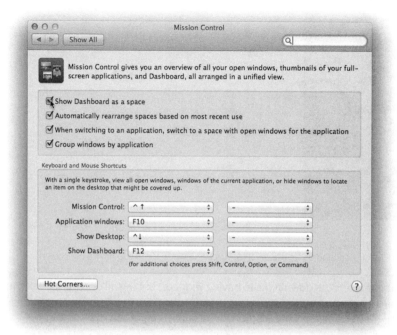

Figure 4-6.
Skipping this step is not optional if you want to pull off this hack.

```
$ killall Dock
```

Your windows might jump around a little after you hit Return, but the Dock is the only process that suffers. Once the Dock reappears, the protocol to get a widget onto the desktop is fairly simple even if it does take the slightest bit of manual dexterity.

Fire up Dashboard using the method of your choice (pressing the Dashboard key, clicking the Dashboard icon in Dock, or using the Mighty Mouse scroll ball), and then click and begin dragging the widget you want to move to the desktop. Now it's time for your inner video-gamer to come out: while you're dragging said widget, press *and hold* the Dashboard shortcut key (exactly which key that is depends what you have it set to in System Preferences→Mission Control), and then release the mouse button. The Dashboard disappears, and the widget now resides on your desktop (Figure 4-7). (If you mess up, the widget disappears from Dashboard but doesn't appear on your desktop; to get the widget back and try again, launch Dashboard and click the + at its lower left.) Repeat for as many widgets as you like or as many as your screen will hold. You can reverse the process by starting to drag the widget from the desktop, then pressing the Dashboard key, and finally releasing the mouse button.

Figure 4-7.
The desktop widget lives! And floats over everything else. Always. Hope you have a big screen...

Naturally, there are some downsides to having widgets running all over your desktop. The first thing you'll notice immediately is that the widgets "float" above all the other windows. Not a big deal if it's a small widget or you have a 30-inch monitor, but you give up a certain amount of screen real estate until you close the widget. Another ramification of widgets floating on the desktop is that they're constantly using your computer's resources. Ideally, Dashboard widgets only suck the computing power down when Dashboard is running (though there have been reports to the contrary in the case of some poorly designed widgets), but if the widget is always running, it's always affecting system performance.

After a while, you might get bored with the widget you moved to the desktop, so you'll want to know just how to get it back *off* your desktop. If you want to take individual widgets off the desktop, the solution is simple but less than intuitive. Simply press the Option key while pointing your cursor in the general vicinity of the widget. A bubble with a white X in its center appears at the upper left corner of the widget (Figure 4-8). Banish the widget by clicking the X (this trick works in Dashboard as well).

Killing a widget in this manner also removes it from Dashboard, so the next time you want to use the widget in Dashboard, you'll have to find it among the available-but-uninstalled widgets and drag it back onto the Dashboard playing field. If you wish to return your system back to the state in which Apple shipped it to you, simply repeat the procedure outlined earlier for entering Developer mode with Terminal, but change YES to NO, like this:

```
$ defaults write com.apple.Dashboard devmode NO
```

You'll still have the widgets you liberated on your desktop (kill them with the Option key as mentioned earlier), but you won't be able to add new ones to your desktop. Your Mac is just like it was when you started.

Figure 4-8.
Banishing a widget that bears bad news!

Quit Dashboard for Real

As great as Dashboard is, some folks just don't like it. And if you don't like it, there's no legitimate reason to keep it around taking up Dock space, using a valuable function key and gobbling up valuable system resources. Sure, you'll be killing one of OS X 10.4's most hyped features, but Apple is up to 10.8 now and no one develops widgets anymore. Plus, this is a completely reversible process, and there's no reason to run Dashboard all the time if you never use it.

You'd think that quitting Dashboard would be easy—but you would be wrong. Simply removing the Dashboard icon from the Dock frees up a little more Dock space but still leaves Dashboard running in the background. To *truly* kill Dashboard and keep it from restarting every time you restart your Mac, it is time for a trip to the Terminal:

1. Open a Terminal window and enter the following command:

   ```
   $ defaults write com.apple.dashboard mcx-disabled -boolean YES
   ```

   As always spelling, spacing, and capitalization all count.

2. Hit Return.

You'd think that would be enough to get rid of Dashboard—but you would be wrong again. At this point, you've set the stage for killing it (it's at the gallows, so to speak), but you haven't pulled the lever. To fully rid yourself of the Dashboard, you have to restart the Dock by typing the following into a Terminal window:

```
$ killall Dock
```

The Dock restarts and, unless you investigate by looking at the Activity Monitor or repeatedly hitting the Dashboard key, you won't be able to tell that Dashboard ever existed.

Unhacking the Hack

At some point you're going to hear about a great new widget and want full Dashboard functionality back. Don't fret: all the steps described above are easily undoable. To get Dashboard running again, open a Terminal window and enter the following command:

```
$ defaults write com.apple.dashboard mcx-disabled -boolean NO
```

Naturally, you'll need to follow that command up with:

```
$ killall Dock
```

Dashboard returns to whatever state it was in when you killed it: the widgets you were running will be running again, and widgets you moved to your desktop will reappear.

To put the Dashboard icon back in the Dock, all you need to do is open up the Applications folder in a Finder window, locate the Dashboard application, and then drag Dashboard's icon back to the Dock.

HACK 21 Turn Your Desktop into a Fount of Useful Info

> The desktop is generally reserved for displaying beautiful Apple-supplied images or pictures from your iPhoto library. This hack explains how to display *useful* information on your desktop with GeekTool.

Your desktop is slacking. While your other applications are off collecting pertinent information and displaying interesting results (even your screensaver can display RSS feeds) the desktop just sits there, rarely changing and providing no input into your daily computing life.

What would be great would be a way to have your desktop display something useful and timely. This concept harkens back to one of the earliest OS X hacks: running a movie as your desktop background. While interesting, those who actually ran movies on their desktops quickly found that not only was the hack processor intensive, it was also very distracting. With this lesson in mind, it is obvious that choosing which information the desktop displays is almost as important as getting the desktop to tell you a little something about what's going on in the world. The ideal type of information for desktop residence would be something that's updated relatively infrequently, isn't of crucial importance (since you won't see it if you have a bunch of windows open), and can impart a vast amount of info at glance.

What fits all the above criteria? Traffic! A quick glance at the route(s) you take to and from work will tell you volumes about what you're likely to face on the commute. You can't personally *do* anything to speed up the traffic flow, but you can change your travel plan if one path looks intractably tangled.

First, it's a good idea to find a traffic cam that displays the area you're interested in. In this example, I-62 at Lovell Road is potential trouble spot for those traveling east or west around the Knoxville area. A quick Google search reveals that there is indeed a traffic cam devoted to that particular spot (no surprise there). For those playing along at home, here's *the URL (http://www.tdot.state.tn.us/cctv/cctvknox/cam02.asp)*.

Once you confirm that the traffic cam is available, it's time to go about getting said image onto the desktop. There are a variety ways to do this, but installing one piece of free software not only makes the process simpler, it also makes it much more adaptable as your cravings for an information-packed desktop grow. Head to the Mac App Store and download GeekTool, an app that lets you make tiny apps for your desktop. These tiny apps are called *geeklets* and can offer a lot of functionality. The ease of getting GeekTool from the App Store is nice, and the price (free) is even better. Once the blue bar disappears from Launchpad, launch GeekTool (Figure 4-9).

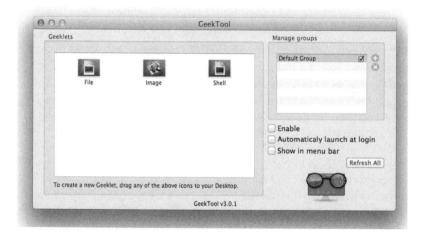

Figure 4-9.
It might look a little intimidating, but GeekTool will make your desktop better.

We've got a video feed we want on the desktop, so let's start by dragging GeekTool's Image icon to your desktop. The result is shown in Figure 4-10.

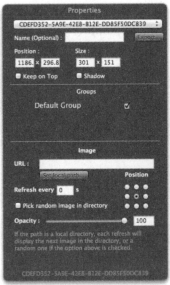

Figure 4-10.
Wow, that looks pretty darn complicated! Don't be put off by the appearance—images in GeekTool are actually very easy to use.

The first thing we need to do is add the URL to GeekTool so it knows where to get the image. Recall that we found a traffic cam earlier, but GeekTool can't pull the image directly from that page. GeekTool wants something that's an image, so in your web browser, right-click the traffic cam feed you want and then select "Open Image in New Tab" (Figure 4-11). Then, in the new tab, copy that URL and you're almost done.

This image is updated every few seconds, so it's a great way to learn about the traffic at any particular moment, but we need to get GeekTool to display it. That's easy: back in the GeekTool Properties box (shown on the right in Figure 4-10), paste the URL into the aptly named URL box and then hit Return. If the URL is valid, your image will show up in the box (Figure 4-12). To make sure the image updates, in the Properties box, enter a number in the "Refresh every __s" box, like 10 if you want a new image every ten seconds.

At this point you're technically done but there are a few tweaks you can make. You can resize the pic by dragging the double-arrow handle in its lower-right corner; use the slider in the Properties box to set its opacity; and drag the image to wherever you want it displayed. You can also tell GeekTool whether you want traffic on top of your other apps or lingering in the background using the "Keep on Top" checkbox in the Properties box.

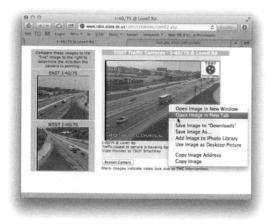

Figure 4-11.
Grabbing the URL of the traffic cam.

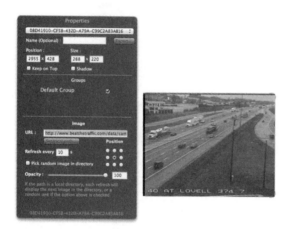

Figure 4-12.
Wow, you've got traffic on your desktop. You should start giving updates to your coworkers and calling yourself the Eye in the Sky.

That's a pretty nifty trick, but GeekTool isn't a one-trick pony. If you want more Geek-Tool goodness, visit *Brett Terpstra's site (http://brettterpstra.com/topic/geeklet)*, or *http://www.macosxtips.co.uk/geeklets*. Remember: you can edit the scripts that others use in their geeklets, so the world is soon to be on your desktop.

5

Make It Automatic

In the olden days, computers promised shorter workweeks and more leisure time (or, as some call free time, naps). It hasn't quite worked out that way. Accountants don't get to use all the time they save from not having to do computations for naps—they just get to use that time for other accounting tasks. That doesn't mean a computer can't save you time or that you should give up the dream. Computers are great at doing things without your supervision, you just have to tell them what to do. This chapter explains some ways to automate mundane tasks.

HACK 22 Getting Things Done with AppleScript

> Everyone wants a clean desktop, but no one wants to perform all the dragging and dropping required to achieve a tidy computing environment. Forget the carpal tunnel–inducing drag-and-drop method: let AppleScript do the work.

Everyone uses their Mac a little differently. Some people are conscientious and put all their documents in the Documents folder, all their pics in the Pictures folder, and all their movies in the Movies folder. Some people don't work that way: they use the desktop just like you'd use a real desktop—as a temporary storage place for whatever you happen to be working on at the time. Still other users use the desktop as a repository for every file they run across during a particular computing session. They don't bother putting anything away until the desktop is cluttered beyond hope.

The old excuse for having a cluttered desktop is that it was the easiest place to find a file. Sure, it looked messy and each one of those icons was actually a little performance-sapping window, but you didn't have to open your Documents folder and hope you put that TextEdit file in there instead of in the Pictures folder or something. At least that was the argument.

With the integration of iCloud and the Finder's slick built-in All My Files option, it's actually a lot faster to properly place files and use All My Files then to make your desktop a digital catchall. But die-hard clutterers toss stuff on the desktop out of habit. They need serious help—the kind of help only an app can provide. As it turns out, the files on the desktop are likely of predictable types, and so they're easily categorized, which means the process of cleaning up the desktop could be easily automated.

You can't say "automation" without thinking of Automator when you're using a Mac, and Automator holds the key to a clean desktop. What would be ideal is an AppleScript that will put everything in the appropriate folder: MP3s in the Music folder, documents in the Documents folder, movies in the Movies folder, etc. Turns out, this is relatively easy to do.

Note: The following script will fail if a file exists in the destination with the same name as the file being moved. Think of it as a safety precaution so that important data doesn't get overwritten.

Creating the Script

To get started on your AppleScript, launch the AppleScript Editor (Applications→Utilities→AppleScript Editor). Here's the script that will identify files on your desktop by their extension and then move them to the appropriate folders. Here's the script we'll be using for this hack (you can either type it in or download it from this book's *catalog page (http://oreil.ly/Mac_Hacks)*):

Note: In the following script, change every instance of username to your actual username (unless your username happens to be username). Your username is the same as the name that graces your Home folder.

```
tell application "Finder"
    set theDesktop to alias ":Users:username:Desktop:"

    --Where to put stuff
    set theMusic to alias ":Users:username:Music:"
    set thePics to alias ":Users:username:Pictures:"
    set theVideos to alias ":Users:username:Movies:"
    set theDocs to alias ":Users:username:Documents:"

    --filetype by extension
    set musicExt to {".mp3", ".aac"}
    set picsExt to {".jpg", ".gif", ".tif", ".tiff", ".png"}
    set videosExt to {".avi", ".mpg", ".mov", ".mp4"}
    set docsExt to {".rtf", ".txt", ".doc"}

    set allFiles to files of theDesktop
    repeat with theFile in allFiles
```

```
            copy name of theFile as string to FileName
    repeat with ext in musicExt
            if FileName ends with ext then
                move theFile to theMusic
            end if
        end repeat

        repeat with ext in picsExt
            if FileName ends with ext then
                move theFile to thePics
            end if
        end repeat

        repeat with ext in docsExt
            if FileName ends with ext then
                move theFile to theDocs
            end if
        end repeat

        repeat with ext in videosExt
            if FileName ends with ext then
                move theFile to theVideos
            end if
        end repeat

    end repeat
end tell
```

Warning: This script works recursively, meaning that any folders (but not drives) on your desktop will be sorted along with any files. So it's a good idea to use this script only if your desktop is cluttered with files, not folders.

A closer look at what's going on here is in order because you'll likely want to modify the script to suit your needs. The following bit of the script invokes the Finder and tells it to look at the desktop:

```
tell application "Finder"
    set theDesktop to alias ":Users:username:Desktop:"
```

Here, the desktop is being defined by the path *:Users:username:Desktop:*. You could change this path to tell the Finder to examine and clean up a different folder. If you wanted to run this script on your Downloads folder, for example, change it to *:Users:username:Downloads:*. Note the colons—in AppleScript, colons replace the more familiar slash (/) that's used when working in Terminal.

The next section of the script defines where the files are going to end up:

```
--Where to put stuff
    set theMusic to alias ":Users:username:Music:"
    set thePics to alias ":Users:username:Pictures:"
    set theVideos to alias ":Users:username:Movies:"
    set theDocs to alias ":Users:username:Documents:"
```

Good Comments Are Good Code

In AppleScript Editor, typing -- indicates a comment; in other words, typing two hyphens tells the editor to ignore whatever follows. While the computer doesn't need the info in comments to figure out what to do, *you'll* need the comments to remember what you did.

You can adapt the script to folders of your choice by changing the paths to different folders. If you wanted your music to end up in a folder called NewMusic within your Music folder, say, you'd tell the script to burrow one level deeper in the folder by adding one more level to the path: *:Users:username:Music:NewMusic:*.

The next section of the script defines which extension belongs to which kind of file:

```
--filetype by extension
    set musicExt to {".mp3", ".aac"}
set picsExt to {".jpg", ".gif", ".tif", ".tiff", ".png"}
    set videosExt to {".avi", ".mpg", ".mov", ".mp4"}
    set docsExt to {".rtf", ".txt", ".doc"}
```

If these extensions aren't sufficient, you can add your own. For example, if you want to include Photoshop files among the files sorted as pictures, you'd simply add ".psd" inside the brackets on the `set picsExt` line.

If you type the script into AppleScript Editor window, you'll end up with a rather bland-looking script as shown in Figure 5-1.

```
tell application "Finder"
set theDesktop to alias ":Users:cks:Desktop:"
-- Where to put stuff
set theMusic to alias ":Users:cks:Music:"
set thePics to alias ":Users:cks:Pictures:"
set theVideos to alias ":Users:cks:Movies:"
set theDocs to alias ":Users:cks:Documents:"
--filetype by extension
set musicExt to {".mp3", ".aac"}
set picsExt to {".jpg", ".gif", ".tif", ".tiff", ".png"}
set videosExt to {".avi", ".mpg", ".mov", ".mp4"}
set docsExt to {".rtf", ".txt", ".doc"}
set allFiles to files of myDesktop
repeat with theFile in allFiles
copy name of theFile as string to FileName
repeat with ext in musicExt
if FileName ends with ext then
move theFile to theMusic
end if
end repeat
repeat with ext in picsExt
if FileName ends with ext then
move theFile to thePics
```

Figure 5-1.
After you spend a little time with AppleScripts, you'll be able to tell immediately that this file hasn't been compiled yet.

You Don't Have to Type in AppleScript Editor

AppleScript Editor is great for *editing* AppleScripts, but it isn't great for *writing* them. Nothing against AppleScript Editor—it just lacks a lot of the tools that coders like to use. So if you have a text-editing program you'd rather use, like TextMate or some other application, feel free to write the script in your preferred editor and then paste or import the code into Apple-Script Editor.

You probably already know this isn't right: scripts are supposed to be color-coded and indented. No problem—simply click the Compile button (it looks like a hammer), AppleScript Editor will work a little magic, and everything will look as expected (Figure 5-2). As a bonus, AppleScript Editor will find any structural errors (unclosed quotation marks, for example) and alert you.

```
set theVideos to alias ":Users:cks:Movies:"
set theDocs to alias ":Users:cks:Documents:"
--filetype by extension
set musicExt to {".mp3", ".aac"}
set picsExt to {".jpg", ".gif", ".tif", ".tiff", ".png"}
set videosExt to {".avi", ".mpg", ".mov", ".mp4"}
set docsExt to {".rtf", ".txt", ".doc"}
set allFiles to files of myDesktop
repeat with theFile in allFiles
    copy name of theFile as string to FileName
    repeat with ext in musicExt
        if FileName ends with ext then
            move theFile to theMusic
        end if
    end repeat
    repeat with ext in picsExt
        if FileName ends with ext then
            move theFile to thePics
        end if
    end repeat
    repeat with ext in docsExt
        if FileName ends with ext then
            move theFile to theDocs
```

Figure 5-2.
AppleScript Editor took that boring wall of text and styled, indented, and colorized the code, making it look like everything was intentional. Amazing!

If you're only going to need this script very occasionally, you could just save it as a script. Then, whenever you want to clean up your desktop, fire up AppleScript Editor and hit the big green Run button. That's a great option for the occasionally untidy, but for desktop abusers it isn't the best idea; those folks need to run the script on a daily basis, and could use a way to run the script with a minimal amount of hassle. If you're in that category, save the script as an application, using the File Format pop-up menu (Figure 5-3). (If you're using Mountain Lion, you have to press the Option key to make the Save As item appear in the File menu.)

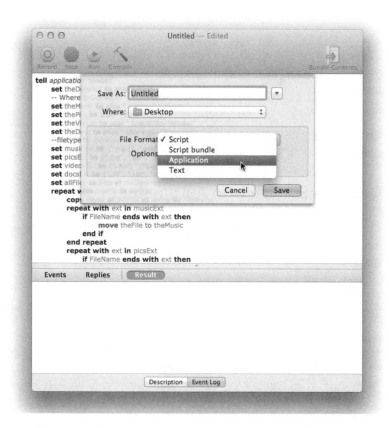

Figure 5-3.
You're creating an application—won't Mom be proud? Maybe not, but your desktop will be clean with just a few clicks.

Name the app something descriptive (Cleaner Upper, say) and save it wherever you wish—except on the desktop, since that's what you're trying to keep tidy! All the necessary files will be generated and packaged with your script, and you'll be able to clean your desktop any time you wish with just a double-click.

Hacking the Hack

If you would like to modify the script to move another file type, such as applications, this is how to change it. In the `--Where to put stuff` section, add this line of code:

```
set theapplications to alias ":Users:username:Applications:"
```

And in the `--filetype by extension` section, add:

```
set applicationsExt to {".app"}
```

And finally, before the final instance of end repeat, add this:

```
repeat with ext in applicationsExt
    if FileName ends with ext then
        move theFile to theApplications
    end if
end repeat
```

As you've deduced by now, you can extend this script to any folder and any app type. Think of it as the moving company of apps.

HACK 23 Create a Service with Automator

You can manipulate text, pictures, etc., more easily from the Services menu. This hack shows you how to add useful features to this menu using Automator.

Automator is Apple's way of making programming easy for anyone who wants to take a few minutes to learn how to do it. There are thousands of pre-compiled scripts on the Web, and Automator is bursting with examples.

One of the underused and underappreciated aspects of Automator is its ability to create services that will show up in the universally accessible Services menu. So let's create a service that does something useful—one that sorts selected text alphanumerically.

To get started, launch Automator (Applications→Automator). When the program starts, it will ask you what type of document you'd like to create. Select Service and then click the Choose button.

On the lefthand side of the new document window, you'll see a list of available actions. You can filter the list by typing in the search field at the top of it. You're after the Run Shell Script action, so type *shell* in the search field, and Automator will filter the list down to just the action you're looking for. Then simply drag the action over to the big empty pane on the right (Figure 5-4).

A Run Shell Script box appears in the formerly empty pane. Above that are a few settings (Figure 5-5). Make sure the "Service receives selected" box is set to "text," and that the "in" box is set to "any application." Then turn on the "Output replaces selected text" checkbox. What you're doing here is telling Automator that the text you select in an application (like Word or TextEdit—wherever the service applies) will be replaced by the text generated by the script you're about to write.

Figure 5-4.
There are a lot of choices in Automator. You could scroll through them all but it's much easier to use the search box. Then simply drag the Run Shell Script action into the pane on the right.

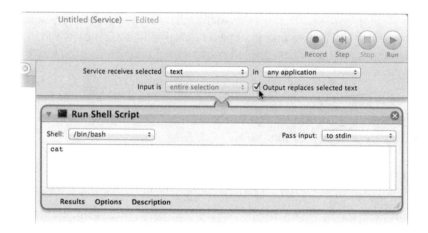

Figure 5-5.
Telling Automator what you want it to do.

Now that you've adjusted the settings, it's time to write the script. We'll just use the default UNIX `sort` command. To do that, leave the Shell box set to "/bin/bash," and the "Pass input" box set to "to stdin." Then edit the text in the Run Shell Script box (where it initially says "cat"), and change it to `cat|sort` (Figure 5-6).

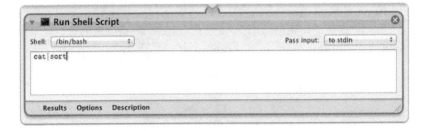

Figure 5-6.
You can't tell, but you're about to do command-line stuff without ever visiting the command line.

What does all that mean?

- /bin/bash is the default shell for OS X.
- stdin (which is short for "standard input") is one of the standard *streams* (the way the computer passes information from the program to the outside world) between the program's environment (where the program runs) and your screen. In other words, the service will take the content you selected and send it to the shell script using stdin. The program then performs its actions on the passed text and sends it back.
- cat is a small program that concatenates (get it?) and outputs files.
- The | character connects cat to sort.
- sort is a program that (not surprisingly) sorts lines of text.

Basically, cat will take the text you select (more on that in a moment) and "pipe" it to the sort command. The service will then replace the selected text with the result.

All that's left to do now is save your new service. Press Command-S and name the service Sort Lines. From now on, in any application where you can edit text, you'll be able to choose [Application name]→Services→Sort Lines to run this script.

An even faster way to use your new service is to select some text and then right-click your selection. At the bottom of the contextual menu, you should see a Services submenu, which is where you'll find your new service. (Note that OS X sorts items in this submenu in strange ways, so if you have multiple services, you might have to look carefully to spot Sort Lines [Figure 5-7].) Select it and OS X will sort the selected text.

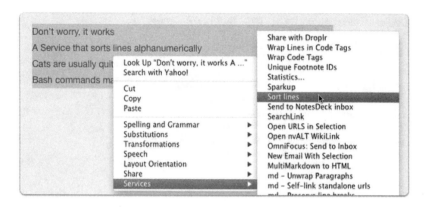

Figure 5-7.
Your service is now available.

When you run Sort Lines on lines that start with letters, it will sort them alphabetically. When you run it on lines that start with numbers, it will sort them numerically. And lines that contain both letters and numbers get sorted first by number, then by letter. Give it a whirl to see it in action!

—Brett Terpstra

HACK 24 Customize the Services Menu

> You know that Services menu that you rarely use? You can make it more useful and have it display things you want to use with this helpful hack.

The Services menu is an underused productivity tool. In fact, you may not even know it's there. It lives in the application menu of each program on your Mac. So in Safari, you find it by going to Safari→Services, in Calendar it's under Calendar→Services, and so on. The Services menu is also a bit of a chameleon: what you see in the menu depends on what you have selected when you open it.

The idea behind the Services menu is solid—quick access to tools you use a lot, specifically tailored to what's currently selected—but the implementation is bland. Apple supplies some services, but they're ones that most folks rarely use. Figure 5-8 shows what the Services menu looks like when text is selected.

Figure 5-8.
The standard services for text. Not the most exciting menu in the world. If only there were some way to make it more useful...

What most people don't realize is that the Services menu is customizable. That means you can add the service you want to use so it will be available to you whenever you need it!

Find the Service You Need

Just knowing something is customizable isn't any good if you don't know how to customize it. You can create your own services (see Hack #23) but, chances are, someone has already created the service you need. (A *service* is a small program that does something useful: transforms text, speaks text, creates an email, etc.) So where can you look to find a useful service? Try an online search for "OS X workflow *capitaliza tion*" where the last word (or phrase) is what you want your Mac to do, such as capitalize every first word of a sentence. You'll likely find several results. (If you're wondering why you'd include the word "workflow" in your search instead of "service," it's because the service file will have a *.workflow* extension.)

Find and Uncompress the File

When you download the service file, it may be compressed, probably as a *.zip* file (if your browser is set to automatically open files or you see a *.workflow* file but no *.zip* file, skip ahead to the next section). You can probably locate the file in your Downloads folder and double-click it to unzip/extract the contents. But, occasionally, you might unwittingly change the download destination or the folder might be jumbled and the file hard to find. If that's the case, you can use Safari or Spotlight to find the file (Figure 5-9). For most third-party services you'll find on the Web, the extracted file will have a *.workflow* extension.

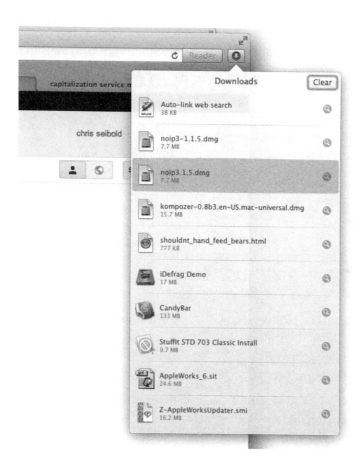

Figure 5-9.
Using Safari to find a downloaded file. Just click on the magnifying glass icon next to the file's name and Safari will take you right to the file. (Note that this only works on files you've downloaded using Safari.)

> *Tip: Want a real-life workflow to play along while you're doing this hack? Head to my website and grab the Markdown Service Tools (http://brettterpstra.com/ projects/markdown-service-tools). They're designed for Markdown text, but there are a lot of tools that you'll find yourself using all the time.*

Move the File

You've found the service you need, you've downloaded it, and you're ready to start using it. You're just a few steps away:

1. Open a new Finder window (press Command-N).

2. Locate your user's Services folder. In Lion and Mountain Lion, do this by pressing and holding the Option key, and then choosing Go→Library. Within that Library folder, you'll see the Services folder.

3. Drag the *.workflow* file from wherever it currently lives into your Services folder (Figure 5-10).

The service is now installed. That was easy!

Figure 5-10.
Moving a service from the download destination to the Services folder. That's where your Mac looks for services, so that's where they have to live!

Using the Service

When it's available, your new service will show up in two places: the Services menu you get by going to *Application Name*→Services (Figure 5-11), and the Services sub-menu of the contextual menu that pops up when you right-click (or Control-click) a file or selected text. (The first time you use the Services menu after installing a new service, you might see a "Building…" message.)

Remember, not all services are available all the time—they only appear when your selected object is something on which they can act. For example, if you've installed a text-modifying service and you right-click a file, that service will not show up in the services menu because it doesn't work on files.

Using the service is as easy as selecting the type of object it acts on (files, text, etc.), and then selecting it either from the *Application Name*→Services menu, or by right-clicking (Control-clicking) your selection and then choosing it from the Services sub-menu. There's one more way to activate the service, though, and it makes accessing your tools very convenient. Keep reading for details.

Figure 5-11.
Your newly added service! Remember that services only show up when they're applicable, so if you don't see the service you added, chances are there's nothing for it to do.

Adding a Keyboard Shortcut

Turns out you can add keyboard shortcuts for Services menu items. To add one for your service, head to System Preferences→Keyboard, and then make sure the Keyboard Shortcuts tab is selected at the top of the preference pane. (Sometimes there's a delay when loading this tab as OS X indexes all of the available applications and services.) On the left side of the pane, click Services, and then locate your new service on the right.

> Note: In the Keyboard Shortcuts preference pane, you can use the checkboxes next to services' names to enable and disable services without having to remove them from the Services folder.

When you find your new service in the list, click its name; an "add shortcut" button will appear to its right (in Lion and earlier, you don't actually see a button, just a blank area; double-click that blank area). Click that button and, when that area turns into a text field (Figure 5-12), press the key combination you want to use to activate the service. Use a combination of modifier keys (Command, Shift, Control, Option) and a letter or number. If the combination is available (not used by another service or existing system shortcut), your new shortcut appears in the text field. If that doesn't happen, try a different combination of keys.

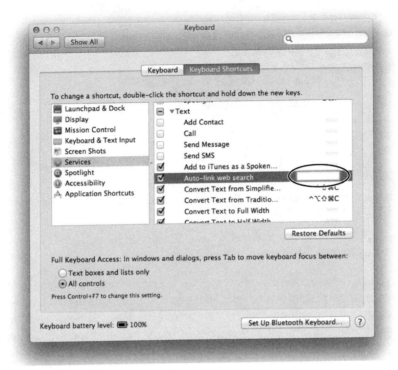

Figure 5-12.
The blank is where you enter a key combination for your service. Keyboard shortcuts aren't manda-
tory, but if you use this service a lot, setting up a key combo can be a real timesaver.

If you see a yellow warning triangle next to your Service, it means that there's another
service or application using that key combination, but it let you add it anyway. This
can cause odd results, but mostly just results in neither shortcut doing anything if
both associated actions are available at any given time. It's safest just to change your
shortcut and avoid the warning.

That's all there is to it. You now have a shiny new service that probably does something
really cool. Select some text or a file and use the menus or your new key combination
to test it out!

—Brett Terpstra

Speed Things Up with Keybindings

> Keybindings let you create keyboard shortcuts that are available in almost any program where you can edit text.

Text input is a huge part of using any computer. Typing emails, writing notes, even putting together books—it's all part of every user's digital life. Fortunately, you can hack your system to make text-entry easier. One of the most interesting and powerful of those is the keyboard-shortcut system that OS X calls *keybindings*. Keybindings assign keyboard shortcuts to commands. (If you've ever used Command-C to copy or Command-S to save, you've used keybindings.) What few people know is that you can create your own bindings. (One exception: you can't create keybindings for Microsoft programs like Word.)

Note: Keybindings are different from plain old keyboard shortcuts because short-cuts only let you assign keystroke triggers to existing commands. But keybindings let you combine commands however you like, and then assign keystroke triggers shortcuts to those combinations. That means you're not stuck with just the commands that the app's creator came up with—you can create whatever command combos are the most useful to you.

On your Mac, you can create a text file in *~/Library/KeyBindings* called *DefaultKey Binding.dict* to which you can add your own custom tricks. If you're working in Finder, the easiest way to get to this directory is to press Command-Shift-G, then type *~/ Library* and press Return. If you see a folder called KeyBindings, open it; if you don't, use Command-Shift-N to create it (make sure to capitalize it the way I've written it here). Next, open up TextEdit (or your text editor of choice) and create a new file. Save it as *DefaultKeyBinding.dict* in the KeyBindings folder you just located or created (you can get to this folder from a Save dialog box using the exact same procedure as above: press Command-Shift-G, and then type `~/Library/KeyBindings`). Now you're ready to start adding your own bindings.

These bindings can include shortcuts for cursor movement; text selection; and deleting, copying, pasting, and inserting text. You can even combine the shortcuts in sequences, which provides a wide variety of possibilities. The *DefaultKeyBind ing.dict* file is in a plain-text PLIST format (see Hack #06), so it's easy to modify in any text editor.

You can see my custom keybindings file at *http://ttscoff.github.com/KeyBindings* to get some ideas. You'll probably want to start with a fresh one, though, and only add the bindings that you need. It's easy to lose track of what you've created if you don't use them often, and using bindings that another application has assigned can lead to confusing behavior in that app. It's best to create bindings one or two at a time and get used to them before getting too crazy. An empty *DefaultKeyBinding.dict* file simply looks like this:

```
{
}
```

You add bindings between the curly brackets. Here's an example binding:

```
"^T" = (capitalizeWord:, moveWordForward:, moveWordBackward:);
```

The first part of any keybinding—the bit before the equal sign—is the key combination that will trigger the action. Here are the symbols you use in this part of the keybinding to represent modifier keys:

∧ The Control key
@ The Command key
~ The Option key
$ The Shift key

These can be used in combination with other modifier keys and regular characters to create shortcuts that won't conflict with default system ones.

Note: You only need to include the Shift key symbol ($) in a keybinding when you can't represent the character that follows it in its Shift-modified form. In all other cases, you can just use the character that you get when typing it holding Shift, such as a capital letter or a number-row symbol. For example, in the sample binding above, ^T represents the key combination Control-Shift-T, since you have to press Shift to type a capital T (if it were written as ^t instead, that would mean you just need to press Control-T). Or if you wanted to use an exclamation point (which you type by pressing Shift-1), you can just use ! in your keybinding instead of $1. But, you can't include arrow characters in a keybinding, for instance, so if you want to include one, you'd instead type an escape sequence such as \UF700 (up arrow). A full list of special-character escape sequences (http://www.hcs.harvard.edu/~jrus/site/cocoa-text.html) is available.

The next part—the bit after the equal sign—is what happens when you type the specified key combination in a text field. It consists of a sequence of commands that will be performed in order. There are quite a few commands available, including cursor movement, text insertion/deletion, and copy-and-paste functions. Jacob Rus has a helpful *list of available commands* (http://www.hcs.harvard.edu/~jrus/site/selectors.html). The sample binding above (the one triggered by pressing Control-Shift-T) capitalizes the word that your insertion point is currently within and then moves the insertion point to the next word when you type. It allows you to put your insertion point at the beginning of a title and then press the key combination repeatedly to capitalize all the words in the title.

One of my favorite and most useful keybindings is a replication of the Command-Return keybinding found in the text editor TextMate. In TextMate, this keybinding allows you to type Command-Return when your insertion point is anywhere within a line to add a blank line below the current paragraph, and your insertion point will jump to the new line without breaking the text in the current line. The keybinding definition looks like this:

```
// TextMate Command-Return (Command Enter)
"@\U000D" = (moveToEndOfParagraph:, insertNewline:);
```

Lines beginning with // are comments and are ignored by the system, but they're useful for reminding you what this keybinding is for. The \U000D part is the code you need to use for Return, as there's no character representation of it. The command sequence, as you can probably tell, just moves the cursor to the end of the paragraph and inserts a blank line. Simply placing these lines of code between the curly brackets in your *DefaultKeyBinding.dict* file will create this shortcut on your system, and it will be available to *any* application the next time you start it. (Applications that are running when you save the file will need to be restarted for it to take effect.)

Along the same lines, here's a keybinding that does the opposite. Pressing Command-Shift-Return will insert a new line *above* the current paragraph and jump to it .

```
// Insert blank line above paragraph (Command Shift Return)
"@$\U000D" = (moveToBeginningOfParagraph:, moveLeft:, insertNewline:);
```

Lastly, you can also nest commands to create sequences. For example, I use nested commands to create Markdown (*http://daringfireball.net/projects/markdown*) links using my clipboard contents. (Markdown is a plain-text syntax created by John Gruber that lets you rapidly create HTML and rich-text documents.) The following code creates a sequence that allows me to copy a URL to my clipboard, select some text, and then type Control-Command-W, then l (that's a lowercase L, not the number one), then c to reformat the selected text as "[selected text](URL from clipboard)," which becomes an HTML link when the Markdown is converted:

```
"^@w" = { // Multi-stroke Markdown command
    "l" = { // Markdown link
        "c" = (setMark:, breakUndoCoalescing:, moveRight:, insertText:,
" ", deleteToMark:, insertText:, " [", moveLeft:, deleteBackward:, moveR
ight:, yank:, moveLeft:, insertText:, "](", setMark:, pasteAsPlainText:, in
sertText:, ")", moveRight:, deleteBackward:, moveLeft:, selectToMark:); //
link with clipboard
    };
};
```

As you can see, following a keybinding definition with another set of curly brackets creates the sequence. Every nested set of curly brackets adds another keyboard shortcut that can be pressed after the parent shortcut. This allows you to add a set of commands that only fire after pressing the parent command, helping to prevent overlap with system shortcuts and other custom shortcuts. The possibilities are vast. You can find out more at *my blog (http://brettterpstra.com/topic/keybindings)* and at the aforementioned GitHub URL. Also, see *"Customizing the Cocoa Text System" (http://www.hcs.harvard.edu/~jrus/site/cocoa-text.html)* for more details on creating your own commands.

—*Brett Terpstra*

HACK 26   Eject iTunes

> You don't have to sacrifice iTunes library size if you're using a MacBook. Learn how to quit iTunes *and* eject the external drive you store your iTunes content on all at once.

I'm going to venture a guess that most of you reading this use a MacBook as your primary Mac, and that your iTunes library has grown too big for its britches. You moved it to an external drive, didn't you? And now you wish there were an easy way to quit iTunes and eject your drive at the same time to bring back that good ol' fashioned "grab and go" feeling that got you using a MacBook to begin with, right? I think I can help.

With a little Automator and a dash of Terminal, you can create a utility that does exactly what I just described, which can make your portable life just a little easier. You can put this utility in your Dock or give it a shortcut with a productivity utility like Alfred or LaunchBar—whatever lets you work the fastest. Let's get started.

Step 1: Quit iTunes

The first thing you want your Automator utility to do is quit iTunes for you, and you just need one action for that. Here's how to set that up:

1. Launch Automator.
2. In the "Choose a type for your document" window, pick Application and then click Choose.
3. On the left side of the Automator window, click the Library heading (if it's not already selected).
4. In the next column to the right, scroll down in the list of actions until you find Quit Application. Double-click it to add it as the first step of the Automator utility you're creating.
5. In the rightmost pane of the Automator window, in the pull-down menu in the Quit Application action you just added, select iTunes.

You've now created a utility that quits iTunes. So far, so good.

Step 2: Tell Automator to Wait

I don't know about you, but iTunes sometimes takes a couple seconds to quit, even on my powerful, maxed out, SSD-slinging Retina MacBook Pro. Maybe it's tidying up some changes I made to the library database, or maybe it's just checking to see if it left the oven on. Whatever the reason, I've been using a Mac long enough to know that if an app is depending on an external drive, you should wait for the app to *truly* quit before you cut it off from that drive. So let's add a slight pause to your action:

1. In the list of actions in the second-to-left column in Automator, find the Pause action and double-click it to add it to your utility.
2. In the rightmost pane, specify how many seconds you want Automator to wait. I recommend a pause of three seconds, but this is really up to you. Enter your best guess as to how much time iTunes needs to do its thing.

Step 3: Eject Your Drive

Now comes that dash of Terminal I mentioned. Automator strangely doesn't have any kind of "eject external stuff" action, so we need to get slightly messy with a single-line Terminal command:

1. In Automator's list of actions, find Run Shell Script and double-click it to add it to your utility. In the main Automator pane, and make sure the Shell menu in the upper-left corner of that action is set to "/bin/bash."
2. In the action's text box, delete any existing text and then add this line of code:

   ```
   *hdiutil eject /Volumes/the name of your external iTunes drive
   ```

You'll need to substitute the name of *your* external iTunes drive into the end of that command.

Step 4: Save Your Utility

You're all set. In fact, if your external drive is connected right now and iTunes is running, try clicking the big Run button in the upper-right corner of Automator's window. If everything's set up right, iTunes should quit and your drive will be ejected.

Now it's time to save your Automator utility as an application that you can fit into your workflow. Go to File→Save, give it a relevant name like "Eject iTunes," pick a convenient location to save it, and be sure the File Format menu is set to Application. When everything looks good, click Save.

Congratulations! To the chagrin of many a music startup and competitor, you just created an, ahem, iTunes killer. Now it's time to actually use it.

Step 5: Make Your Utility Useful

You could place your new iTunes killer in the Applications folder and then drag it to your Dock for easy access. Or, if you're *really* feeling lazy, you could just put it on the desktop and launch it from there. But there are fairly easy ways to assign this utility a shortcut so it's just a keystroke away.

In System Preferences→Keyboard→Keyboard Shortcuts, you can create a new Application Shortcut by choosing Application Shortcuts in the lefthand list and then clicking the + button. Then browse to your new utility and assign it a shortcut that will make OS X launch your utility and run that series of commands no matter what you're doing or what app you're using.

Or, if you use one of the Mac's popular productivity utilities like Alfred, LaunchBar, or Quicksilver, they each have a variation on the theme of assigning a shortcut to any file or folder. In my favorite, Alfred, you do it by going to Preferences→Hotkeys. You can also tinker with Alfred's Extensions panel, where you can create bundles of *multiple* apps to open or close with a single shortcut.

However you decide to work your new iTunes killer into your workflow, I hope it saves you at least a little time fumbling around with quitting the app and then ejecting the drive it depends on. After all, those little bits of time do add up.

—*David Chartier*

6

Fun with Unix

Unix is what hides behind the pretty face of OS X. All those nifty graphics are powered by command-line programs that remain inscrutable to the vast majority of Mac owners. But you're not the vast majority, you're a *Mac Hacks* reader, so don't let the power of Unix go to waste. Once you take a few steps into the Unix world, you'll never look back.

HACK 27 Harmless Unix Tricks

> Unix is the core of OS X, but to get at it you need the command-line interface, which terrifies a lot of people. This hack demystifies the command line by showing you the fun that's baked in!

Unix was originally intended to be used from a text-only terminal console, and many of its features are still accessed via typed commands. These days, OS X users never have to use the command line to get everyday work done. (In early versions of OS X, firing up the command line was sometimes required to empty Trash!) So why would anyone want to bother with something as arcane as the command line?

For hardcore hackers, the answer is obvious: to harness the power of OS X's underlying system. But the command line isn't just for the geekiest among us; it's a useful tool for everyone. Not only can otherwise unchangeable parts of OS X be modified via the command line, but in certain situations, the command line actually works better than the graphical user interface.

The easiest way to get to the command line is via an application called Terminal (you can find it in your Mac's Utilities folder). When you launch Terminal, you're presented with a *shell*, Unix-speak for a program that waits for your commands and executes them, sort of like OS X's Finder. In this shell, you can navigate, copy files, create directories, and modify files in a nongraphical, generally nonintuitive, completely un-Mac-like but powerful way.

Almost all Unix features are configurable (which is how Apple engineers managed to shoehorn it into OS X), so you actually have some choices when it comes to the shell.

The default shell is called *bash* (short for "Bourne Again Shell"), but there are plenty of other options. For most people, it's wise to stick with bash to ensure compatibility with the scripts you'll see throughout this book and with scripts you'll find online.

Quick Hack: Changing Your Shell

If you've steadily upgraded from earlier versions of OS X, you may find that the default shell Terminal uses is tcsh instead of bash. That's because tcsh was the default shell until Panther was released, and that preference was saved as you upgraded. To change the default shell in Mountain Lion to bash (or to switch from bash to another shell), head to System Preferences→Users & Groups. After clicking the lock icon to authenticate, right-click or Ctrl-click on the account name in the left side of the pane where the accounts are listed. A menu with a single option appears: Advanced Options. Click it, and the Advanced Options window appears. You can change the shell by clicking the down arrow next to the "Login shell" field.

Time to get up and running with Unix. Launch Terminal (Applications→Utilities→Terminal). Once it's running, you'll see a *prompt* something along the lines of:

```
computer:~ username$
```

Where *computer* is the name of your Mac, and *username* is your login name. (This prompt is endlessly configurable. In this book, we'll just use $ to indicate the command prompt. So when you see $ in the following commands, remember that you don't need to type it in.) This prompt is a Unix representation of the current *directory* (that's the Unix term for "folder"). The tilde (~) tells you that you're in your home directory, and the $ represents the command prompt. You can prove this by typing:

```
$ ls
```

and then hitting Return. Wow, that list exactly mirrors your Home folder. Figure 6-1 and Figure 6-2 show the differences (and the similarities) between the Unix way and the Mac way.

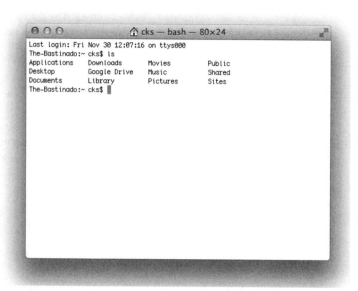

Figure 6-1.
The home directory's contents as displayed by Terminal.

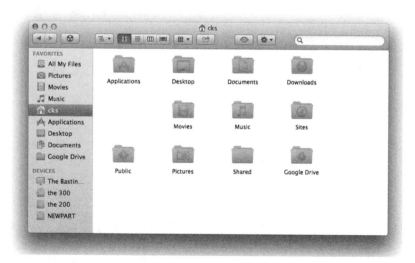

Figure 6-2.
The home directory's contents as displayed by the Finder.

Now that the Terminal is running, it's time for the fun stuff. Sure, you won't accomplish anything important by trying out these tricks, but they'll help alleviate any fear you may have of the Terminal. Here's a quick list of (arguably) fun stuff you can do with the Terminal:

Watch Star Wars Episode IV.

In Terminal, type:

```
telnet towel.blinkenlights.nl
```

Press Enter and you'll be treated to the movie shown in Figure 6-3.

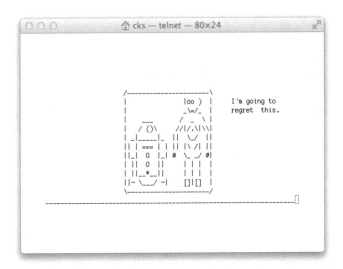

Figure 6-3.
Star Wars on your Mac, in ASCII. (The downside of this is that, if the ASCII version sucks you in, sooner or later you'll watch the movie versions and that will, inevitably, lead to Jar Jar Binks. Apologies in advance.)

Get some mental help from Eliza the built-in psychotherapist.

Type:

```
emacs
```

This launches a Unix program called—you guessed it—emacs. Hit the Esc key, then type X (capitalization matters), and then type doctor. Now vent your frustrations to Eliza (Figure 6-4).

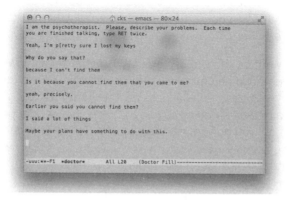

Figure 6-4.
Eliza isn't the most insightful psychotherapist around, but her hourly rate is low and her patience knows no bounds.

Note: Emacs can do more than help you through the rough times in life. You can also use it to play games. Instead of typing **doctor**, *type* **snake**, *for a classic snake game;* **dunnet** *for a text adventure game; or* **tetris** *for, well, a Tetris-type game.*

Get the Terminal to talk to you.

Type:

```
say -v Fred Mac Hacks makes a great gift for any occasion
```

That's not just an interesting trick—that's solid gift-giving advice! But you're not limited to that; your Mac can actually say just about anything. The say -v part tells your Mac to say something, the Fred part tells it which voice to use, and the rest is the text you want it to say. As long as the text is all on one line, your Mac will speak it (that means you can't hit the Return key when typing the text). All this leads to tricks like the following. Turn up your speakers and type:

```
say -v Pipe Organ da da da dum dun da dum da da
```

Quick Hack: Easy Help from Terminal

If you're using Terminal, you might be wondering where its Help option lives. For the Terminal *program*, it's where you expect: at the top of your screen. But that doesn't do you much good if you want to know about the application you're using *within* Terminal.

For example, if you want to know about grep, the seemingly all powerful search utility, you won't find helpful information in Terminal's Help menu. But all is not lost: programs you launch via the Terminal (cp, grep, imagemagick, etc.) all include *manual pages*, a.k.a. *manpages*. Manpages are instructions that tell you how to use the program. To read the current application's manpage, type $ man *programname*. For example, $ man rm will bring up a page telling you all about the rm program, with examples.

One final, semi-useless trick: change the look of the shell. OS X comes with a bunch of different Terminal emulators. You can find them in Terminal by choosing Shell→New Window. These emulators don't change how Terminal works, just how it looks.

Okay, you're not scared of the Terminal anymore and you want it to do something useful. Tighten up those Terminal typing gloves because here we go!

It's likely you've had a program hang before and used the Force Quit option found in the Apple menu to kill off the misbehaving application. The trouble is that there are a lot more processes running on your Mac than are revealed in the Force Quit window. You can see all the running processes using the top command in Terminal. Simply type **top** at the prompt, and then hit Return (Figure 6-5)

If you open up the Force Quit window and compare it to the output of **top**, you'll note that **top** reveals *many* more processes than Force Quit. If something isn't behaving properly, or if you just want to kill off a process that Force Quit won't let you get at, it's the Terminal to the rescue. Note the PID number of the process you want to quit and then either hit Q (to quit **top**) or open a different tab in the Terminal by choosing Shell→New Tab (a new tab is much more useful if you plan on halting multiple processes), and then type **kill** followed by the PID number. For example, if you wanted to kill off **top** (which doesn't show up in the Force Quit menu), simply type **kill** **43171** and then hit Return (note that this number is likely to be different on your computer and will probably be different each time you run whatever application you're trying to shut down). Voilà—**top** is no longer running.

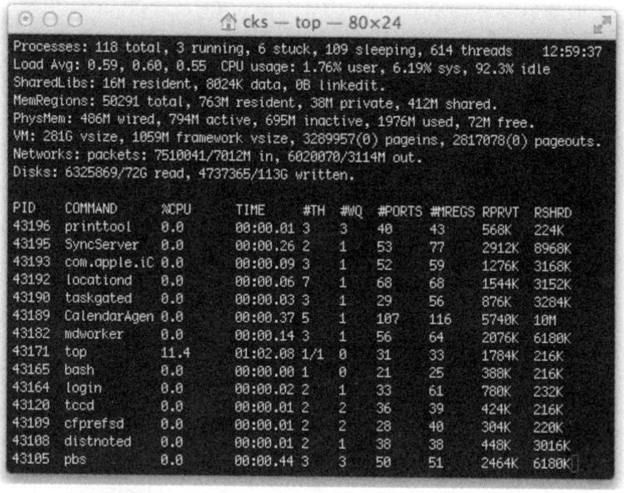

Figure 6-5.
The result of the top command: all the processes your Mac is running and associated stats!

Now that you're armed with the `kill` command and a way to watch things in the Terminal, you can track down those pesky performance drainers and banish them to the digital ether!

Tip: What's that you say? You love the idea and functionality of **top** *but loathe the very notion of firing up the Terminal? Today is your lucky day: every Mac ships with a cool GUI version of* **top** *called Activity Monitor. Just dig into Applications→Utilities and fire it up. All the goodness of* **top** *with pretty icons everywhere. (Here's a fun experiment: fire up* **top** *and Activity Monitor at the same time and see which one requires more from the CPU. On my machine, Activity Monitor requires roughly four times the resources of* **top***.)*

HACK 28 Install Homebrew

> The Mac App Store is full to bursting with apps made specifically for OS X, but there are even *more* great apps your Mac can run with just a little bit of help.

When OS X was first released way back in 2001, one reviewer remarked that Apple had "hidden UNIX really well." The thought was that UNIX was a powerful computing system for the hardcore folks out there and not suited for home computers. That made some folks wonder, "Hey, can I still get the power of UNIX on my Mac?" The answer is yes—and if you give it a chance, you'll really like it.

Alas, most people don't give it a chance. They take one look at what is takes to install a program like The Gimp on OS X and think "Well, the price is nice but installing all that? No way." Even if they do go to the trouble of installing an app that doesn't require OS X, then they have to worry about keeping it updated and other app-management tasks. It all seems like too much. Why isn't there some easy way to install new programs and look for updates? Also, if all this software that doesn't run natively on your Mac is so great, why hasn't someone made it easier to use?

Turns out people *have* noticed that problem and have been working on solutions. While there's more than one program that aims to make nonnative apps run on the Mac more easily, Homebrew is a great one to start with.

Prepare for Homebrew

One of the neat things about Homebrew is that it takes care of dependencies for you. For example, program X might rely on program Y and program Z, so to install program X, you have to realize that they rely on the other two programs and install those, too. It can be a bit of a headache, and that's a great reason to use Homebrew. In this example we'll be using ImageMagick, which has dozens of dependencies. You *could* chase all of them down by hand if you wanted to, but Homebrew will do all that for you. Neat!

Another great reason to install Homebrew? It has minimal dependencies. All you need is a copy of Xcode (free from the Mac App Store) and the Command Line Tools extension. Download Xcode (a 3.5+ GB download) from the Mac App Store for free. Once you've done that, launch the application, agree to its terms, and then choose Xcode→Preferences. In the Preferences window, click the Downloads tab, and then click the Install button next to Command Line Tools (where the status bar is in Figure 6-6). You'll be asked to authenticate, and once you do, the download will begin.

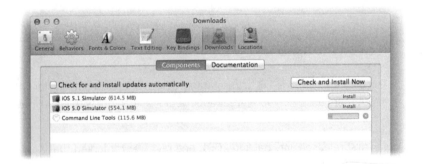

Figure 6-6.
Xcode alone isn't sufficient—you need the Command Line Tools, too. These used to be a standard part of the Xcode download, but now you get to jump through an extra hoop to get them.

After you've installed Xcode and the Command Line Tools, you'll want to install or update your XQuartz installation. (XQuartz is the windowing environment used by a ton of applications that aren't OS X native.) It came preinstalled on older versions of OS X, but in Mountain Lion, it isn't installed. If you already have XQuartz, launch it and install the latest updates for it. If you don't, head to Applications→Utilities→X11 and follow Apple's instructions for installing XQuartz.

Install Homebrew

Installing Homebrew is simply a matter of typing a single line into Terminal:

```
ruby -e "$(curl -fsSkL raw.github.com/mxcl/homebrew/go)"
```

Before we run this command, let's take a look at what it will do:

- `ruby` is a programming language built into your Mac. This command starts Ruby, and the `-e` tells Ruby a command is coming.
- `curl` stands for cURL, a command that fetches data from a server.
- `-fsSkL` is a set of flags that tell cURL when (and when *not*) to report errors, use progress bars, and so forth.
- `raw.github.com/mxcl/homebrew/go` tells cURL where to get Homebrew from.

Note: It turns out that the line of code you use to install Homebrew is the same line you use to uninstall it. So if you have Homebrew installed and need to get rid of it, type that command in and Homebrew will say it's already installed and give you a command to uninstall it.

Once you type that in and hit Return, you'll see information about what Homebrew is going to do. Once you've digested all of the changes Homebrew is going to make, press Return, and then type in your administrator password and hit Return yet again. It will take a few moments, but Homebrew will complete the installation process on its own.

When the process is complete, Terminal displays two instructions: it says to run the command `brew doctor` before you install anything, and to type `brew help` now. Typing `brew help` and then pressing Return displays some quick examples and troubleshooting tips that you should take a look at. The `brew doctor` command tells you about the installation. When you run this command, if Homebrew sees anything it doesn't like, it will let you know (Figure 6-7).

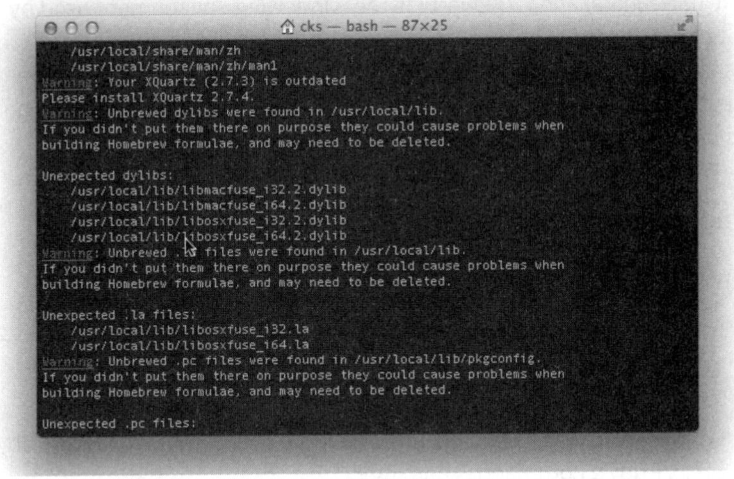

Figure 6-7.
Homebrew isn't seeing what it expected, so it's letting the world know something isn't right. It specifies the location of the offending files (in this case, /usr/local) so you can find and delete them.

In my case, Homebrew wasn't pleased about an old installation of the now deprecated MacFuse, so I manually deleted the files Homebrew listed. Once you delete any offending files, you can run `brew doctor` again and you'll see the message "Your system is raring to brew." So let's get brewing!

Tip: If you're loathe to navigate to the offending files using Terminal and don't want to turn on invisibles (by default, the usr folder—whose name is short for "Unix system resources"—is invisible in OS X), use the Finder instead. Choose Go→"Go to Folder" and you can see whatever folder you wish. In this case, typing in /usr/ local gave me access to the folder holding the suspect files so I could manually delete them.

There are a ton of apps you can install with Homebrew. One useful app is ImageMagick, which lets you do all sorts of nifty image manipulation so you can impress your friends, and Homebrew is a great way to install and manage it. Simply open a Terminal window and type:

```
brew install imagemagick
```

Homebrew takes care of the rest (Figure 6-8).

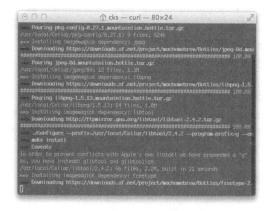

Figure 6-8.
Now you have a cool command-line image editor to play with, and you installed it with one line in Terminal instead of chasing various apps all day long.

Once the installation is over you've got ImageMagick. Well, maybe not. Look for any errors. My particular install said ghostscript was missing. ImageMagick needs ghost-script? But how can a person easily install ghostscript? Oh, yeah! Here's how:

```
brew install ghostscript
```

Now ImageMagick is ready to roll! See Hack #30 to learn how to use it.

HACK 29 Get Things Done Safely with the Command Line

Once you're relatively comfortable with the command-line interface, you'll want to do more with it. This hack takes you down the path to command-line proficiency.

Navigating Around Your Mac

Killing processes with the command line is great fun and empowering (Hack #27), but that example doesn't even *begin* to hint at all the command line's abilities. The first order of business is deciding how to move around using the command line. It isn't as intuitive as the GUI of OS X, but the process is straightforward. Try launching Terminal and typing this (remember, $ represents the command prompt; you don't actually need to type it in):

```
$ cd Documents
```

That command changes the *working directory* to the Documents folder of your home folder (cd is short for "change directory"). Your working directory is the one you're "in" at the moment; you can think of it as analogous to the active Finder window. You can see the results of moving to this directory by typing:

```
$ pwd
```

This command (short for "print working directory") makes Terminal display the path to the current destination: */Users/username/Documents*. (In Unix and many programming languages, *print* doesn't refer to printing text on a page; it just makes something appear onscreen—in this example, the current working directory.)

To get back to the home directory, type:

```
$ cd
```

This command is a lot like Dorothy's red slippers—it takes you back to your home directory no matter *where* you are in Unix space. You can, naturally, string things together. If you wanted to get to your iPhoto library, just keep extending the pathname of where you want to end up. To wit:

```
$ cd Pictures/iPhoto\ Library
```

There are a couple of things to note here. If you want Unix to understand where you want to go, you can't skip ahead and type only iPhoto\ Library; you'll have to follow the path from the directory where you currently sit (in this example, your home directory). Secondly, if the name of your destination contains a space, you have to replace the space with "\" (a forward slash and then a space). (It's enough to make you want to use underscores!)

Navigating backwards a single level is easy enough: two dots tell Unix to move up to the parent directory:

```
$ cd ..
```

If you're not a big fan of moving about using the command line, you can always use a nifty OS X feature that automatically completes the path. Simply type cd at the command prompt, followed by a space, and then drag a folder from a nearby Finder window over to your Terminal window. Your Mac will automatically fill in the path to that folder. For example, typing cd, then a space, and then dragging the iPhoto Library folder onto the Terminal window results in (on my Mac, anyhow) the following:

```
ElChupacabra:everything cks2$ cd /Users/cks2/Pictures/iPhoto\ Library
```

Hitting Return takes me to the desired directory:

```
ElChupacabra:iPhoto Library cks2$
```

Quick refresher: The stuff before the $ is useful because it tells you where you are. It lists your computer's name (ElChupacabra, in this example), the directory you're currently in (iPhoto Library), and your username (cks2).

Creating Directories and Working with Files

Now that you know the fundamentals of traveling about using the command line, we can move on to creating *directories* (the Unix term for "folders"). The command to create a directory is `mkdir`. On its own, `mkdir` doesn't do anything; it needs the name of the new directory, too. Type:

```
$ mkdir machacks
```

Whatever directory you were in before now has a new folder in it called machacks. Does this mean you can only create directories in whatever directory you're in at the moment? Of course not. You can use the navigation method we used earlier to choose any directory you want. Simply replace `cd` with `mkdir`, and the new directory can be created in the place of your choosing. This command, for example:

```
$ mkdir ~/Documents/machacks
```

Results in a folder called *machacks* in the Documents folder.

But what good is a directory without files in it? None at all, so now it's time to learn how to move files around. In Unix, you do that with the `mv` command. Here's what to do if you wish to move a file named *monk.tif* from your working directory into the newly created *machacks* folder:

```
$ mv monk.tif machacks/
```

The command moves the specified file into the *machacks* folder. You can also use `mv` to rename a file:

```
$ mv monk.tif machacks/monknew.tif
```

That changes the name of *monk.tif* to *monknew.tif* and also moves the file to the *machacks* folder. But you could just as well have kept it in the same location and changed the name by typing:

```
$ mv monk.tif monknew.tif
```

Of course, you don't always want to move a file; sometimes you just want to *copy* it. In Unix, the command for copying a file is `cp`. You have to specify the name of the file and the name of the copy:

```
$ cp monk.tif monkcopy.tif
```

This results in the original file *monk.tif* and an identical file called *monkcopy.tif* residing in the working directory. That's great and all, but most of the time you want the file copied to some other location. No problem. Just type:

```
$ cp monk.tif machacks/monkcopy.tif
```

That creates a copy of *monk.tif* called *monkcopy.tif* and deposits it in the *machacks* folder.

Tip: It's easy to forget that names don't always translate from the Finder to Unix. In Unix, the file extension is visible even if you saved a file with the Hide Extension option turned on. It's technically possible, though rare, to find files without extensions. That probably won't happen to you, but if it does, you've been warned. If you find yourself wondering why you can't copy a file that's clearly present in the Finder, use the ls *command to see if the name you're typing matches the name the command line is looking for.*

You've generated a directory and created some superfluous files. But who wants a bunch of worthless files lying around? Time to get rid of them!

Warning: We are about to invoke the rm *command. This is the time to remember that in Unix spelling, spacing, and capitalization all count. If you forget that, you might accidentally delete the wrong file.*

Before using the rm command (short for "remove"), it is a good idea to make sure you know where you are and what you're about to remove. To see a list of all the files in the working directory, type ls (short for "list") and then hit Return. Until you feel very confident in your command-line skills, run the ls command before the rm command so you can see what files are in the working directory before you banish them for eternity.

Time to get rid of that useless *monkcopy.tif* file. Type:

```
$ rm monkcopy.tif
```

Bam, *monkcopy.tif* is gone! And I mean *gone*—don't look for it in the Trash, because it's not there. It's been obliterated from your machine. So don't use rm unless you want to *completely* get rid of a file.

You can extend the rm command by specifying multiple files you want to delete. Simply put a space between the filenames. For example, this command deletes both *monk.tif* and *monkcopy.tif*:

```
$ rm monk.tif monkcopy.tif
```

You can include as many files as you wish, and they'll all be gone as soon as you hit Return.

Quick Hack: Make Terminal Warn You

The cp, mv, and rm are commands that give people new to Terminal pause. They're only two-letter commands, but they can be incredibly destructive. For instance, cp and mv will overwrite any files with the same names in the target directory without warning. This can be a real problem when you're moving files to a backup location; your old backups will be overwritten without a peep from Terminal. The rm command can be even more worrisome because those two letters are the Unix equivalent of saying goodbye forever.

The good news is that all three commands support the -i option, which will prompt you (in the case of cp and mv) if any files are going to be overwritten and (in the case of rm) which file is about to be deleted. In Terminal, type **rm -i filename** to use this feature. For example, if you're about to use rm to remove *monkcopy.tif* and type **rm -i monkcopy.tif**, Terminal will warn before it erases *monkcopy.tif*. This isn't a set-it-and-forget-it deal: you'll need to add the -i each time you use one of the commands if you want Terminal to warn you. (The -i bit is called a *flag*, and when used in conjunction with the rm, cp, and mv commands, it causes Terminal to warn you before it deletes data.)

Fancy Command-Line Moves

Moving files and creating directories is useful, but it's time to step things up a notch. It turns out that there's more power in these commands than is apparent from the way you've been using them.

In general, commands have *arguments* and *options* (a.k.a. *flags*). Arguments are usually the file you want the command to act upon (in rm monkcopy.tif, for instance, the argument is *monkcopy.tif*), and options are ways to specify how the command should work. Options vary from command to command. You can find a list of the options for any particular command by typing man (short for "manual") followed by the command you're interested in. For example, typing man ls returns a list of the various options you can invoke when using the ls command. (When you're done looking at the manual page, hit Q and you'll be back to a shell you can type in.)

It's one thing to read the list of the options; it's another to actually *use* them. Let's try stringing together a command, an option, and an argument. Pick a folder and type:

```
$ ls -F /usr/libexec/
```

You've specified a command (ls), an option (-F), and a folder to inspect (/usr/libexc/). Thanks to the option you supplied, ls won't just return a list of all the files; instead, it'll return a list in which directories are identified with a trailing / and executable files are identified with an *. Here's the partial output of that command:

```
ApplicationFirewall/  gdb/      rexecd*
CCLEngine*            getNAME*  rlogind*
InternetSharing*      getty*    rpc.rquotad*
MiniTerm.app/         gnurmt*   rpc.yppasswdd*
```

As you can see, the -F option modifies the behavior of the ls command. But there's more to adding options and arguments. You can string them together like so:

```
$ ls -F -a ~/Desktop/Chapter_4 ~/Desktop/bboah_bu
```

In my case, that command roots through a folder called *Chapter_4* and a folder called *bboah_bu* on my desktop and returns the results according to the ls command's -F -a flags (-a tell ls to list files that start with a ., which are usually invisible).

Finally, it turns out that there are a lot of hidden programs on your Mac. The Finder won't reveal them, but you can run them from the command line. One program included on the Mac is Diff, which can compare documents and show you the differences between them (particularly useful when you are updating an old file and a trick I wish I had remembered when writing *OS X Mountain Lion Pocket Guide*!).

The syntax for Diff is: diff *firstfile secondfile*. To make the differences easier to spot, we can make Diff display the output in two columns by adding the -y flag after the diff command. The actual command looks like this:

```
diff -y pathtofile1 pathtofile2
```

That will generate two columns showing you the difference between the two text files you're comparing. The thing about Diff isn't that it's so interesting; it's that it's such a good example of a command-line program. There are a lot of them, and they generally work the same way: command, flags, file(s). For a list of all the commands that are available to you, visit *this page* (*http://ss64.com/osx*). You'll be amazed.

HACK 30 Manipulate Images with ImageMagick

If you followed along with "Install Homebrew" (page 151), then you installed ImageMagick. Time for that hard work (well, okay—that single line of code in Terminal) to pay off.

ImageMagick is a free, open source image-editing program that has an amazing amount of power. With minimal effort in the Terminal, you can add watermarks, resize pictures, create animated GIFs, change file types, and much, much more. How much more? Even *ImageMagick's website* (*http://www.imagemagick.org*) doesn't list them all.

If you played along with "Install Homebrew" (page 151), you already have ImageMagick installed so there's no good reason to *talk* about what ImageMagick can do—you can just try it out! Before you get started, create a folder full of image files. Make sure these are copies of other files or files that you don't care if they get changed permanently, because this hack is here to show you the power of ImageMagick, not to refine your images to the standards of fine photographers! (ImageMagick is perfect for fine photography, it's just that the *Mac Hacks* folks don't have the skills of a fine photographer.)

For the purposes of this hack, I created a folder called *Feed ImageMagick*. Said folder contains a copy of the all the images from *Mac Hacks* thus far and a bunch of other pics I had lying about from other projects—around 275 files of mixed types, with a median file size of about 100 KB, and a max file size of 7 MB. Nothing too troublesome, but still a nice test of ImageMagick.

ImageMagick isn't a single application that does one or two things; it's actually a collection of different applications that each do something powerful to graphics (these are called *dependencies*, and they're one of the big reasons Homebrew is so neat). So while you won't see the term "ImageMagick" included in any command in this hack, everything the hack uses depends on ImageMagick.

To start, you need to launch Terminal and then change the directory you're in to the directory with the photos you want to use. In my case, the folder is on my desktop, so I typed:

```
cd /Users/cks/Desktop/feed/testpics
```

Alternatively, you can type **cd**, then drag the folder into the Terminal window, and then hit Return to accomplish the same thing.

Now that we're in the proper directory, we can use ImageMagick to create a montage. Type:

```
montage page41.jpg page42.jpg twopages.jpg
```

Montage tells your Mac to cram two pictures together; **page41.jpg page42.jpg** tells it which pics to use; and **twopages.jpg** tells it what to name the output file. All this results in Figure 6-9, which is a new file named *twopages.jpg* that's stored in the current directory.

Figure 6-9.
A pretty plain montage, but creating it with ImageMagick was much faster than doing it by hand.

Let's spice it up a bit and really challenge the montage function. Try this:

```
montage page30.jpg page31.jpg -geometry 500x500 pohno.jpg
```

In this case, `page30.jpg` and `page31.jpg` are the files we want glued together; `-geometry` `500x500` is how large we want the individual pics to be in pixels (montage won't stretch them but will, if necessary, shrink them to fit); and `pohno.jpg` is the file we want the result output to. The result is a much bigger and better pic.

There are plenty of other things you can do with ImageMagick's montage function. You can add borders, control how the images are laid out, and even add a label to each pic. Let's try it:

```
montage -label %f -frame 5 -geometry +4+4 page3.jpg page4.jpg page5.jpg
page6.jpg fancy.jpg
```

`-label %f` tells montage to add a label to each pic that's the same as the pic's filename; `-frame 5` tells montage to add a 5-pixel frame around the combined image; `-geometry` `+4+4` tells montage the preferred tile and border size; and `page3.jpg page4.jpg page5.jpg page6.jpg` are the source files I want to use. Finally, `fancy.jpg` is what I want montage to name the resulting file. The result is shown in Figure 6-10.

Figure 6-10.
This is getting absolutely useful.

There's a lot more you can do with the montage command. Someone could likely write a book about it, but there's no better way to learn about it than playing it. If you ever get confused, remember that typing `man montage` will show you the manual page for the function.

Let's use montage one more time, just for fun. Montage supports wildcards, so:

```
montage *.jpg -geometry 50X50 whathaveidone.jpg
```

This tells montage to cram every JPEG in the current directory into a single, um, montage. The resulting abomination looks like Figure 6-11.

Figure 6-11.
That's just disturbing.

If all ImageMagick did was make montages, it would be called Montage. So let's check out some of the other cool stuff ImageMagick can do. Imagine you want to create some thumbnails for your website. In that case, mogrify might be your friend. Let's try it on all the JPEGs:

```
mogrify -resize 256x256 *.jpg
```

This command resizes all the JPEG files in the current directory to 256×256 pixels. (Remember when you were warned to use test pics for this? It's a good thing you listened because mogrify just overwrote all the files it acted on.) You can also use mogrify to change file types, as in:

```
mogrify -format jpg *.gif
```

That command changes all the GIFs in the directory to JPEGs.

Mogrify is powerful, but many times you *don't* want to overwrite the images you want to change. In such cases, the convert tool is useful. It's nondestructive so try it out! For example:

```
convert page31.jpg page31.png
```

Transforms a JPEG into a PNG. That's great—but boring. How about some actual image manipulation?

```
convert page31.jpg -resize 50% onehalfpage31.jpg
```

This command takes the file named *page31.jpg*, reduces it in size by 50%, and creates a new file named *onehalfpage31.jpg* that contains the new, smaller image.

You can also rotate images with convert:

```
convert page31.jpg -rotate 25 ropage31.jpg
```

Which rotates *page31.jpg* 25 degrees and outputs the resulting file as *ropage31.jpg* (Figure 6-12).

Figure 6-12.
Timber!

These are nifty tricks, but how about creating a GIF with ImageMagick? We're not talking changing a file's type—we're talking about *making* one of those animated GIFs that every site had in 1998. With ImageMagick, it's easy.

First we want some numbered GIFs (the numbering makes everything easier). We already have a bunch of sequentially numbered JPEGs, so let's use mogrify to turn them into GIFs:

```
mogrify -format gif page*.jpg
```

This command turns JPEGs named *page somenumber.jpg* into GIFs. If you have a lot of files, you can watch mogrify work in the Finder. Just open up the folder where the images are and select Cover Flow view. As the file types change, Cover Flow view updates.

Once the files are converted, let's animate them:

```
Convert -delay 20 -loop 0 page*.gif animatespage.gif
```

If you open the resulting file (*animatepage.gif*) with Preview, you'll just see all the frames. But open it with Safari and you'll have a nice animated GIF.

All these examples just scratch the surface of what ImageMagick can do without the overhead of a GUI image editor. For more on what ImageMagick can do for you, visit *the Usage page* (*http://www.imagemagick.org/Usage/*). You'll be impressed!

HACK 31 Customize the Dock with Terminal

> You don't have to put up with the Dock's default behavior—you can keep all its functionality (and even add some) while bending the Dock to your will.

When it was initially introduced, the Dock was controversial. People have by and large become accustomed to it, but that doesn't mean they necessarily like it. If you're one of the people who grudgingly puts up with the Dock, you've probably already played with the settings in the Dock preference pane. If you still find the Dock wanting, you might find it a little more tolerable once you tweak it with Terminal.

Highlight that Item

When you open a folder or stack from the Dock, there's no visual feedback to tell you what item you're about to open unless you use the keyboard. If it's useful for the keyboard, wouldn't it also be useful for your trackpad/mouse? It's easy to lose the cursor against a dark background or black icon; this tweak fixes that problem. Launch Terminal and type:

```
defaults write com.apple.dock mouse-over-hilite-stack -boolean yes
```

Hit Return. And as with all of these tips, you have to relaunch the Dock to get this change to take effect, so follow it with:

```
killall Dock
```

In addition to giving you more feedback when working with stacks, this hack also makes lists and grids easier to navigate, as shown in Figure 6-13.

Figure 6-13.
Now you'll know what you're pointing at even when using the mouse and not the keyboard. (In this case, the cursor is over the FaceTime icon.)

Was that not for you? Turn it off with:

```
defaults write com.apple.dock mouse-over-hilite-stack -boolean no
```

Followed by:

```
killall Dock
```

Get Rid of the Glass

Some folks find the look of the reflective "glass" used in the Dock to be overdone and somewhat garish. If you're one of them, banish the eyesore with:

```
defaults write com.apple.dock no-glass -boolean yes
```

Which is (as you already guessed) followed by:

```
killall Dock
```

And the 3-D effect and the glass will be gone, as shown in Figure 6-14.

Figure 6-14.
Easier on the eyes? Easier to tell which apps are running, at least. This is one change the *Mac Hacks* lab is keeping.

Want to go back to the windshield look? No problem:

```
defaults write com.apple.dock no-glass -boolean no
```

Of course, that command won't do anything until its partner command comes along for the ride:

```
killall Dock
```

Add a Recent Applications Stack

You know that there's a nifty and useful Recent Items entry in the Apple menu, but remembering to use it is a bit of a chore, since you're used to using the Dock for launching, right? Turns out you can add a Recent Applications stack to the Dock and save yourself some time! In Terminal, type:

```
defaults write com.apple.dock persistent-others -array-add '{ "tile-data" =
{ "list-type" = 1; }; "tile-type" = "recents-tile"; }'
```

Isn't there something we're forgetting? Oh yes:

```
killall Dock
```

Now you'll have a Recent Applications stack (Figure 6-15)!

Figure 6-15.
The more you can keep stuff clustered in one area, the less time you'll spend mousing around.

To undo this tweak, we have to use a new technique: drag the stack to the trash.

Organize Your Dock with Spaces

Some people love organization, but there just isn't a lot you can to do organize the Dock. Sure, you can put things in a preferred order (though the Finder and Trash are exceptions), but that's only so interesting. What if you could add empty spaces to your Dock so you could group similar apps together? Let's do it. Type:

```
defaults write com.apple.dock persistent-apps -array-add '{"tile-
type"="spacer-tile";}'
```

Then use that loyal follower:

```
killall Dock
```

That's it. For every space you want to add, simply repeat these two commands. In Figure 6-16 two spaces have been added.

Figure 6-16.
The blank spaces were added by Terminal. You can use as many as you wish and organize your Dock as you see fit.

To get rid of the spaces, banish them from the Dock by dragging them to the Trash.

Have the Dock Display Only Running Apps

Icons are on the Dock so you can easily launch the programs they represent, but if you use an alternative method to launch programs (such as Spotlight or Quicksilver, then you don't really need those icons on the Dock. You can keep the Dock's clutter to a minimum by forcing the Dock to only display icons for running applications. In Terminal, type:

```
defaults write com.apple.dock static-only -bool true
```

Look, over there in the bushes! It's:

```
killall Dock
```

Your new, slimmed-down Dock includes only the apps that are currently running (Figure 6-17).

Figure 6-17.
Now that's a minimalistic Dock!

Sounded good on paper but don't like it in action? Undo it with:

```
defaults write com.apple.dock static-only -bool false
```

And, making its final appearance in this hack:

```
killall Dock
```

7

Lock Down that Mac

One supposes that a Mac connected only to a power source, in a secure location, and without network access would be perfectly safe. But it would also be practically useless. The way the world works demands that your Mac be online, and the way you *watch* the world demands it, too. There's no reason that this has to be an inherently unsafe proposition. This chapter explains how to lock your Mac down and safely go about your daily business with some peace of mind.

HACK 32 Achieve Network Anonymity

> While you're bouncing around on the Internet, the Internet is keeping an eye on you. This hack explains how to jump around the Web without giving away information about yourself or your computer using free tools and services.

You know that when you visit a website, you're giving up information about yourself. This might be something you can live with or it might be something you can't abide. There's no way to know unless you're aware of how much information you're giving up when you visit a site or connect to another computer. Turns out you can find out what info you're giving out by visiting *Panopticlick* (*https://panopticlick.eff.org*) and clicking the site's Test Me button. Figure 7-1 shows the type of results you'll see.

Figure 7-1.
You leave behind a lot of information when you browse the Web. Is it too much?

The nifty tool you just used is brought to you by the Electronic Freedom Foundation. The results might worry you a bit, but you probably don't need to fret too much. While you'll likely be told your browser fingerprint is unique, it's a big jump from that to someone actually being able to identify your computer as the source.

That noted, websites can use the information you broadcast and learn quite a bit about you and your habits with *cookies*. Cookies are little packets of information stored by your browser that can let a website know that you've been there previously and how you want things configured. That seems innocuous, but there are also *tracking* cookies that track every site you visit. As you can imagine, that level of information could reveal information you'd rather keep to yourself. Don't worry—taking care of cookies is easy.

Control Those Cookies

If you're worried about cookies, head to Safari→Preferences→Privacy. You'll see a Re-move All Website Data button, which wipes out *all* your cookies. However, this is prob-ably a bit extreme for most folks, so instead, try inspecting all the cookies in Safari manually by clicking the Details button. This will bring up a list of all the cookies and other information stored by your browser. You can delete the information on a case-by-case basis, as shown in Figure 7-2.

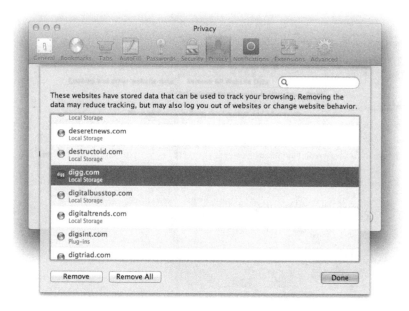

Figure 7-2.
Deleting cookies one at a time. It's cumbersome, but the result will be more to your liking.

After you've finished deleting the little bundles of tracking that you no longer want, click Done. Back on the Privacy tab, in the "Block cookies" section, you have a decision to make about the future: do you want to only accept cookies from sites you navigate to (the default setting, "From third parties and advertiser"), stop accepting cookies altogether (Always), or make like a famished moppet and accept every cookie sent your way (Never)? It's your choice, but the default option works well for most users. For the security minded, Always is the preferred setting.

If you're not satisfied with that level of control, you can go completely incognito by using an *anonymizer*. These online sites route your network traffic through their servers, leaving the impression that their associated IP address was the point of origin. Several sites provide this service, such as *Anonymouse (http://www.anony-mouse.org)*, shown in Figure 7-3. A Google search for "anonymizer" will get you a bevy of other options.

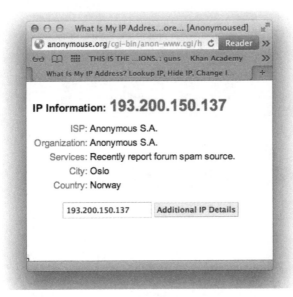

Figure 7-3.
The closest this computer will ever come to Oslo is the Norway exhibit at Epcot, but that's where the IP address it's currently using points to!

While using Anonymouse or a similar web service seems like an ideal solution, there are some drawbacks. Since these sites anonymize people, shady types sometimes exploit them for spam and such. Many websites are wise to this, so you'll likely run into a ton of captchas you wouldn't usually have to deal with.

The second problem is that most of these anonymizers handle HTTP requests only. That's fine when you want to browse the Web, but not so great when you want to transfer a large file, because such files are generally handled by a different protocol (FTP). So if you want to transfer a big file—like a song, for example—you won't be helped by an anonymizer.

If the little inconveniences and the (unlikely) possibility of ne'er-do-wells compromising your information when using a web-based anonymous proxy are too much to bear, it is time to think about Tor.

Unlike a web-based anonymizer, which makes it look as if all your traffic is emanating from its server, Tor works by routing your traffic through *numerous* other computers. It aims to keep you anonymous by making your path very hard to follow. Imagine the connection from your computer to a particular site as a piece of string. It's trivially easy to follow that string from a data-harvesting site back to your computer. But with Tor, the string doesn't point back to your computer; it points back to *another* computer, which points back to yet another computer, etc. Put differently, Tor transforms your connection from a single string to a ball of twine with 20 ends hanging out in every direction.

Tip: Some sites block requests from known anonymous servers. Because Tor routes your Internet traffic through any number of different servers, you're much less likely to be blocked when using Tor than when using an anonymizer.

To start using Tor, simply head to *the download page* (*http://www.torproject.org/ download*) and grab the browser bundle. This will get you browsing anonymously in no time (you'll need to have Firefox on your Mac). Once the download is finished, double-click it and you'll be informed of your success (Figure 7-4).

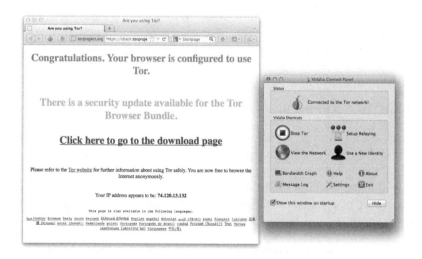

Figure 7-4.
Tor will automatically fire up a browser and nifty control panel when you launch Vidalia. You're browsing anonymously in seconds.

You can now safely browse the Internet using Tor (Tor does the legwork of anonymizing your data; Vidalia provides the graphical interface to control Tor). But before you start, read the "Want Tor to really work?" section at the bottom of the download page. It includes five really good suggestions for protecting yourself while browsing with Tor.

Warning: Tor offers an easy path to anonymity, but it doesn't do anything at all for privacy. Using Tor is a little like going to a foreign country and streaking: no one knows who you are, so you're anonymous, but anyone who cares to look can see you running about in the nude. In other words, all your data sent over the network is easily peered at and analyzed by the person running the Tor server (specifically, the exit node) that the information passes through. So while Tor is great for helping you be reasonably anonymous, it's not a good idea to use Tor to send out any critical unencrypted data.

Now that you can safely browse the Net, you might wonder about other ways you connect to the Net and how to anonymize those connections. For example, if you use Messages (formerly known as iChat), you might want to make those communications untraceable. You can do that with Tor, but it takes a little configuring. You can find information on how to Tor-ify individual applications and protocols at *the wiki page* (*http://tinyurl.com/bloa875*).

HACK 33 Monitor Your Network Traffic

Everyone worries about someone secretly accessing their machine over the network, but not as many people worry about just what their Mac is sending out over the network. Learn how to keep an eye on the data going into *and* coming out of your Mac.

Using Mac OS X's Firewall

When you load a program on your Mac, you usually do so for a specific reason. For example, if you're into photo management, you install a piece of software to manage your photos. What most people *don't* knowingly do is load software on to their computer knowing that the software will use your always-on Internet connection to phone home and report that status of the program to the company that produced the software.

Usually the check-in with the corporation's servers is completely innocuous—the software is just checking for updates or getting help topics. But other times, the call back to home isn't as benign. The program could be checking to see if your copy of the software is valid, or it might be relaying information you'd rather not broadcast. Of course, not all software does this. Some programs are completely upfront about when and why they check in with home base. But other programs check with more stealth.

While it's easy to sympathize with a software company's desire not to have its titles pirated, it's a headache when legitimate use of a program is blocked by the company's antipiracy efforts. To put a face on this problem: User CKS has multiple Macs and rarely bothers quitting a program. On more than one occasion, he has been prevented from using a particular program on one machine because another instance of the program is running on another machine (Microsoft Office is one example of a program that does this). So even though User CKS is only attempting to actively use one copy of the software, he's prevented from doing so because the program has been phoning home.

Denying users use of legitimately obtained software isn't just annoying, it also means that the software is communicating to another computer somewhere without the user's knowledge. In some cases, it's just another computer on your network, as when the running copies of a program compare license keys. But in some cases, this communication is with a server somewhere else—and that's a little disconcerting. If a program is calling home without your knowledge, you don't really have any idea what information the program is actually sending. This is something you'd probably like to put a stop to.

If you want more control over the data entering and leaving your Mac, what you're really after is a *firewall*. A firewall separates the Internet from your computer and, depending on which firewall you use, it can be customized to meet your needs. As you can probably imagine, customizing a firewall can either be so superficial as to be worthless or so arcane as to be indecipherable. What most users would like is just a little more control with a minimal amount of effort.

OS X comes with a built-in firewall that is turned off by default. Why is that the default setting? Because chances are that your Mac is behind the firewall that's part of your router, so having the OS X firewall off makes for easy connections with all your other Apple devices.

But that doesn't mean you have to *leave* the OS X firewall turned off. If you use a laptop and hop onto a lot of different networks, you'll likely want to turn the firewall on. It's easy to do: just head to System Preferences→Security & Privacy→Firewall. Once there, click the lock icon, authenticate, and then (on the Firewall tab) click the Turn On Firewall button (Figure 7-5).

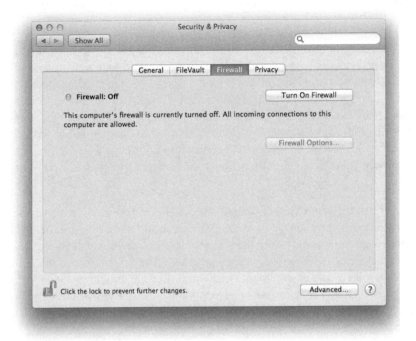

Figure 7-5.
The default Firewall setting in OS X is off, which means your Mac will listen to and chat with anyone (or anything).

Just turning on your Mac's firewall doesn't seem to do much except light up the green circle next to Firewall: On. There's more going on, you just won't see it until you click Firewall Options. On the pane that appears (Figure 7-6), you can set access on a per-app basis or even block *all* incoming connections. You can go as crazy as you want configuring everything, and once you're done you can rest safely knowing your Mac is better protected.

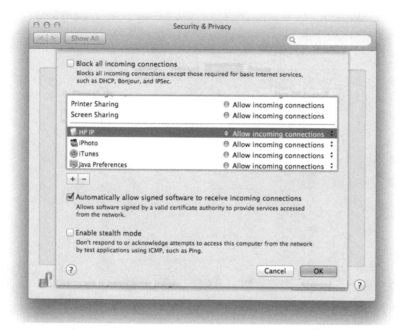

Figure 7-6.
OS X's fully adjustable per-app firewall. You can tweak this list anytime, ensuring that only the connections you want to allow are made.

Quick Hack: Enable Stealth Mode

This hack is about limiting the information leaving your Mac, but since you're adjusting the firewall settings anyway, you might want to consider enabling stealth mode. This won't stop your Mac from sending information out, but any other computer that tries to contact your machine will receive no response—essentially telling the other machine that nothing at all resides at your IP address. To turn stealth mode on, head to the Security & Privacy preference pane, click the Advanced button in the Firewall tab, and then turn on the "Enable stealth mode" checkbox. Why would you want to do this? Well, if someone is looking for a receptive host computer and yours doesn't respond, they'll look elsewhere.

More Information with Private Eye

You can secure your Mac as tightly as you'd like with the built-in firewall, but that only gives you control over what apps can connect to outside connections, not what they can connect *to*. What an app is connecting to is easily as interesting whether or not it's making connections, so a tool to see what an app is up to on the Net would be ideal.

Fortunately such a tool exists and (happy day) it's free. It's called Private Eye and you can download it *here* (*http://radiosilenceapp.com/private-eye*). Once it's installed, launch Private Eye and look at what the gumshoe can do for you (Figure 7-7).

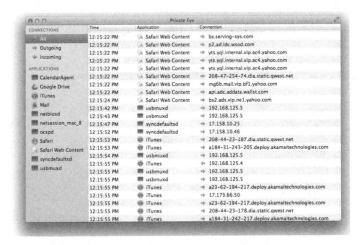

Figure 7-7.
Private Eye in action! You can see whether data is inbound or outbound, which app is using it, and where the data is headed. Here, usbmuxd is sending info to an iPhone through a WiFi network (the IP associated with the only iPhone on the WiFi network is 192.168.125.5).

Private Eye reveals a lot of info that you can filter by using the sidebar on the left side of the window. If you're worried that Private Eye is going to constantly scan your data's comings and goings, worry not—Private Eye only works when its program window is open. If you see that a program is sending out data and you don't think it needs to be doing that, note what program it is and find a replacement.

So now you know how to stop network traffic with the firewall that's built in to OS X, you know how to monitor the traffic and where it's going with Private Eye, and you're probably wondering about the next logical step: how to tell what data your computer is sending and/or receiving?

How Is Data Sent?

Turns out that when your computer communicates over a network, it uses a technique called *packet switching*. It's an old concept in the computer world, but a very useful one. What it means is that, instead of sending a movie (for example) as one giant file to your Mac, the file is chopped up into packets of a suitably small size. These packets are then sent to your Mac where they're decoded and stitched back together all so you can watch that Oscar-nominated film without dragging yourself to the local art-house theater.

MAC HACKS

It isn't much of a trick to see the exact data your computer is sending out: all you need is a packet analyzer and a little time. There are plenty of packet analyzers for OS X, but one of the easiest to use is Cocoa Packet Analyzer. While this tool lacks some bells and whistles that other packet analyzers offer, it's easy to get up and running and will introduce you to the world of packet analysis. To get the app, head to *the TastyCocoaBytes download page (http://www.tastycocoabytes.com/cpa).* (The app is also in the Mac App Store, but that version won't capture packets, so be sure to get it directly from *TastyCocoaBytes (http://tastycocoabytes.com).*)

Once Cocoa Packet Analyzer is installed, fire up the app and click the Capturing button. When you do, you'll see a pane where you choose which interface you want to capture the packets from. The Interface field will give you a variety of interfaces to choose from; you'll usually want to select en0 (Ethernet) or en1 (WiFi) depending on whether your Mac uses a wired or wireless Internet connection. Once you've made your selection, click the Start button, authenticate, and watch Cocoa Packet Analyzer grab those packets (Figure 7-8)!

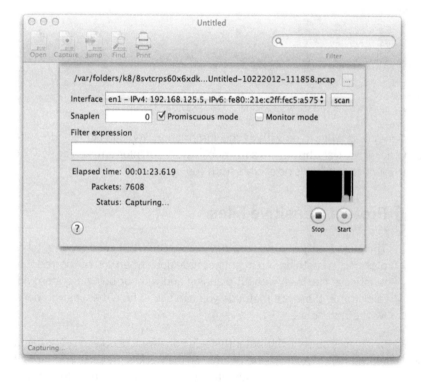

Figure 7-8.
Cocoa Packet Analyzer capturing packets. Don't worry, it isn't intercepting the packets, it's just copying them, so feel free to use your Mac as you usually would while CPA is running.

Once Cocoa Packet Analyzer has run for what you feel is a reasonable amount of time (meaning you've collected enough packets to play with), click Stop. You'll be in captured-packet nirvana! (See Figure 7-9.)

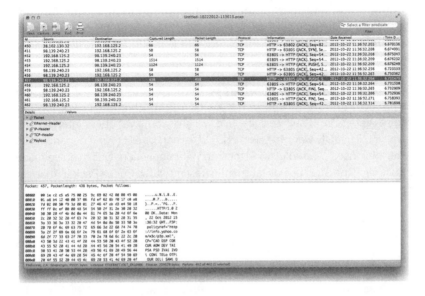

Figure 7-9.
Captured packets, which let you see what your Mac was sending and receiving.

The question now is what to do with all this information. You can actually do quite advanced packet analysis, but that's a full book's worth of information. For now, be happy that your network holds no secrets from you.

HACK 34 Protect Sensitive Files

There are plenty of ways to secure files in OS X, but good security takes planning, something you might not have done when you ran across that must-save file. Even without planning and without being a system administrator, there are methods you can use to hide the files you don't want others to see.

There are probably files on your computer that you don't want people to see. It might be financial information, embarrassing poems, or the world's greatest invention. It really doesn't matter what it is—if it's something you don't want others to see, you need to know the tricks to keep other eyeballs off your work while keeping the data accessible to you.

The most obvious solution to this problem is simply taking proper security procedures: use strong passwords, multiple accounts, encrypt everything with FileVault, etc. Taking those steps will provide a great deal of security for your files, but most people don't bother to—or can't—take all those steps. For example, if you work on a shared Mac in an office with lax security procedures, the system administrator might have everyone working off the same account. Or, if you use your computer around the house, you likely have it set to auto login and family members just come and use the Mac as they wish without separate, secured user accounts.

Many (probably most) users get by using their Macs in this fashion, and it usually isn't that big a deal. If your computer mates at work aren't interested in delving into the Mac and your family members are using your home machine mainly for web surfing, everything will probably be okay. That isn't to say that one account for everyone can't lead to serious problems—it surely can, particularly if it's an administrator account. It's just that most people don't run into insurmountable problems.

A problem people *do* run into when using a shared Mac is one of keeping their really private stuff *truly* private. Say you've found a video you want to share with your friend, just to see their reaction. If you save it to your desktop as a file called *reallyfunnyvi deo.m4v* or *supergross.mp4*, there's a good chance someone else won't be able to resist the temptation to take a look. But some things just don't go over well at work or at home. You need to hide that file.

The Quick and Easy Way: Bury It in Your Library

Probably the easiest way to hide files is simply to put them somewhere no one (not even Spotlight) is likely to look. If you're logged in as an administrator, you can make this place just about anywhere you want: in the system library, deep in an application package, or in a fake account you set up. These are all great places, but ones that require authentication to use. For nonadmin users, their user library comes to the rescue. The user library is a pretty boring place, and shoving a file somewhere inconspicuous inside it is likely to keep your plans secret (see Figure 7-10).

Note: In Lion and Mountain Lion, the user Library folder is hidden (even better!). To see it in the Finder, click the Go menu and then press the Option key.

Make It Disappear

When OS X first came out, one of the common reactions among computer critics in the know was that OS X hid its Unix roots very well. What they meant was that, while OS X is based on a system that had been around forever (in computer years, anyway), not much of the text-based Unix came through. The thing is, all that Unixy stuff is still there; you just can't see it. OS X manages to hide the files from view, so the end user is presented with a clean GUI to play with. One of the ways OS X achieves this is by making a lot of files invisible. Visibility of a file or folder is controlled by a bit that is set

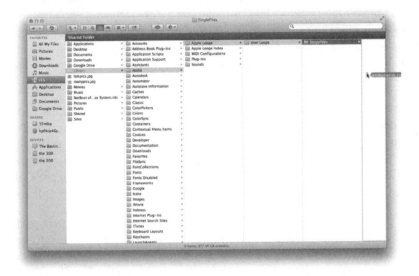

Figure 7-10.
Even Spotlight won't know.

to either visible or invisible. You can edit the bit by hand, rendering formerly invisible files visible or vice versa. Fire up the Terminal and type:

```
setfile -a V testfile.txt
```

Where *testfile.txt* is any file you want hidden. To make the file visible again, in the Terminal, type:

```
setfile -a v testfile.txt
```

That's right: the only difference is whether the v is capitalized or lowercase V, but it makes *all* the difference.

You can still open an invisible file, but you'll need to use Terminal to do so because it's mighty hard to click something represented by zero pixels. Try:

```
open testfile.txt
```

This command doesn't just work for individual files, it works for folders (directories) as well—with one important difference: with individual files, you have to toggle their visibility, but use this trick on a folder and you can store visible items inside the invisible folder and those files remain invisible to everyone else. To get at the files in an invisible folder, in the finder, select Go→"Go to Folder."

Alas, Spotlight will still index the contents of the invisible folder and that, obviously, won't do. Exclude the hidden folder from Spotlight by opening Spotlight's preferences

(System Preferences→Spotlight). Click the Privacy tab and then add the folder you want hidden to the list of places you don't want Spotlight to search (Figure 7-11). Simply click the + sign below the list and then navigate to the directory you want to keep under the radar.

Figure 7-11.
Keeping Spotlight from searching specific locations is a necessary step when hiding files.

Since it's a directory, you can toss any files you want into the hidden folder without switching the files' visibility with Terminal. The files won't be visible because they're in an invisible folder, but they're *technically* still visible because you haven't changed their visibility setting. Confusing? Yes. If it helps, you can think of it as sort of like Harry Potter's cloak: Harry isn't actually invisible, so if you're with him under the cloak you can see him, but no one *outside* the cloak can see him. (The Invisible Woman, on the other hand, she's just plain invisible.) To access the files in the Finder, press Shift-Command-G or choose Go→"Go to Folder." Type in the path to your folder (such as **~/worlddomplan1**), and you'll be able to browse the files in your favorite GUI manner.

How hard will these files be to find? Using either method (hiding individual files or a whole folder) will defeat a Spotlight search, but things could get dicey if the folder or files get too large. You don't have to put the files or folder in a particular spot, but wherever you put them, their size will be the giveaway and people may notice that if they sort the disk by file size. No one is ever going to notice a few kilobytes being taken up by a small directory, but if you're slapping Blu-ray rips of *Honey Boo Boo* into a hidden folder, that will likely be discovered if someone is trying to save some drive space.

Hiding Files in a Disk Image

Perhaps a more elegant way to hide files on the fly is with an encrypted disk image. This hack works on two levels. The first level is social engineering: we'll name the disk image something so boring that no one will want to look at it. Second, we'll password-protect the data so if someone does try to take a peek, they'll need a password. Will it be safer if you bury the disk image? Probably, but you can let it sit right on the desktop if you play your cards right.

To get started, launch Disk Utility (Applications→Utilities→Disk Utility) and then click New Image. Now here's the crucial naming part. You'll want a name so impossibly boring that no one would ever want to look at the disk image. How about *Principia_Latin_Version*? That should keep the files from being looked at anywhere outside a university physics building. If you happen to be trying to pull this hack off in a physics building (like I once did), a better choice is probably *PORNO* or *interpretive_dance_reviews*. The important thing is to know the types of people likely to be using the computer and to adjust the name accordingly (see Figure 7-12). Type the appropriate name in the Save As box.

After that, pick an appropriate size. The default size is 100 MB, but obviously you'll want something big enough to hold all the files, so change the size to suit your needs. Finally, choose your encryption method and pick a good password. Type the password twice and ensure the "Add to Keychain" box is *unchecked* because, unless you've changed the defaults, Keychain will automatically type the password in for you, which is obviously self-defeating in this case.

After the image is created, the disk will auto-mount. Drag any files you wish to the disk and then eject the disk. The *.dmg* you created will remain, but the files inside won't be visible with a Spotlight search, and anyone trying to open the *.dmg* will be required to enter the password you created.

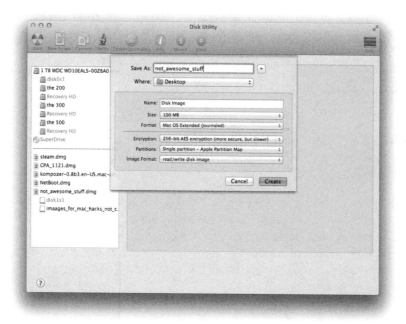

Figure 7-12.
Creating an encrypted *.dmg*.

It's Better to Be Better

Thanks to an easy-to-use feature of OS X called FileVault 2, you can encrypt your Home folder.

> *Note: In Mountain Lion, FileVault 2 is just called FileVault. In Lion, it was a big deal so Apple made sure you knew it was FileVault 2. It's still a great feature, and still technically FileVault 2, but OS X Mountain Lion simply refers to it as FileVault.*

Once encrypted, it can't be accessed, even if the firmware password is removed or your hard drive is stolen. In fact, your Mac's disk is ciphered with XTS-AES 128 (Advanced Encryption Standard with 128-bit key), and files can't be read if the correct password isn't provided. (You enable FileVault 2 on a user-by-user basis; each person's password will allow them to access their own disk.)

Tip: This is a good time to point out that having very different passwords is a really good idea. Say you've set your firmware password to "Letmein" and your administrator password to "kn030213zOO#4.fgh." Even if someone compromises your firmware password, they still have to figure out the other password. Far too many people will use the same password with minor variations over and over and this is definitely not the time you want to do that.

To enable FileVault 2, go to System Preferences→Security & Privacy and click the FileVault tab. Click the bottom-left lock icon to authenticate and change settings. Then click "Turn on FileVault."

At this point, you'll get a long recovery key (OS X calls it a "safety net") that you can use if you forget the password (see Figure 7-13). Write down this key and keep it in a safe place. When you click Continue, you'll get the option to store the recovery key with Apple by filling out a form. It's a good idea to take Apple up on this offer (remember, if you store the key on your Mac and forget the administrator password, you won't be able to retrieve the key).

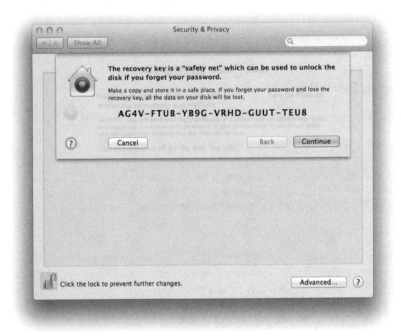

Figure 7-13.
A FileVault 2–supplied recovery key.

Once you enable FileVault 2, things change a bit. All the files in your Home directory will be encrypted and will be automatically deciphered after you login. Sounds processor intensive, right? Actually, it isn't—this feature is almost transparent to the user (so you shouldn't notice your computer running any slower) and provides great protection against people accessing your files.

HACK 35 Encrypt a USB Drive

You know how to encrypt your hard drive (Hack #34), but what if you want that same level of safety when you're physically transporting files? This hack shows you how to encrypt a USB drive (or other portable drive) with state-of-the-art security.

The preferred method of sharing files is Dropbox or iCloud. Those sites work well unless the files are large or you've got a ton of them. In either of those cases, you'll want to consider transferring the files by hand—by physically carrying them from one place to another.

The first thing you'll need to pull this off is an appropriately sized drive that's either blank or doesn't have any important info on it (since you're going to erase it before encrypting it). Flash memory has become very affordable in recent years (a 16 GB flash drive can be had for under 10 bucks), so finding a drive large enough for your data shouldn't be a problem unless you're rendering the next Pixar movie.

> Note: This hack is written with a USB flash drive in mind, but this technique works with just about any drive.

Once you've got a portable drive, it's time to mount it on your Mac (that's the geeky way of saying "jam the drive in the USB slot"). Once you've done that, you'll see it in the sidebar of a Finder window or on the desktop (depending on how your preferences are set).

If you've been reading this book in order, you can guess what the next step is; if you haven't (it's *your* book, after all, so read it however you wish), the utility you need to password protect your drive is Disk Utility (Applications→Utilities→Disk Utility). Upon opening Disk Utility, you'll be presented with a window resembling Figure 7-14.

Figure 7-14.
Disk Utility lists all the drives connected to your Mac, so proceed with caution. This Mac, for example, has one internal drive with three partitions and the USB drive inserted into the USB slot. Note the different look of the icons representing the drives.

Warning: Fortunately, Disk Utility won't allow you to mess up the startup disk. But you can suffer catastrophic data loss on any of the other drives you have connected to your Mac if you try this process on the wrong drive.

Once you've picked the right drive, you've got a decision to make. Do you want to encrypt the *entire* drive or partition the drive and encrypt only part of it? In this hack, we'll encrypt the entire drive, but this process will work on just part of the drive, as well (see Hack #03 for more on partitioning drives).

To get the process rolling, click the name of the drive you want to encrypt, and then click the Erase button at the top of the righthand pane as shown in Figure 7-15.

Among the various settings, you'll find a world of new options in Format menu:

Mac OS Extended (Journaled)
Mac OS Extended (Journaled, Encrypted)
Mac OS Extended (Case-sensitive, Journaled)
Mac OS Extended (Case-sensitive, Journaled, Encrypted)
MS DOS (FAT)
Ex FAT

You'll want to choose either "Mac OS Extended (Journaled, Encrypted)" or "Mac OS Extended (Case-sensitive, Journaled, Encrypted)." Which option is right for you? That depends. The difference between the two options isn't as big as you might imagine. The case-sensitive option means that OS X will pay attention to the capitalization (upper- and lowercase) of names, whereas the non-case-sensitive option doesn't discern between j and J, for example. To put a finer point on it: if you choose case-sensitive, you'll be able to put a folder called Pictures inside a folder called PICTURES; if you choose the other option, OS X will see the two folders as having the same name

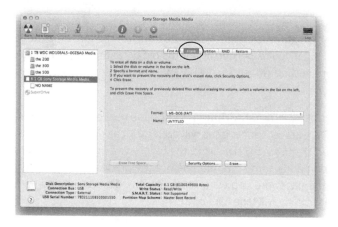

Figure 7-15.
This drive is selected at the mount point (the highest level of the drive), but you could select any drive in the left column. For example, if you wanted to encrypt just one partition of your hard drive, you'd select that partition.

and won't let you nest them. This isn't a huge issue for most people, but knowing what behavior to expect can save you headaches down the road. So just choose the format option that best suits your organizational habits.

Now it's time to let your creative side shine through: you get to rename the drive to something meaningful (or, barring that, something entertaining). Simply type the new moniker in the Name field. Once you've done that, it's time to step into the past. What was on the drive before you decided to use it as a secure device? If you just bought it from your local USB Drive Shoppe, go ahead and click the Erase... button. But if you've previously stored sensitive data on the drive, you'll want to consider *securely* erasing the drive.

Why Should You Care About Erased Data?

When you're about to erase the data from a drive, you might be wondering why you should bother securely erasing it. It turns out your computer is lazy. If you just tell it to erase the data, it only erases the *reference* to the data, which is kind of like ripping the table of contents out of a book and imagining that no one will bother looking at the actual pages. When you want the data to be truly gone, you have to securely erase the drive instead. You might think that this involves simply deleting all the data on the disk, but the method your Mac uses for this procedure is counterintuitive: your Mac erases the disk by writing over the existing data (kind of like using a black Sharpie to redact info on sensitive documents).

To securely erase the drive, click Security Options. You'll get a nifty slider that lets you decide whether your Mac should be lackadaisical about the previous data or go full on cold war and overwrite the data *seven times*. With a USB stick or other nonmagnetic memory, once is enough; but if you're worried about the old data, the only drawback to choosing the maximum setting (Most Secure) is that the erasing process takes slightly longer.

Whether you choose to invoke the Security Options or not, the next step is the same: time to erase the drive. Click Erase... and a pane will drop down asking if you're sure you *really* want to proceed (Figure 7-16). This isn't the binary yes-or-no pane you're likely used to; this pane demands some attention before the process can move forward. To proceed, enter the password you want to use for the drive twice and then click the Erase button. Disk Utility will take care of the rest.

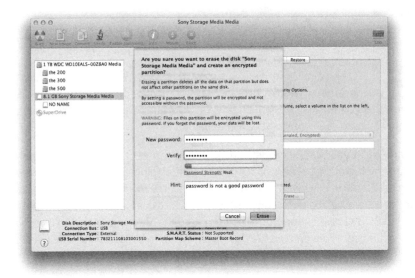

Figure 7-16.
The disk is about to get erased and encrypted. Note that Disk Utility is judgmental and will rate your password.

The process could take some time depending on the settings you choose and the size of the disk. You don't want to remove the disk while the formatting process is going on, so Disk Utility displays a tiny bar in the lower-right part of the pane indicating its progress. (For reference, on a 2009 iMac, an 8 GB USB stick was securely erased, encrypted, and formatted in less than 30 seconds.)

Using Your New Drive

Once the drive is encrypted, you can use it in the same fashion you've always used it. The big difference is that now you'll see something like Figure 7-17 when you attempt to mount the drive. Type in the password correctly and you can use the drive as you wish. Type in an incorrect password and the window will shake and you'll be denied access.

Figure 7-17.
Hope you remembered your password. If you didn't, you can use the Show Hint button to give your-self a hint—if you remembered to add one when you encrypted the disk, that is.

Beyond the Hack

An encrypted portable drive sounds great, but the privacy-minded among us will quickly object that, while the password protection is great if you just lose the drive, the password isn't very good if someone wants the data out of you. The problem is that, while nefarious types can't get at the data directly, they might have access to *you*. Sure, you've memorized an unbreakable, 128-random-character password that can't be brute-forced with all the computing power in the world. But it if they decide to use the password-cracking algorithm known as "a t-ball bat to the knees," that password won't last long.

The easiest way to avoid such complications is to not physically transport any sensitive data. Unfortunately, that isn't always an option. When you have to physically move data, a little misdirection can help. What if you could use a completely normal drive and partition part of it to be invisible? For example, you could partition a 4 GB drive into a visible 2 GB section and an invisible 2 GB section. That way, anyone examining the drive would likely assume you had a 2 GB drive with nothing interesting on it.

That's the idea behind TrueCrypt, which can do a lot of nifty things including make a partition invisible so you always have plausible deniability. To get started, head to *the TrueCrypt download page (http://www.truecrypt.org/downloads)* and download the version for OS X. (TrueCrypt is free but the team accepts donations; don't be afraid to make one!)

Add Physical Security Measures to Your Mac

> You've protected your Mac from the networks you use; now protect it from people who can touch it!

With Mountain Lion, Apple introduced a new feature called Gatekeeper that allows you to specify what apps your Mac can run based on where you procured them. You can, for example, set your Mac so that it will refuse to install an app that isn't from the Mac App Store (to adjust these settings, head to the General tab of the Security & Privacy preference pane). Like sandboxing (wherein apps are run separately from the operating system) and permissions, these steps help protect your Mac from malicious and/or inept developers.

Protecting your Mac from developers and network intruders is one thing, but your Mac isn't safe without *physical* protections, too. Physical access to your Mac means that someone could steal it or—if you've left the default settings in place—simply turn it on (or wake it from sleep) and access files. Obviously, stealing your Mac doesn't require a password—and until you set one, neither does waking your Mac. So how can you achieve maximum security for your precious files? The best option is never to lose physical control of your computer, but that method can be unwieldy (especially in the shower). This hack shows you steps you can take to protect your Mac and files from someone with physical access.

You want your data to be safe from crashes, user error, and prying eyes. Time Machine or solid backups have you covered for the crash and user-error scenarios, but you want more security than that. So just how do you protect your Mac from the nosey? There are four different solutions, and they're described in the following sections.

Security Cables

Most Macs feature a security slot (which is specially designed to accept a security cable), and you can find cables and locks specifically designed to use this slot, making your Mac impossible to steal without cutting the cable. But some Macs (MacBook Airs and MacBook Pro Retinas) don't have security slots because there simply isn't room in their minimalist design. Does that mean that fans of Retinas and utra-light Airs are stuck bathing with their machines? Nope—if you're lucky enough to own one Apple's cutting-edge laptops, you can find various solutions ranging from lockable protective cases to clever cables. The site *Maclocks site* (*http://www.maclocks.com*) is one good place to find them.

Screensaver/Sleep Password

Protecting your computer from unauthorized "borrowing" is a good idea, but it doesn't protect your *data* from those with physical access. This scenario is familiar to many of us: you work in an office but spend a lot of time away from your desk. When you leave your desk, you likely leave your Mac on so you can skip the tedium of a restart. Your Mac is just sitting there, alone, defenseless against the hordes who might want to steal all your hard work and take credit for it! Even if you have honest coworkers who help orphans fill out college applications, there will still be at least one joker who will mess with your computer just for kicks. You don't want that.

Quick Hack: Mac Pranks

This hack is telling you how to secure your Mac, but it isn't really helping your coworker secure *their* Mac. So it might occur to you that it would be fun to be the jerk who plays pranks while you remain unprankable (computer-wise, that is—your car can still get filled with packing peanuts). There are a ton of good Mac pranks, but one of the better ones is a simple prank called *iPanic* (*http://namedfork.net/ipanic*). It simulates a kernel panic by displaying the kernel panic screen and telling folks to restart (you quit iPanic with the predictable Command-Q). You can get your victim to start a fake kernel panic with whatever nefarious scheme you want to use: set it as a startup item, change its name and icon to some app they use all the time (Hack #18), etc. Great fun for everyone (well, at least for you), but be prepared to confess quickly because it does get very frustrating for the person who needs to use the Mac. (It's also not considered cool to install iPanic on your home computer to convince your significant other that your Mac is beyond hope and that it's time to buy a new one.)

The simplest solution is to set a screensaver/wake-from-sleep password. Just open System Preferences, open the Security & Privacy preference pane, authenticate by clicking the lock icon, and then, on the preference pane's General tab, tick the box labeled "Require password [some time interval] after sleep or screen saver begins" (Figure 7-18).

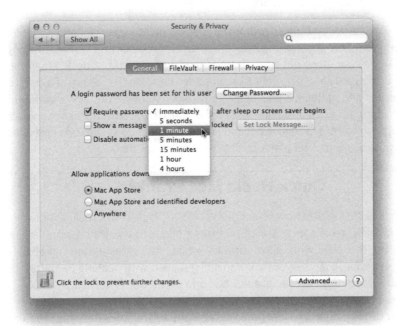

Figure 7-18.
You have several intervals to choose from here, ranging from immediately to four hours in the future. In general, the shorter intervals are more cumbersome and safer, while the longer intervals require less input from you but offer less protection from others.

Quick Hack: Pick a Good Password

The following passwords aren't any good: qwerty, 123, letmein. So now that you know three bad passwords, you might be wondering how to pick a better one. There are plenty of tips and techniques from misspelling real words (try substituting letters with symbols), to using your favorite book title (M@C #2CK$ 2o!3), to using a random number generator. These are good methods, but they don't provide any feedback about your password choice. Fortunately, OS X is here to help.

Once Password Assistant is running, OS X will helpfully volunteer suggested passwords, or rate one you've entered (see Figure 7-19).

So what's the difference between a good and bad password? Since Password Assistant is running, it is an opportune moment for an experiment! Figure 7-20 shows a good password; Figure 7-21 shows a bad password.

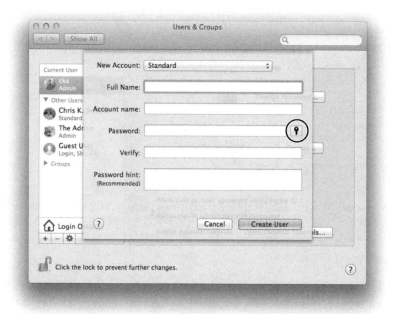

Figure 7-19.
Whenever you stumble across the tiny key symbol (circled), you're one click away from Password Assistant. Click the key icon and OS X will start judging your password.

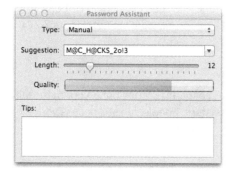

Figure 7-20.
Mixing symbols, upper- and lowercase letters, and numbers adds up to a great password. Don't use this particular one, though—it's been in a book and probably added to a hash table (a list of passwords used to crack systems) somewhere.

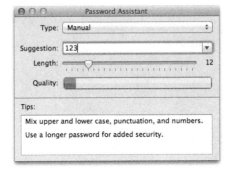

Figure 7-21.
OS X is laughing at this choice of password, it is just too refined to say so. Pick something better or let OS X generate a better one (use the drop-down menu to have OS X suggest passwords).

Login Password

Does a screensaver password make your Mac any safer? Yes, if the person wants to casually poke about on your machine, but your Mac isn't really any safer from someone even slightly determined to get access. The screensaver password can be avoided by restarting the Mac (holding down the power button for a few seconds is the simplest way to do so, and everyone knows about the power button). Once your Mac restarts, the malefactor will have free rein. So you also need to make your Mac ask for a password at every login. To do that, go to System Preferences→Users & Groups. In the Accounts pane on the left, select your username and then click Login Options. Click the lock icon and authenticate, and then set "Automatic login" to Off (Figure 7-22).

Firmware Password

You've locked your computer down against the casual interloper, but is your data really safe? Not if the person after your data is persistent. People can still access your files with one of the following methods:

Target Disk mode

1. Connect two Macs with a FireWire or Thunderbolt cable.

2. Restart the one whose data you want to access.

3. Press T just after the startup sound.

4. The target hard drive will appear on the other Mac's desktop.

Single-user mode

1. Reboot the Mac that contains the data you wish to access.

2. Press Command-S after the startup sound.

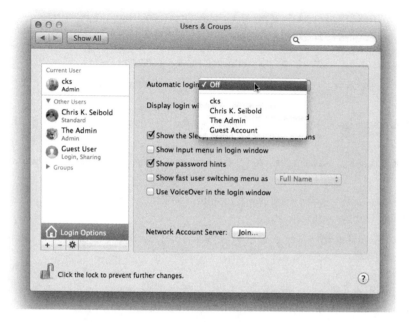

Figure 7-22.
Disabling auto login is one security step you should definitely perform unless you live alone in some place completely inaccessible by any other human.

3. Enjoy root privileges (if you know how to use the command line).

Password reset

1. Hold down Command-R while booting the Mac whose password(s) you want to reset.
2. Select Utilities→Terminal.
3. Type **resetpassword** at the prompt.
4. Select the user whose password you want to reset.
5. Choose a new password.

As you can see, once someone has physical access, there are several ways to get around your password machinations. Surely there's some way to protect your Mac against intrusions of these sorts. There is: set a firmware password.

Warning: Unless you are serious about security, be very careful when applying a firmware password. If you forget your firmware password on a 2011-model Mac or newer, you'll have to go through Apple to get your computer functioning again.

Setting a firmware password will:

- Block the ability to start up from an optical disc (using the C key).
- Block the ability to start up from a NetBoot server (using the N key).
- Block the ability to start up in Target Disk mode (using the T key).
- Block the ability to start up in verbose mode (pressing Command-V during startup).
- Block the ability to start up in single-user mode (pressing Command-S during startup).
- Block a reset of parameter RAM, also known as PRAM (pressing Command-Option-P-R during startup).
- Make your Mac ask for a password to enter the Startup Manager (accessed by pressing Option during startup).
- Block the ability to start up in Safe Boot mode (pressing the Shift key during startup).

Once you've decided to set a firmware password, you have two ways to do it. The standard method is to boot using the Recovery HD partition. To do that, simply hold Command-R while booting. Once your Mac has booted and OS X Utilities is running, head to the Utilities menu and choose Firmware Password Utility. Follow the onscreen instructions to set a firmware password.

The nonstandard method is preferable if you've done Hack #06 and don't want to reboot your Mac. Open Disk Utility (make sure you've added the option to see all partitions per Hack #06) and, in the list on the left, select Recovery HD (Figure 7-23).

Once the Recovery HD partition is selected, mount the partition by clicking the blue Mount button at the top of the Disk Utility window. Once it's mounted, the name of the disk will turn from being grayed out to black.

Time to head to the Terminal! In a Terminal window, type:

```
open /Volumes/Recovery\ HD/com.apple.recovery.boot/BaseSystem.dmg
```

Press Return, and your machine will tell you it's opening the *.dmg* (the place where the recovery system is stored). Then you'll be presented with the contents of the Recovery HD partition (Figure 7-24).

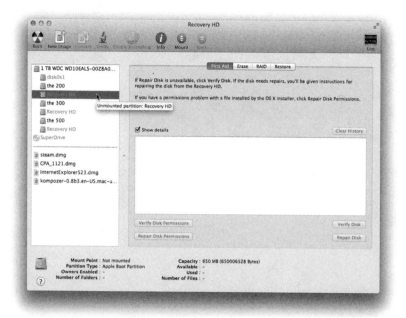

Figure 7-23.
Selecting the Recovery HD partition. (Your Mac probably won't have multiple partitions, so don't worry if this picture doesn't exactly match what you see.) If you don't see Recovery HD, you either haven't enabled Disk Utility's debug menu, haven't turned on the option to see all partitions, or you're missing the Recovery partition. You can either enable Disk Utility's debug menu (Hack #06) or restart your Mac while holding the Option key, and then choose the Recovery partition (if you don't see a Recovery partition, reinstall OS X).

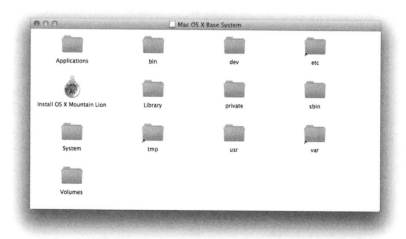

Figure 7-24.
The Base System, the minimal OS X system your Mac uses in Recovery mode.

All that's left is to navigate to the Firmware Password Utility: in the Mac OS X Base System window, go to Applications→Utilities→Firmware Password Utility. Then simply follow the onscreen instructions to add a firmware password for your Mac (Figure 7-25).

Figure 7-25.
Setting a firmware password to protect your Mac and your data.

8

Other OSes

Your Mac can do a lot that might not be readily apparent. It can control all the Apple devices you own, emulate a Wii system, and host a Minecraft server. Using your Mac for all these nifty things will get you wondering what other cool and unthought-of uses your Mac might have.

HACK 37 Run a Minecraft Server on Your Mac

Learn how to run your own Minecraft server for a select group of kids (or adults) on your Mac.

Imagine this *purely* hypothetical situation: you're a den leader for the Cub Scouts, and you find yourself asking the kids what they're interested in. As a good den leader, you listen intently, and when one of the scouts says that the coolest thing possible would be a scouts-only Minecraft server, you start to think to yourself, "Hey, now there's something I could put in my book!" When every other scout agrees that that would be the coolest thing ever, and factoring in that the winter holidays are coming, you realize a Minecraft server wouldn't only be fun for the scouts—it would be blessed relief for the parents, too. So you realize you need to get busy.

The first thing to contemplate when setting up a Minecraft server is what machine you're going to run it on. I have a first-generation Intel MacBook Pro that I decided to donate to the cause. You don't have to have a dedicated server—your main Mac can likely run a Minecraft server—but if you've got a spare computer laying around that's used infrequently, why not put it to work?

Before you get started, you might want to check your expectations against the reality of the situation. Head to *Can I Host a Minecraft Server?* (*http://canihostami-necraftserver.com*) and type in how much memory your machine has (get that figure from the Apple menu by selecting "About This Mac") and connection speeds [from *SpeedTest.net* (*http://www.speedtest.net*)] into the form. The site will then spit out a result. Figure 8-1 shows the results for the scouts' server.

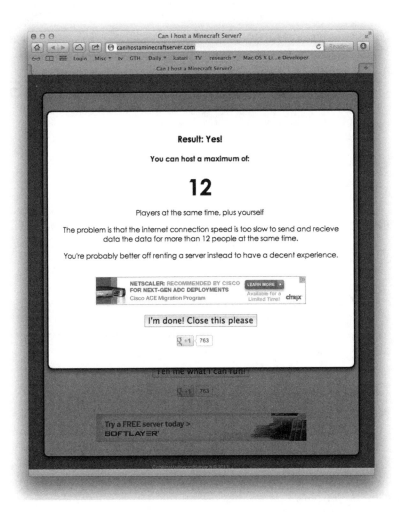

Figure 8-1.
Twelve players isn't many, but it's sufficient for the needs of the scouts. If you want to go bigger, talk to your ISP or rent a server. (For the record, a 12-person Minecraft server runs about $13.00 per month at one place I checked. For that kind of dough, the scouts would be on their own.)

Armed with that knowledge, it's time to start getting things installed. First, install any updates for your Mac (go to the Apple menu and choose Software Update). Once your Mac is up to date, it's time to make sure your Mac has the language that Minecraft requires: Java. Java used to be a standard part of an OS X install, but it hasn't been part of OS X since Mountain Lion's summer 2012 update. Since the Mac I'm using for the server is running OS X Snow Leopard, it has Java, but your situation might be different. A trip to Terminal should tell which version of Java your Mac is running (if it's running one at all)—just type:

```
java-version
```

Warning: Java isn't secure, which is why it doesn't ship with Macs and the Department of Homeland Security recommends deleting it. But they're usually talking about running Java in browsers. In the case of a Minecraft server, Java won't be running in a browser so you're a little safer. This warning may make you not want to install Java at all but if you want to run a Minecraft server, you're going to have to put up with Java.

Quick Hack: Install Java in Mountain Lion

If you're running OS X Mountain Lion and want to join the Java party, a quick trip to the Terminal will solve your Java-free lifestyle. In a Terminal window, type **java** and then hit Return. You'll see a message telling you Java isn't on your Mac and then, weirdly, your Mac will automatically install Java.

The building blocks are now in place, so it's time to get a Minecraft server installed. Head to *the Minecraft download page* (*https://minecraft.net/download*) and download the multiplayer server file (*minecraft_server.jar*). Next create a folder for your Minecraft server to live in (name it something creative like "Minecraft"), move the downloaded file to that folder, and get ready to have some fun with the shell script.

Open TextEdit and type the following:

```
!/bin/bash
cd "$(dirname "$0")"
exec jave -Xmx1G -Xms1G -jar minecraft_server.jar
```

Then save the TextEdit file as *start.command* in the same folder you saved the Minecraft server software you downloaded earlier. (You may have to hold down the Option key in order to get the Save As command to appear in TextEdit's File menu.)

You've created a script, and now that script needs to be made executable. To do that, open a Terminal window and type:

```
chmod a+x
```

Then drag the *start.command* file you just created into the Terminal window and hit Return. This makes the file executable. Now, in the folder you created earlier (maybe you called it Minecraft), double-click the *start.command* file and watch your new Minecraft server run—with lots of errors (Figure 8-2).

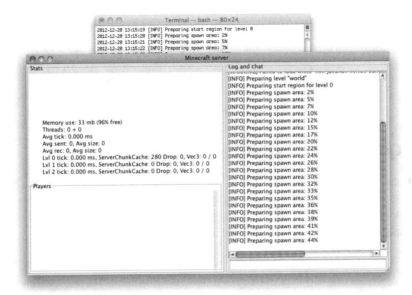

Figure 8-2.
Your Minecraft server is running at this point. Unfortunately, it's not running very well. To make it useful, you'll need to configure it.

You've come a long way and the kids are probably screaming at this point, but there's not a lot left to do. Quit the Minecraft server (Command-Q works) and get ready for the last few steps.

The first thing you have to do is called *port forwarding*. This lets your Minecraft server see the outside world and lets the outside world see your Minecraft server. Just how you do this will vary depending on what kind of router you have, but the general process is as follows: specify ports, specify protocol, specify end point, enable all the changes you made. Here's the specific process I used on my Cisco router in Knoxville, Tennessee:

1. Open the router's configuration page.
2. Head to the Applications and Gaming tab.
3. Add Minecraft to the Application name column.
4. Set External Port to 25565.
5. Set Internal Port to 25565.
6. Set Protocol to TCP.
7. Set IP Address to the address of your sever (found in System Preferences→Network).
8. Check the box labeled Enabled.

Your process will be different, but the port number will be the same. When I was finished, the setup on the scouts' router looked like Figure 8-3.

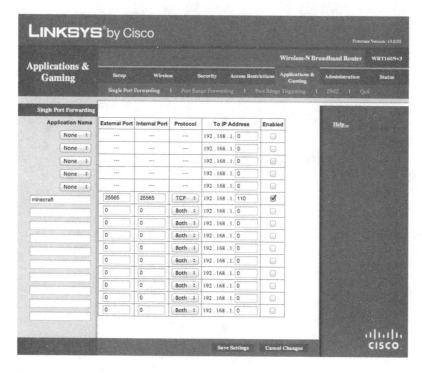

Figure 8-3.
A successfully set up router. Now people can play Minecraft on your server. Well, they could if they knew where to go...

At this point, you're actually done—you've gone through all the steps to host Minecraft on your Mac. All you really need now is the external IP address of your Mac (the address the outside world uses to find your Mac). You can find this information on your router, or you can use any number of websites to discover your external IP address. The easiest way is probably to do a Google search for "external IP address."

With that information in hand, you're ready to test out your Minecraft server. Double-click the *start.command* file you created earlier (the Minecraft folder you created earlier will have a lot more files in it now than it did before) and wait for the Minecraft server to load. At this point, a scout was recruited to beta-test the server; I supplied him with the external IP address and the resulting conversation is shown in Figure 8-4.

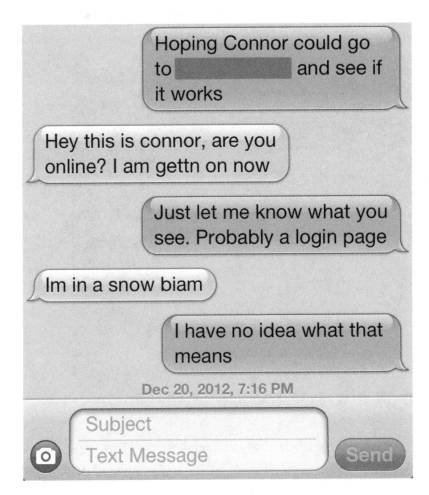

Figure 8-4.
If you don't know Minecraft, this conversation won't be understandable. Translation for the Minecraft impaired: I'm playing on a snowy world so the server worked perfectly.

Everything is running perfectly so you can just quit, right? Sure you *can*, but there's some stuff you could do to make everything better. The first time you ran the Minecraft server, a configuration page was generated, and you'll get a lot of options when you open up that file (see the next section to learn how to change some settings). You'll also want to consider using a No-IP or similar service (see Hack #15) to convert your IP address to a name and make it easy to find.

Configuring Minecraft

What you want to configure is completely up to you. In this case of the scouts, there are a few things I configured before turning the kids loose on the server. To configure the server, you'll edit the *server.properties* file located in the *Minecraft* folder you made earlier. Open this file with a text editor and you can change anything to the right of the = sign. If you don't know a setting does, leave it alone. For the scouts, I changed the following lines:

- `level-name=world` to `level-name=Flaming Arrow Patrol` (the kids picked the name). Changing that value sets what the world is called.
- `max-players=20` to `max-players=6` This limits how many people can play at one time.
- `white-list=false` to `white-list=true` This limits who can use the server.
- `motd=A Minecraft Server` to `motd=Welcome Scouts. Go do some math` This value is just a *message of the day* (get it?).

The only setting that needs a little more explanation is the `white-list` one. This setting lets you control who's allowed to use your server. After you change this setting as described above, open the *white-list.txt* file found in the Minecraft folder you created, and type the Minecraft usernames of the people who are allowed to use the server. Save the file and if they aren't on the list, they won't be playing!

Going Further

That's a great setup for a group of kids, but if you're serious about Minecraft you can go a lot further. You could set up a daemon so the server will automatically start, jack up your bandwidth for more players, use No-IP to make your server easier to find, and a host of other changes. But for the scouts, this configuration should be sufficient and fun.

—*Chris Seibold, Connor Langford, and Nathaniel Seibold*

HACK 38 Play Wii Games on Your Mac

Who says Macs aren't gaming machines? Discover how to put your Wii games on your Mac!

If you ask a child what the greatest video game of all time is, they'll either say *The Legend of Zelda: The Wind Waker* or they'll answer the question incorrectly. Whether they answer correctly or not, there's a good chance that you'd like to play Zelda (and other Wii games) in hi-def on your razor-sharp Mac monitor. The good news: you can! The bad news: you'll also need a PC.

Why do you need a PC if you're going to play the games on your Mac? Your Mac can't run the games from the Wii disc directly; it has to run them from a ROM (read-only memory). Your Mac also can't copy the necessary data from the Wii disc. But a PC that's equipped with a compatible drive can perform all those tasks. And since you want to be respectful of copyrights, you'll only want to use ROMs for the games you own. Explaining how to pull it off with a PC, like one you probably have at work, is beyond the scope of this hack but the most common way to pull it off is to use Raw-Dump (find it with a Google search). While your PC extracts the data you need, you can get your Mac ready to use a Wii emulator so you can play Wii games in glorious HD.

When people think about Wii emulators, they usually think of the super-popular Dolphin, which has been around awhile, supports multiple systems (Windows, OS X, Linux), and is free. What's not to love? Aim your browser to *the Dolphin Emulator download page* (*http://www.dolphin-emulator.com/download.html*) to get a copy of Dolphin. There, click the top Download link for Mac OS X. The next screen is a little weird because the link you want is kind of hidden under an ad. Aim for the circled area (Figure 8-5).

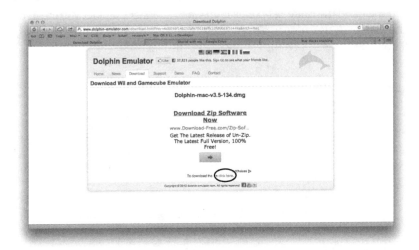

Figure 8-5.
The very small "click here" is actually the download link. Everything else is an ad to confuse and stymie those in a hurry.

Warning: Some gamers have experienced crashes with any version of Dolphin above 3.5.0. If you experience trouble don't hesitate to trash your copy of Dolphin and download version 3.5.

Once Dolphin is downloaded (as you'd expect, it comes in *.dmg* format), double-click the file to expand. When the installation process is finished, you'll have a program that's ready to go! Well, ready to go as much as an emulator without any games can be.

You need games! As mentioned earlier, you'll have to extract the data on a PC and then move it to your Mac. The 10-year-old intern employed by *Mac Hacks* was fearful that the process might damage the games somehow and only allowed your humble author to use GameCube games. That's okay—the process is the same as for Wii games, it just isn't quite as fulfilling to pull this trick off with a 12-year-old game.

In any event, once you have the ISO files, create a central repository for them on your Mac. You could find and open them one by one when you want to play, but if you keep all the games in one spot, all your options will show up when you start Dolphin. But first you'll need to tell Dolphin where to look. Launch Dolphin, and then double-click where it says "Doubleclick here to browse for files..." (Figure 8-6, background). Find the directory (folder) where you've stored your ISO files and Dolphin will add them to its home screen.

Figure 8-6.
You could use Dolphin's Open command each time you want to play a game, but adding a directory with all your Wii (and/or GameCube) games will give you much quicker access to them.

Once you've added the directory, all the games located there will be displayed in Dolphin. It's actually a really nifty way to jump from game to game. Just select a game and then click play (Figure 8-7)!

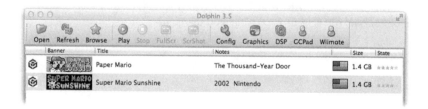

Figure 8-7.
A meager collection of games displayed very nicely by Dolphin. You'll notice that the icons and buttons don't look very OS X-ish but don't let that bother you—Dolphin adds a lot of fun to your Mac.

Once you've got your games loaded up and ready to play, you'll want to familiarize yourself with the controls. Otherwise, poor Mario won't be able to do a thing. Click Dolphin's GCPad button (short for "GameCube Pad") to see how everything is laid out. In this case, we're using a keyboard so we'll select that option and see which button does what (Figure 8-8).

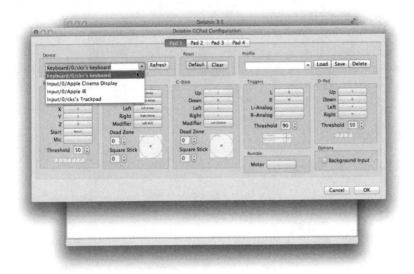

Figure 8-8.
You don't have to use the keyboard, but when you're writing a book, it's the handiest option. The drop-down menu lists all the options that are currently available, even ones that won't do much, like a second monitor.

If you want to use a real Wii Remote (a.k.a. Wiimote) with Wii games, click Dolphin's Wiimote button instead. In the dialog box that appears, choose Real Wiimote in one of the numbered Wiimote fields, and then click Refresh and push 12 on the Wiimote simultaneously. The Wiimote will vibrate to let you know you're connected. You'll definitely want to use the sensor bar for games, so check out Hack #51 for the skinny on using a sensor bar with your Mac.

All that's left to do is fire up *Paper Mario: The Thousand Year Door* and let the intern have some old-school fun (Figure 8-9) while you take a nap.

Figure 8-9.
Everything works and you're playing games on your Mac. Lots of fun for you and the family!

HACK 39 Manage Your Devices with Profile Manager

> In Mountain Lion Server, you can use Profile Manager 2 to control all your Apple devices from one computer.

Profile Manager first appeared in OS X Lion Server as the Apple-provided tool for managing Apple devices, including mobile device management (MDM) for iOS-based devices as well as profile management for OS X–based computers, including Mac-Books, MacBook Airs, Mac Minis, Mac Pros and iMacs running Mac OS X 10.7 and up. In OS X Mountain Lion Server, Apple has added a number of new features to Profile Manager, most notably the ability to push certain types of apps to mobile devices.

In this hack, we're going to set up Profile Manager 2 from scratch. If you're upgrading to OS X Mountain Lion Server (10.8 Server) from OS X Lion Server (10.7 Server), you can find upgrade instructions at *this Krypted.com page* (*http://krypted.com/mac-os-x/upgrading-to-mountain-lion-server*).

Preparing for Profile Manager

Before we get started, let's prep the system for the service. This starts with configuring a static IP address and properly configuring a host name for the server. In this example, the IP address will be 192.168.210.135 and the hostname will be mlserver3.pretend-co.com. We'll also be using a self-signed certificate, although it's easy enough to generate a CSR (certificate signing request) and install it ahead of time. For the purposes of this example, we have installed Server from the App Store (and done nothing else with Server except open it once so it downloads all of its components from the Web) and configured the static IP address using the Network preference pane. Next, we'll set the hostname using scutil using Terminal (Applications→Utilities→Terminal):

```
sudo scutil --set HostName mlserver3.pretendco.com
```

Then the ComputerName:

```
sudo scutil --set ComputerName mlserver3.pretendco.com
```

And finally, the LocalHostName:

```
sudo scutil --set LocalHostName mdm
Now check changeip:
sudo changeip -checkhostname
```

The changeip command should output something similar to this:

```
Primary address = 192.168.210.135

Current HostName = mlserver3.pretendco.com

DNS HostName = mlserver3.pretendco.com

The names match. There is nothing to change.

dirserv:success = "success"
```

If you don't see the message telling you that the names match or the success message, you might have some DNS work to do next, depending on whether you'll be hosting DNS on this server as well. If you *will* be hosting your own DNS on the Profile Manager server, then the server's DNS setting should be set to the server's IP address (Figure 8-10). To manage DNS, start the DNS service and configure it as shown in the DNS article (*http://krypted.com/mac-os-x-server/managing-dns-using-mac-os-x-mountain-lion-server*) I linked previously.

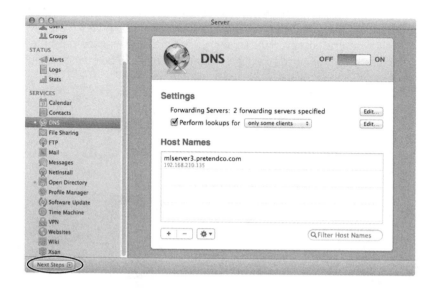

Figure 8-10.
A properly configured DNS Server.

Provided your DNS is configured properly, `changeip` should work. If you're hosting DNS on an Active Directory–integrated DNS server or some other box, then just make sure you have a forward and reverse record for the hostname/IP in question.

Now let's open the Server app from the Applications directory. Here, use the Next Steps drawer (circled in Figure 8-10) to verify that the Configure Network section states that "Your network is configured properly" as shown in Figure 8-11.

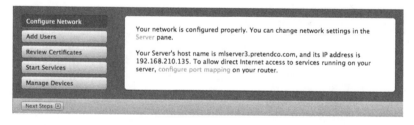

Figure 8-11.
Good news—your network is configured properly.

Profile Manager is built atop the web service, APNS, and Open Directory. Therefore, let's close the Next Steps drawer, click on the web service, and hit start. While not required for Profile Manager to function, the web service can be helpful. We're not going to configure anything else with this service in this hack, so as not to accidentally break Profile Manager. Don't click on anything while waiting for the service to start. While the indicator light can go away early, note that the web service isn't fully started until the path to the default websites is shown (the correct entry, as shown in Figure 8-12, should be */Library/Server/Web/Data/Sites/Default*) and a View Server Website link is shown at the bottom of the screen. If you touch anything too early, then you're gonna mess something up, so while I know it's difficult to do so, be patient (honestly, it takes less than a minute—wait for it...wait for it...there!).

Figure 8-12.
Configure the web service.

Once the web service is started and good, click the View Server Website link at the bottom and verify that the Welcome to Server page (Figure 8-13) loads.

Figure 8-13.
Welcome to the OS X Server default website.

Setting Up Profile Manager

On the Welcome to Server page, click the Profile Manager link. On the page that appears (Figure 8-14), click the Configure button.

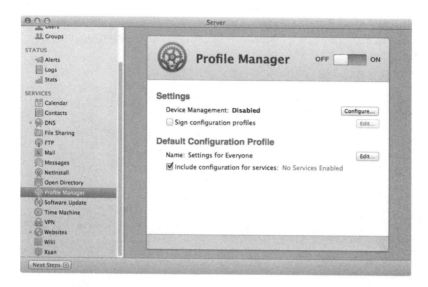

Figure 8-14.
Configure Profile Manager.

The first screen of the Configure Device Management assistant appears; click Next.

Assuming the computer is not yet an Open Directory Master or Replica, and assuming you wish to set up a new Open Directory Master, select "Create a new Open Directory domain" on the Configure Network Users and Groups screen. Then click Next.

On the Directory Administrator screen, provide the username and password you'd like the Open Directory administrative account to have. (Note that, in this example, this is going to be an Open Directory Master, so this example diradmin account will be used to authenticate to Workgroup Manager if we want to make changes to the Open Directory users, groups, computers, or computer groups from there). Once you're done entering the correct information, click Next.

On the Organization Information screen, enter your organization's name and administrator's email address. Keep in mind that this information will be in your certificate (and your CSR if you submit that for a non-self-signed certificate), which is used to protect both Profile Manager and Open Directory communications. Click Next.

On the Confirm Settings screen, make sure the information that will be used to configure Open Directory is set up correctly. Then click Set Up.

The Open Directory Master is then created. (Even if you're tying this thing into some-thing like Active Directory, this is a necessary step.) Once Open Directory is set up, you'll be prompted to provide an SSL Certificate. This can be the certificate provided when Open Directory is initially configured, which is self-signed, or you can select a certificate that you have installed using a CSR from a third-party provider (Figure 8-15). At this point, if you're using a third-party Code Signing certificate, you'll want to have installed it as well. Choose a certificate from the Certificate drop-down list, and then click Next.

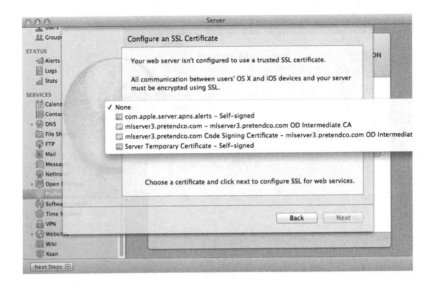

Figure 8-15.
Choose an SSL certificate.

If you're using a self-signed certificate, you'll see a message warning you that the certificate isn't signed by a third party. Click Next if this is satisfactory.

You will then be prompted to enter the credentials for an Apple Push Notification Ser-vice (APNS) certificate. This can be any valid AppleID, but it's best to use an institutional AppleID (e.g., push@krypted.com) rather than a private one (e.g., charles@krypted.com). Once you have entered a valid AppleID username and pass-word, click Next.

Provided everything is working, you'll see a message stating that the system meets the Profile Manager requirements. Click the Finish button to complete the assistant.

When the assistant closes, you will be back at the Profile Manager screen in the Server application (Figure 8-14). There, click the "Sign configuration profiles" checkbox. The Code Signing Certificate screen then appears (Figure 8-16). Here, choose the certifi-cate you want to use, and then click OK.

Figure 8-16.
Unless you're using a third-party certificate, there should only be one certificate in this list. If you are using a third-party certificate, import it here by choosing Import.

Back on the Profile Manager screen, if you host all of your services on the one server (Mail, Calendars, VPN, etc.), then leave the "Include configuration for services" check-box checked; otherwise, uncheck it. Now that everything you need is in place, click the big On/Off switch to start the service, and then wait for the service to finish start-ing. (The indicator stops spinning when the setup and startup processes are com-plete.) Once started, click the Open Profile Manager link and the login page will open (Figure 8-17). Administrators can log in to Profile Manager to setup profiles and man-age devices.

Figure 8-17.
Log in using administrative credentials.

The URL for the Profile Manager configuration page in OS X Server (for *mlserver3.pretendco.com*) is *https://mlserver3.pretendco.com/profilemanager*. Use the Everyone profile (Figure 8-18) to automatically configure profiles for services installed on the server if you want them deployed to all users. Use custom profiles for everything else.

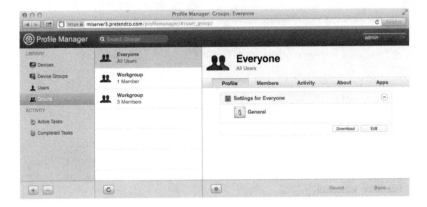

Figure 8-18.
Configure the Everyone profile.

Enrolling into Profile Manager

To enroll devices for management, use the URL *https://mdm.pretendco.com/MyDevices* (replace the hostname with your own). Click the Profiles tab to bring up a list of profiles that can be installed manually (Figure 8-19). You need to install a Trust Profile in order for the client to enroll, so click the Install button for the Trust Profile and complete the installation process.

Once you're done, click back to the Devices tab and click the Enroll button and complete the enrollment process for the client (following the defaults will suffice).

On the devices, you'll then be prompted to install the profile. In iOS, tap Install, then Install, and then Done. In OS X (Figure 8-20), click Continue, and then Install.

Once enrolled, you can wipe or lock the device from the My Devices portal. Management profiles from the MDM server are then used. Devices can opt out of management at any time.

Figure 8-19.
Installing the Trust Profile.

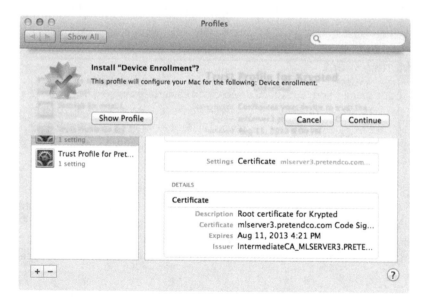

Figure 8-20.
Installing the profile in OS X.

If there are any problems when you're first getting started, you can always run the *wipeDB.sh* script that resets the Profile Manager (a.k.a., devicemgr) database. To do that, run the following command in OS X's Terminal application:

```
sudo /Applications/Server.app/Contents/ServerRoot/usr/share/devicemgr/back
end/wipeDB.sh
```

Automating Enrollment and Random Management Tips

The two profiles needed to set up a client on the server are accessible from the Server app's web interface. Saving these two profiles to a Mac OS X computer then allows you to automatically enroll devices into Profile Manager using Apple Configurator, as shown in *this previous article (http://krypted.com/iphone/using-apple-configurator-for-automated-enrollment)*.

When setting up profiles, note that the username and other objects that are dynamically populated can be replaced through a form of variable expansion using payload variables in Profile Manager. For more on doing so, see *this article (http://krypted.com/iphone/using-payload-variables-in-profile-manager)* .

Device Management

Once you've got devices enrolled, those devices can easily be managed from a central location. The first thing we're going to do is force a passcode on a device. In this case, it's an iPad. We're going select the device in Profile Manager's admin portal (Figure 8-21), located at *https://servername/profilemanager* (in this case, *https://mdm.pretendco.com/profilemanager*).

On the right side of the admin portal, click the Profile tab, and then click the Edit button (circled in Figure 8-21). Doing so opens the "Settings for [device name]" screen (Figure 8-22), where you can configure a number of settings. There are sections for iOS devices, OS X–specific settings, and settings applicable to both platforms. Let's configure a passcode requirement for an iPad. In the lefthand column, click Passcode, and then click Configure.

Figure 8-21.
Edit the settings for a device.

Figure 8-22.
Configure your passcode policies.

In the Passcode settings, check the box for "Allow simple value," and then set the "Minimum passcode length" to 4. (I find that with iOS, 4 characters is usually enough as it'll wipe long before someone can brute-force that.) Click OK to commit the changes. Once configured, click Save. On the "Save Changes?" screen, click Save. A few moments later, the device prompts you to set a passcode (Figure 8-23).

Figure 8-23.
Enter an appropriate passcode on the device.

The next thing we're going to do is push an app. To do so, first find an app in your library that you want to push out. Right-click (or Control-click) the app and select "Show in Finder." (You can copy the app from your library or browse to it at the location it is in later.) Then, in the admin portal, click an object to manage (in this example, I selected a group called Demo), and then click the Apps tab. There, click the cog icon and select Edit Apps (Figure 8-24).

Figure 8-24.
Lock, wipe, or add apps to a device over the air.

On the Add Apps screen that appears, click Upload and then browse to the app we found earlier. The app is then uploaded and displayed in the list. Click Add to add that

MAC HACKS

app to the currently selected (highlighted) group. Next, click Done, and then click Save and an App Installation dialog box will appear on the iOS device you're pushing the app to (Figure 8-25).

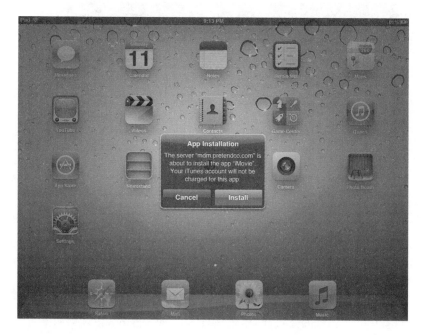

Figure 8-25.
Tap Install to add apps to a device.

In the App Installation dialog box on the iPad, click the Install button and the app will instantly be copied to the last screen of apps on the device. Tap on the app to open it and verify that it works. If the app opens, then it's safe to assume that you've run the App Store app logged in as a user who happens to own the app. You can sign out of the App Store and the app will still open. However, you won't be able to *update* the app; if you try to, you'll see a "You are not signed in" dialog box.

This brings up an interesting limitation of how Profile Manager interacts with the App Store: it kinda doesn't. To push apps to elementary school iPads in a one-to-one deployment (where each user has their own device), either use Apple Configurator (if I wanted to burn up a VPP code per student per year) or I could use iTunes (a labor-intensive process of restoring an iPad per computer rather than a parallel process). But either way, I'm gonna stay away from Profile Manager for apps.

So if you push an app to a device and the user taps on the app and the screen goes black, then make sure the app is owned by the AppleID signed into the device. If the app is owned by that ID, have the user open the App Store and update any *other* app, and then see if the pushed app opens.

Finally, let's wipe a device. In the Profile Manager admin portal, click a device and then, from the cog menu at the bottom of the screen, select Wipe (Figure 8-26).

Figure 8-26.
Wipe a device (be careful!).

On the Wipe screen, select the device and then click the Wipe button again. The iPad then says Resetting iPad—and just like that, the technical walkthrough is over.

Note: For fun, you can use the admin portal to wipe your iPad from the iPad itself.

Conclusion

So where are all these new features of Profile Manager that justify a new version number? To quote Apple's Profile Manager 2 page:

> Profile Manager simplifies deploying, configuring, and managing them all. It's one place where you control everything: You can create profiles to set up user accounts for mail, calendar, contacts, and messages; configure system settings; enforce restrictions; set PIN and password policies; and more. Because it's integrated with the Apple Push Notification service, Profile Manager can send out updated configurations over the air, automatically. And it includes web-based administration, so you can manage your server from any modern web browser. Profile Manager even gives users access to a self-service web portal where they can download and install new configuration profiles, as well as clear passcodes and remotely lock or wipe their Mac, iPhone, or iPad if it's lost or stolen.

Wait, it did that before... Which isn't to say that Profile Manager isn't an awesome tool for the money. Apps such as Casper MDM, AirWatch, Zenprise, etc., all have far more options, but aren't as easy to install, nor do they come at such a low price. Profile Manager is a great option if all the tasks you need to perform are available within the tool. If not, then it's worth a look, if only as a means to learn more about the third-party tools you'll ultimately end up using. One thing I can say is that Profile Manager is a little faster and seems much more stable—in fact, *Apple has now published scalability numbers (http://support.apple.com/kb/HT4780?viewlocale=en_US&locale=en_US)*, which they have rarely done in the past. You can also implement newer features with it, including Gatekeeper and Messages.

—*Charles Edge*

9

Networking Hacks

WiFi has become the networking standard for homes, which is good because it saves people a lot of trouble (imagine running CAT-5 cable from one end of the house to the other). But just because a network is wireless doesn't mean you don't have to manage it. You'll want to secure the network, maximize the signal, and massage the network so it performs the way you want it to. This chapter explains how.

HACK 40   Optimize Your WiFi

> OS X is keeping secrets from you! And one of those secrets is a nifty app you can use to resolve WiFi issues and have network fun.

If you click the Wi-Fi menulet in your Mac's menu bar, you don't get a lot of info: a list of nearby networks with a checkmark next to the one you're connected to. Not that exciting or, really, very informative. But click the same menulet while holding down the Option key gives you a whole slew of options (Figure 9-1).

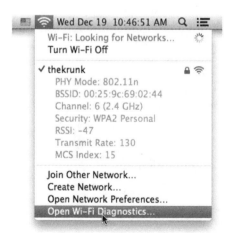

Figure 9-1.
Wow, more information than ever! Plus there's a link to a secret, super nifty app.

Let's take a moment to demystify what the-menulet is telling us. Here's what the grayed-out info under the name of your current network means:

- **PHY Mode** tells you what mode the network is using (b, g, or n).
- **BSSID** is the MAC (Media Access Control) address of the router.
- **Channel** is the channel your Mac is using (wireless routers use multiple channels to send the signals back and forth).
- **Security** indicates what type of security the network is using.
- **RSSI** indicates the strength of the wireless signal.
- **Transmit Rate** is the rate your wireless router is working at.
- **MCS Index** tells you which modulation scheme your router is using.

Tip: After you Option-click the Wi-Fi menulet, you can get this same info about networks you're not connected to by pointing your cursor at the network's name in the list. The info pops up in a yellow box.

All that is nifty information, but you want even more info—you want to know *everything*. So select Open Wi-Fi Diagnostics and let's get going!

Once Wi-Fi Diagnostics is up and running, you have some obvious choices (Figure 9-2).

Figure 9-2.
Three choices for your WiFi fun. But which one is for you?

MAC HACKS

If you choose Create Diagnostic Report, your Mac will check out your Network Services, scan networks within earshot (antenna shot?) of your Mac, run some diagnostic tests, and then monitor your WiFi performance—and it does all of these things without intervention. All you have to do is select the Create Diagnostic Report radio button and click Continue. You'll be asked for your password; after you enter it, OS X will go about testing your WiFi and generating a report (this can take some time). When Wi-Fi Diagnostics is done working, the Continue button will turn blue. Click it (you'll have to authenticate again) and a report will be generated and saved to your desktop. While you'll end up with a lot of nice logs, the usefulness of the report isn't apparent to the average computer user.

The same goes for the other two options here: Turn on Debug Logs and Capture Network Traffic. You'll capture a lot of nice data (even other WiFi networks' data when capturing network traffic), but making sense of the data isn't for the fainthearted.

Does that mean that Wi-Fi Diagnostics is a bust? Nope. Remember how the app was hidden? Turns out the app has a ton of hidden functionality, as well. So instead of choosing one of the three options Wi-Fi Diagnostics presents you with, select File→Network Utilities (or press Command-N). Once you do that, you'll see a brand-new window with four useful tabs (Figure 9-3).

Performance is the first tab, and that's probably the one you'll gravitate to—after all, you need to know just how well your WiFi is working, right? The Performance tab includes a real-time graph of signal strength versus noise, and a separate graph showing network traffic. In the signal-strength graph, the yellow line represents signal strength, and the green line represents noise. It's kind of a weird scale if you're not used to, it but closer to zero means the signal is stronger (we're dealing with negative numbers here).

Note: The signal-strength graph is in dBm, which is a measure of decibels (dB) to a milliwatt (usually abbreviated as mW, but shortened to just m in this case). Zero dBm is 1 milliwatt, but the typical power your Mac receives will be −10 to −60 dBm (around 100 microwatts).That's not a lot of energy, but it's enough to transfer your data.

If you're not satisfied with your WiFi network's performance, the signal-strength graph updates in real time, so you can try different locations (sometimes a small change can make a big difference), different channels, and other tricks to bump up your WiFi performance.

The other tabs in Network Utilities aren't quite as exciting. The Wi-Fi Scan tab shows all the nearby networks (even hidden ones), and the Bonjour tab lists the locally connected devices (printers and other Macs). Finally, the Tools tab gives you access to commonly used network tools like Ping and Traceroute, among others; but these same

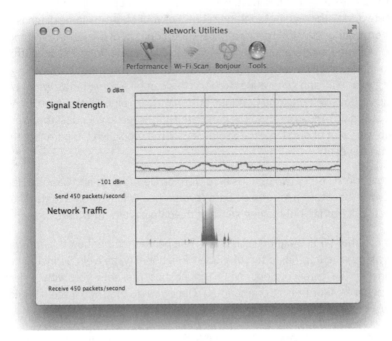

Figure 9-3.
The helpful Performance tab. In this example, signal strength is roughly 45 dBm and noise is 95 dBm, a difference of 50 (a difference of over 30 between signal and noise should be a great WiFi setup).

tools are all also available in Terminal with their requisite manual pages. If you're interested in a particular tool, open up Terminal and type **man** *nameoftoolyou'reinter estedin*.

Make Wi-Fi Diagnostics Easily Available

You could stop here—after all, it's easy enough to access Wi-Fi Diagnostics using the technique explained above. But why not make your Mac a better place and put a Wi-Fi Diagnostics *alias* where you expect apps to be—in the Application folder! (An alias is a link to the original item—the icon *looks* like the item and clicking it will launch or open the original item, but the original item hasn't been moved.) To do that, first we'll need to find the location of Wi-Fi Diagnostics. Spotlight is no help, because it doesn't index the folder where Wi-Fi Diagnostics resides. Time for a little folder burrowing.

The Wi-Fi Diagnostics app is in your Mac's Core Services folder, which you can find in the Library folder of your Mac's System folder. That's pretty confusing so let's type out the path explicitly: *[Computer]/[Startup Drive]/System/Library/CoreServices*. Follow that path (Figure 9-4) and you'll find the Wi-Fi Diagnostics app.

MAC HACKS

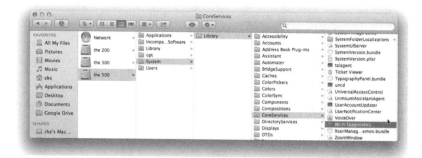

Figure 9-4.
It takes a bit of digging, but you can find the Wi-Fi Diagnostics app. And once you find it, you're free to do just about anything you want with it.

Once you find the app, right-click its icon and select Make Alias. Because the app is in the CoreServices folder, you'll have to authenticate with an administrator's name and password before OS X will let you make the alias. It's not that you're doing anything dangerous; it's just that OS X wants to keep the CoreServices folder unchanged. And the CoreServices folder *will* remain unchanged because, after you create the Wi-Fi Diagnostics alias, you'll move it somewhere you have easier access to it (the Applications folder is a good choice). Even if you forget and leave the alias in the folder, don't worry: nothing bad will happen.

HACK 41 Secure Your Wireless Network

It seems that everyone has a wireless network, but not everyone is willing to take the steps necessary to secure that network. If your network is completely open, people can intercept your packets and see exactly what you're doing over your network. Don't let this happen to you: secure that network!

Nothing is more convenient than the near-ubiquitous wireless network: the 802.11x protocols fill the airwaves around us, put the "mobile" in mobile computing, and give everyone a reason to seriously consider a laptop. When out and about, an unsecured hotspot is a pathway to free Internet usage; at home, strangers mucking about on your network or leeching your bandwidth isn't as appealing.

Before starting the process of locking down your network, taking the time to investigate who's using it can be a revealing exercise. The process is simple; all it requires is a quick trip to the command line, where you type:

```
$ ifconfig
```

This command returns the seemingly inscrutable output shown in Figure 9-5.

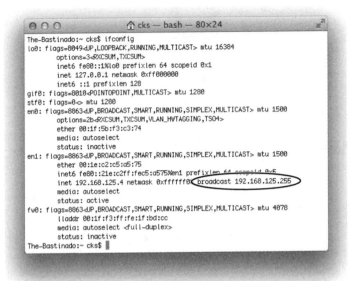

```
The-Bastinado:~ cks$ ifconfig
lo0: flags=8049<UP,LOOPBACK,RUNNING,MULTICAST> mtu 16384
        options=3<RXCSUM,TXCSUM>
        inet6 fe80::1%lo0 prefixlen 64 scopeid 0x1
        inet 127.0.0.1 netmask 0xff000000
        inet6 ::1 prefixlen 128
gif0: flags=8010<POINTOPOINT,MULTICAST> mtu 1280
stf0: flags=0<> mtu 1280
en0: flags=8863<UP,BROADCAST,SMART,RUNNING,SIMPLEX,MULTICAST> mtu 1500
        options=2b<RXCSUM,TXCSUM,VLAN_HWTAGGING,TSO4>
        ether 00:1f:5b:f3:c3:74
        media: autoselect
        status: inactive
en1: flags=8863<UP,BROADCAST,SMART,RUNNING,SIMPLEX,MULTICAST> mtu 1500
        ether 00:1e:c2:c5:a5:75
        inet6 fe80::21e:c2ff:fec5:a575%en1 prefixlen 64 scopeid 0x5
        inet 192.168.125.4 netmask 0xffffff00 broadcast 192.168.125.255
        media: autoselect
        status: active
fw0: flags=8863<UP,BROADCAST,SMART,RUNNING,SIMPLEX,MULTICAST> mtu 4078
        lladdr 00:1f:f3:ff:fe:1f:bd:cc
        media: autoselect <full-duplex>
        status: inactive
The-Bastinado:~ cks$ ▌
```

Figure 9-5.
Plenty of information here, but much of it is unintelligible at this point. Still, this output gives us part of the IP address (circled) we need for the next step in this hack.

While the window is packed with useful information, the only part of interest for the current purpose follows the word "broadcast," as shown in Figure 9-5. That's the IP address of your wireless network and the bit of information we need to perform the next test. Back to the command line and another simple line of code:

```
$ ping -c2 -i30 192.168.125.255
```

Tip: This method won't help you to find all network interlopers because not every computer will respond to a ping request (if you've enabled stealth mode on your Mac, this trick won't catch it). But using a ping command has the advantage of being quick and easy.

What the command accomplishes is straightforward: the computer sends out a data packet, and all the computers using the network send back a packet. It's the command-line version of "Can you hear me now?" (Only not nearly as annoying.) The -c part specifies the number of packets to send, and the -i part indicates the amount of time you want your computer to wait for responses. In this example, two packets were sent, and 30 seconds was allowed for a response. The result is as follows:

```
server:~ cks$ ping -c2 -i30 192.168.1.255

PING 192.168.1.255 (192.168.1.255): 56 data bytes
```

```
64 bytes from 192.168.1.101: icmp_seq=0 ttl=64 time=0.159 ms

64 bytes from 192.168.1.1: icmp_seq=0 ttl=64 time=2.124 ms

64 bytes from 192.168.1.109: icmp_seq=0 ttl=64 time=186.949 ms

64 bytes from 192.168.1.110: icmp_seq=0 ttl=64 time=188.489 ms
```

In this case, the result is just what I expected: there are three devices on the network (plus the router). Usually there are more devices on this network, but since it's late at night, the various iPod Touches and iPads are sleeping. Remember that a lot of devices can legitimately be on your network, so don't be surprised if your list is much, much longer.

You might not be able to tell if someone who shouldn't be is using your network. If you've only got a few devices, you'll likely notice an interloper. But if you're like a lot of people, you've got *dozens* of things going over the network—iPhones, iPads, TVs, Macs, game systems, iPod touches, and so on—which means that trying to suss out the IP that doesn't belong could be rough. That's all the more reason to lock down your network and change the password on a regular basis. The method you choose to protect your network is up to you (of course). Some methods are less work and offer less protection; some methods are more work and make your network *seemingly* secure but are still crackable; and at least one method (which is a fair amount of work) is considered secure. The following sections take a look at your various options.

Quick Hack: Access Your Router

Most wireless security happens inside your wireless router. Typically, users access their router through their browser of choice. Of course, it doesn't do you any good to know that you can control your router through your browser if you don't know your router's IP address. You can obtain this data using the ping command (as described earlier in this hack) and analyzing the results (one of the returned IP addresses will be your router—usually the shortest). Let's make it even easier with a short list of the default IPs for most common routers:

- AirPort: 192.168.2.1
- Linksys: 192.168.1.1
- D-Link: 192.168.0.1
- Belkin: 192.168.2.1

That list obviously doesn't cover every router, but chances are it will cover yours.

Basic Steps

There are a few steps to consider taking even if you decide not to close your network to interlopers. First, you should give the network a new name. Routers come factory-set with names like Linksys or D-Link—names like that practically scream "use me first—my owner hasn't taken the time to customize me." So changing the name of your network to something more meaningful (or silly) is a good idea, and kind of fun to boot (Figure 9-6), like wearing a Los Pollos Hermanos T-shirt.

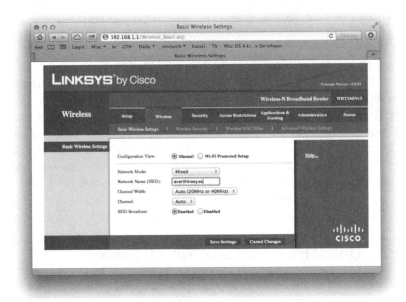

Figure 9-6.
Give your network a custom name—the more individualized and descriptive the better.

Even more important than giving your network a new name is changing the password for your router. The default administration settings for wireless routers are easy to find on the Internet, so there isn't any problem gaining access to your router if you don't change its password. It is also a good idea to turn off remote management so ne'er-do-wells won't be able to do incredibly nasty things to your router over your wireless network (see Figure 9-7).

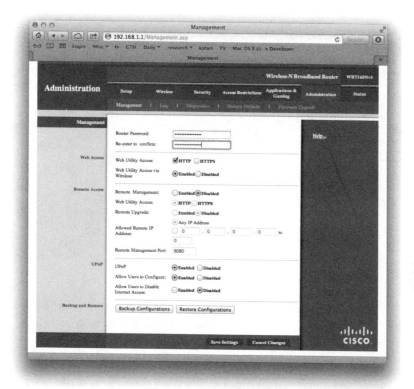

Figure 9-7.
A few small tweaks make your wireless network a better and safer place.

Disable SSID Broadcast

One of the easiest ways to add a modicum of security to your network is to tell your browser not to broadcast its *service set identifier* (SSID), which is the name you gave your network or the default name set at the factory. When looking for an unsecured network to jump on, most people just pick a name associated with an unsecured access point (your Mac displays a lock next to secured access points). With no SSID being flung through the air, most people will overlook your network because if you're not broadcasting an SSID, your network won't show up in their list of choices. It keeps very lazy folk honest because it takes an extra step to find your network! Turn off SSID by accessing your router configuration page (Figure 9-8).

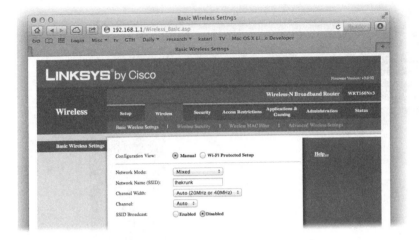

Figure 9-8.
Turning off the SSID with a Linksys router.

How can you join your network if you can't see it? To join or rejoin the network, head up to the main OS X menu bar, click the AirPort menulet, choose "Join Other Network," and then type the network's name.

How much security does not broadcasting the SSID offer? Not a great deal. There are a variety of programs that can detect the unbroadcasted network name (there's even an app built into OS X that lets you do this), and once the name is known, the network is completely unprotected. That said, if you live in a sea of unprotected hotspots, turning off your SSID is probably enough to make the opportunistic leeches look elsewhere.

Restrict MAC Addresses

Most routers allow you to restrict access by only letting certain computers and devices onto your network. Routers decide which devices to allow by checking each device's *media access control* (MAC) address. If you decide to filter the people allowed on your network by MAC address, the first thing to acquire is the MAC addresses of the devices you want to allow. For Macs connecting to the router wirelessly, you'll need the MAC addresses of their devices. To retrieve this information, head to System Preferences→Network→Wi-Fi→Advanced (see Figure 9-9).

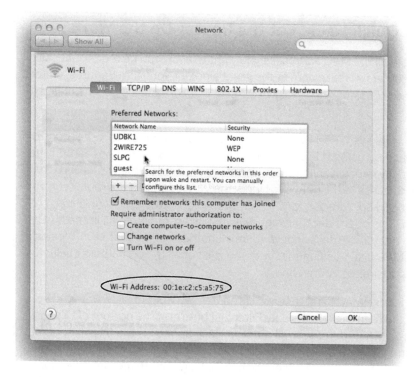

Figure 9-9.
Your WiFi MAC address, important information if you plan to use MAC filtering on your wireless network.

Once you've compiled that information, enter the MAC addresses of the devices you want to allow on your network. The place you enter this information varies depending on your router, so you'll have to go to your router's configuration page to discover where to enter it.

MAC address filtering is tougher to crack than simply turning off the SSID broadcast, but it isn't *much* tougher. Many programs capable of discovering a hidden wireless network can also sniff *packets* (small bits of data sent from your computer to the network and vice versa). Since your MAC address is sent with each packet, and since the communication is unencrypted, if someone wants to get on your network, all they need to do is spoof their MAC address to match yours. On the other hand, adding MAC filtering to a nonbroadcasting SSID increases the hassle factor of using your network—and the hassle can easily chase away slackers trying to get a free ride to the Web.

Quick Hack: Let the Router Do the Work

Typing in all the MAC addresses you want to allow can be tedious. Luckily, some routers will take care of the grunt work for you! Tom Sgouros, editor of *The Big Book of Apple Hacks* (O'Reilly, 2008), explains how he pulled it off:

"I use a Linksys WRT54G wireless router. I logged on to the router control web page by using a browser to open up 192.168.1.1 and opened up the network by removing all the restrictions. Then I fired up the two laptops that needed access to the network. Under the Wireless tab of the router control page, I clicked Wireless MAC Filter, then clicked the Edit MAC Filter List button. This opens another window with places for you to fill in the MACs. But at the top of that window, there's another button that says Wireless Client MAC List. Clicking that gets you a list of all the computers currently making a wireless connection.

"Click Enable MAC Filter for each computer you want to allow onto the network, and then click the Update Filter List button at the bottom of this window. The MAC addresses will automatically appear in the filter list. Scroll down that page and click Save, and all the computers will be saved. Now, make sure that you've checked the box that says only to permit listed computers to access the network, then click Save, and you're done."

Add WPA2

With the lightweight security measures out of the way, we can turn our attention to methods that don't simply obfuscate the network but actually encrypt its traffic. To put a finer point on the difference: if you use one of the previous methods, your network may be difficult to find, but all its traffic will be sent in plain text, so anyone who bothers to intercept your traffic can follow exactly what is going on with very little work. Adding WPA2 to your network makes it much more difficult to see what's actually being transmitted over your network.

Your router likely has several security protocols built in, leaving you to wonder which one is best for your particular needs. Unfortunately, most of the security protocols with your router have been compromised by nefarious types, leaving WPA2 (short for WiFi Protected Access II) as the only sensible option. Once you've decided to go with WPA2, you have to decide which version of it is right for you. Most routers come with two versions: WPA2 Personal and WPA2 Enterprise. The difference isn't trivial: WPA2 Personal relies on a pre-shared key (you can get on the network if you know the password) (Figure 9-10), while WPA 2 Enterprise relies on network clients logging in with a username and password. WPA2 Personal is your best bet for a home network.

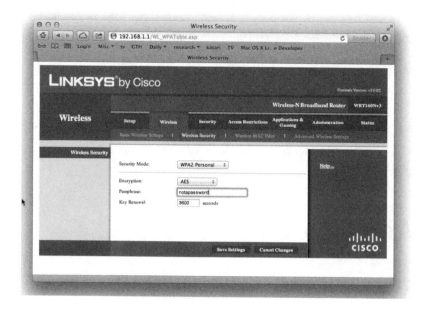

Figure 9-10.
WPA2 Personal is the one you want for your home network because it provides both ease of use and security.

Now that you've made your choice, the good news is that the work is almost done. The bad news is that the process isn't as straightforward as you would expect. With most routers, you can type any password you wish into the WPA2 shared key field. For example, if I set a password to "qwerty," the router will happily accept that key. But trying to enter that key to gain access to the router via WiFi won't work—OS X won't let you enter any password that's less than eight characters. Why? It turns out that OS X is smarter than your router. The WPA2 specification demands a key length of between 8 and 63 characters. Your router wasn't smart enough to tell you that, but OS X is. Now that you know that, all you have to do is choose an 8-character (or longer) password and enter it in your router's settings. If you're successful, a small lock icon should be displayed next to the name of your network when you're browsing nearby wireless networks.

At this point you're feeling pretty good. You've locked your WiFi down so freeloaders can't surf for free. But there's one more thing to consider—the security of your password. A password like 123GOVOLS is memorable, but it's also very vulnerable. WPA2 networks aren't susceptible to the tricks that WEP networks are, but they *can* be compromised by *dictionary attacks* (where passwords are tried from a table of common passwords and words). How devoted are people to trying a zillion network passwords to see if any of them work? Visit *www.renderlab.net* (*http://www.renderlab.net/projects/wpa-tables*) where you can find a rainbow of tables (useful for cracking) that range up to 33 GB in size.

So why not make a really good password? You won't be entering it often, your Mac will remember it for you, and you'll be secure in the knowledge that it will take a really long time to crack your network. A quick trip to *this page* (*http://www.random.org/strings*) gives you access to a tool that generates random sequences of letters, numbers, or a mix of the two (Figure 9-11). Length is crucial: a randomly generated passphrase of 14 letters is considered very secure, so set the page to output just such a string.

Figure 9-11.
The passwords generated by this page are tough to crack—you can't find any of them in a dictionary.

You'll have to really reach to find some obvious phrase or pattern in any of the generated strings. This means they're hard to crack but also very difficult to memorize. Fortunately, ease of memorization isn't a big deal when you're setting a WiFi password, since you'll only have to enter it once on each Mac you use.

Once you've generated and chosen a string, write it down. Store it in OS X's Keychain app or somewhere else safe. Paste the new pre-shared password into the appropriate spot on your router's configuration page and then save the new setting. The router will restart, safe from prying eyes and bandwidth leeches.

To get your Mac back on the network, select the network you've secured and enter the password into the required field.

Unhacking the Hack

You've changed your network's name and password, hidden its SSID, crammed a completely random 14-letter phrase in as a WPA2 password—and then forgotten or lost every scrap of information you used for the settings. If you try to unplug your router hoping the defaults will be restored, you're going to be stymied. So how can you get your router back when you've been blocked by your own security?

Don't worry: your router hasn't become a brick of plastic, circuitry, and electronics. Most routers have a recessed reset button that you can press with a pencil tip or paperclip to return your router to its factory defaults. Hit the reset button and you can start the process all over again.

HACK 42 Use Your Mac as an Access Point

> In case you're feeling generous, this hack shows you how to share an Ethernet connection with your iPad- and iPhone-using friends via WiFi.

Your Mac is a sharing machine! Plug in a printer, and it can share that; toss some files into your Public folder, and users can get to them over the LAN. Want to run a site from your Mac? No problem. But the sharing doesn't end there: you can even go so far as to share your Internet connection with those around you who can't connect, or with your wireless gaming console.

The situation where you might want to share your Internet connection without access to a router seems a bit suspect at first. Just where are you going to be that doesn't have an Internet connection? And if you have an Internet connection, why would you want to share it; heck your laptop is already connected!

It seems an unlikely scenario until it happens to you—then it seems like Apple really knew what it was doing when it added the ability to share your Internet connection via the Network preference pane. Typically, the scenario goes something like this: you're in a hotel room or some other not-home place where you can get Internet via an Ethernet cable but not wirelessly. Of course, you're sharing the room, and the other person also has a laptop. Naturally, you both want to hop on the Internet at the same time. Instead of the predictable knife fight over who gets to use the sole Ethernet hookup, hook up your Mac and use it to *share* the Internet connection.

That's the most common way to use this hack, but not the only one. Some ISPs give you a modem but don't really require that you use it; the Internet connection will work just as well if you plug the Ethernet cable straight in to the back of your Mac. The obvious downside of this method is that you can only connect one device. With this hack, you can use your Mac as an access point so you can get rid of the router and associated cables.

Pulling Off the Hack

The good news is that this is a very easy trick to pull off. The bad news is that the process includes an ominous warning that may frighten the uninitiated. So let's get initiated.

Head to System Preferences→Sharing and configure the preference pane as required for your particular situation. In this example, an Ethernet connection will be shared over WiFi (Figure 9-12). The specific setup you'll want will depend on your particular situation. No matter what configuration you desire, you have to perform this step before OS X will let you turn on Internet sharing.

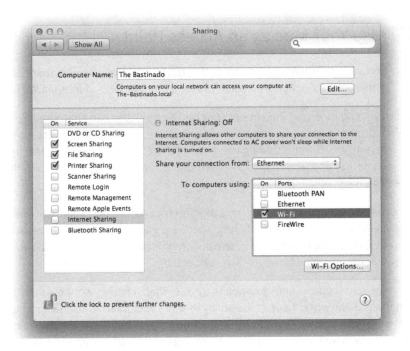

Figure 9-12.
You have to tell your Mac how you want to share the Internet before OS X will let you share it. Sharing options vary by machine—for example, those with newer Macs will find options for Thunderbolt that aren't shown here.

The exact procedure depends on how you want to share the Internet connection. In the case of sharing it over WiFi (likely the most common scenario), you get to make a few choices you won't have to make when choosing other configurations. To proceed, click the Wi-Fi Options button. As shown in Figure 9-13, you'll be able to decide whether or not to rename your network (the default name is the same name as your computer), what channel you want to use, and whether your network should require a WPA2 password. Note that you'll only have to make these decisions (as mundane as they may be) if you click the Wi-Fi Options button; otherwise OS X will just go with default values.

Figure 9-13.
Options for sharing your Internet connection via WiFi. The exact options you're presented depend on the configurations you are using; you won't see options exactly like these unless you are sharing from Ethernet to WiFi.

Once you've got everything set up the way you want, it's time to start sharing that connection. This is where the ominous warnings begin. Instead of simply checking the box next to Internet Sharing and having the sharing begin, you get a stern warning that you're about to mess up everyone's Internet settings and instructions to contact the system administrator (Figure 9-14).

The chances of you breaking the Internet are slim to none, so go ahead and click Start in the warning box to start the sharing process. You'll know you're successful when the AirPort menulet changes from its usual broadcast icon to a quarter pizza slice with an up arrow (see Figure 9-15).

That's all there is to it. You can now hook up any device you would *usually* hook up to a router to your Mac instead and enjoy all the benefits of connectivity.

Figure 9-14.
The warnings are spooky and you probably shouldn't do this at work but it's your home system, so go ahead! Don't worry—you won't break the Internet.

Figure 9-15.
Now you're sharing the Net! iPhoners, iPadders and others can all rejoice that their data plan can remain unscathed while they consume bandwidth.

10

Multimedia Hacks

There's a story, perhaps apocryphal, that upon being offered the design for the Apple I, an executive at Hewlett-Packard mused that he couldn't see a use for a home computer except to store recipes. That comment is both insightful and shortsighted all at once. Recipe storage is a great use of a computer, but what the executive missed (because of his lack of imagination) was the progression of things. Macs can still hold recipes but they can also hold music, TV shows, and movies. With drives always increasing in size, your Mac can process and play multimedia files. The future wasn't just recipes—the future meant that computers could store and play anything that could be digitized. This chapter explains some ways to make your multimedia experience even better.

HACK 43   Turn Your Mac into a DVR

> Just about every program that shows up on your TV screen is hiding somewhere on the Internet, but finding them can be tricky. Let your Mac do the hard work of finding the shows you want to see.

One of the ads currently being shown on cable TV tells of the woes of a family where more than one person wants to record a show to a DVR. Apparently the yearnings of various family members to record their own shows for later viewing is a major source of domestic frustration.

It doesn't have to be this way. You can bag all the shows you want to see on your Mac and let the other members of your household war over whose shows are going to be recorded on the cable box. All you need is a deliciously focused and easy-to-use program and a BitTorrent client.

The really neat thing about catching shows on your Mac? Even if you miss a show, you're only a few clicks away from seeing the episode on your computer. In fact, after reading this hack, you'll discover you can do more than just catch that single missed episode: you can grab shows automatically and watch them at your leisure. By now you're ready to get started, so let's jump on in.

Get the Apps

This hack relies on *torrents*, which are the data part of the BitTorrent peer-to-peer filesharing protocol. Torrents are a way to access all kinds of digital content, and you can accomplish everything in this hack in a less straightforward but more flexible manner with a general-purpose torrent search application. However, if all you're interested in is TV shows, then the unimaginatively named application TVShows 2 is the way to go. This app takes the trouble out of torrents, and since it's free, there's no reason not to give it a whirl. To get your copy, point your browser to *this page* (*http://www.tvshowsapp.com*) and download the wonder of television-show-grabbing goodness.

While TVShows 2 makes *finding* television programs easy, it can't *download* them. For that you'll need a BitTorrent client. TVShows 2 recommends a free client called *Transmission* (*http://www.transmissionbt.com*), but you're free to use any client you're comfortable with. In fact, if you're already using another BitTorrent client, TVShows 2 will default to that client. To install Transmission, simply download it and then click the downloaded file.

Install TVShows 2

TVShows 2 is different from most of the apps you download. Instead of getting a *.zip* file or the app, you get a file named *TVShows.prefPane*. Double-clicking it results in a dialog box asking for permission to add a preference pane (Figure 10-1).

Figure 10-1.
Don't worry—TVShows 2 isn't going to do anything evil to your Mac, so go ahead and click Install. Note that you can choose a system-wide install ("all users") or single-user install ("this user only").

Once you give TVShows 2 permission to add a preference pane, the System Preferences window will restart and you'll be treated to the new TVShows preference pane. Click the pane's icon and then, in the program's window, follow the giant white arrow and click Add Show. There are tons of them, so filter your options using the search box (Figure 10-2).

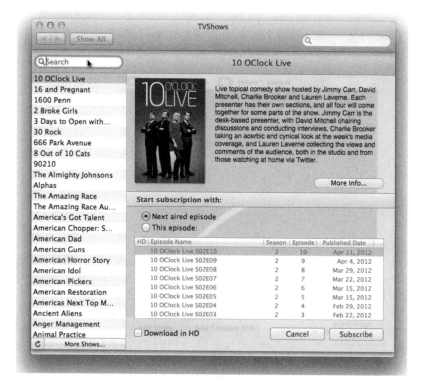

Figure 10-2.
TVShows 2 will find a lot of shows. Specify the one you want by typing the name of the show in the upper-left corner.

Once you've made a selection, your BitTorrent client takes over and starts downloading the episode you want (Figure 10-3). Or, if the episode you're after hasn't aired yet, TVShows 2 will wait patiently and download the show when it airs.

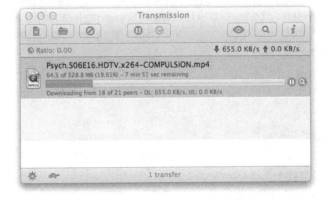

Figure 10-3.
Transmission is downloading the requested episode. By default, the show gets stored in your Downloads folder, something you'll want to change if you're going to be doing this often.

Note: You don't explicitly launch or quit TVShows 2. You just tell it what shows you want via its preference pane, and then it takes care of the rest.

Downloading a single episode is great and all, but there are some settings you probably want to change if you plan on using TVShows 2 a bunch. The first thing to consider is the quality of the shows. (No, not the quality of the shows *themselves*, but the quality of the file encoding.) As is always the way with these things, higher quality means longer download times and larger files; lower quality means quicker downloads and smaller files. Everyone does the HD thing now, so in the TVShows window, click the Preferences tab and then turn on the "Download HD versions by default" checkbox. While you're there, make your life a little easier by dedicating a folder for your downloads using the "Episode save location" pop-up menu, and tell TVShows to make individual folders for each show by checking the boxes next to "Save each show in its own folder" and "Create season subfolders."

Note: High definition can be somewhat hit and miss with some cable companies. And if you can't get cable or satellite TV at all you might find yourself without the HD experience everyone has been raving about. Fortunately, you can use TVShows 2 to get HD content wherever you can get broadband. Couple TVShows 2 with a high-definition TV set or monitor, and you have nearly unlimited HD content whenever you want it.

Once TVShows 2 tells Transmission to do the downloading thing, you're on your way to never-miss-an-episode nirvana. The main problem you may encounter is that, while some episodes play no problem, others won't play on your Mac at all. The no-problem episodes are *.mp4* files, while the stubborn ones are *.mkv* files. Don't worry, there's a quick fix for this. Head to *VideoLAN* (*http://www.videolan.org/vlc*) and download VLC, an open source media player that will play files that OS X can't. (You'll find yourself using VLC not just for TV shows but also for other troublesome media in the future.)

HACK 44 Master Torrents

> Downloading huge files is easier and speedier with BitTorrent. This hack explains how to use your Mac to participate in the downloading fun.

Who can forget Napster, the once-ubiquitous file-sharing program that made university servers slow to a crawl and ignited the RIAA lawsuit revolution. Napster is gone but file sharing is still around and more prevalent (and useful) than ever.

In the standard P2P (peer-to-peer) model, computer A contacts computer B to download a specified file. The method works fine for relatively small files like songs but runs into snags when it comes to larger files. For example, imagine trying to download a 4 GB Linux distribution from another single user. What happens in that scenario? First, most ISPs cap upload speed, so if you were to choose someone using an ISP with a 512 Kbps upload speed cap, you could expect to spend at least 9 hours downloading the file. Were you to download the same file at the maximum speed allowed by your ISP, the same download would take a comparatively short 2 hours (or even less depending on your ISP).

The solution to this problem is obvious now that someone has devised one: instead of a single client downloading a file from a single host (the standard manner in which downloads work), what if everyone participated in both the uploading and downloading of the file? In other words, instead of the standard client-host relationship, all parties interested in a file could upload the bits they have on their computer while downloading pieces of the file they are missing.

The concept sounds nifty, but how can you download just part of a file? This is where the Internet comes in. As opposed to the P2P model employed by now-defunct sites like *LimeWire* (*http://limewire.com*), the *torrent* model locates easily downloadable bits of the files out there on the Internet. A BitTorrent client can grab these slices of files from different sources and knit them together when the download is complete. So a file is split into an arbitrary number of segments. You download segments a, b, and c, stitch them together into a complete file and then share (or *seed*) the file with other downloaders. In this scenario, everyone shares the burden of bandwidth so no one person gets stuck with all the overhead.

If that system seems a bit convoluted, that's because it is. The preceding description is an idealized version, a near-communistic "from each according to his abilities, to each according to his needs" deal. The reality is that BitTorrent has been refined so that the obvious objections (like "How can I upload anything if I haven't downloaded anything yet?") have been overcome, and the result is a very fast and reliable way to download large files.

The protocol has proved popular and, according to some estimates, torrents now comprise a quarter of all web traffic. That shouldn't be a surprise. Because torrents are generally used to transfer large files, downloading a single movie can easily surpass the bit count of all your other online activities for a single day.

If you're already using torrents, you (obviously) already have a torrent client. If you don't, there are a huge number of choices for OS X, from the official *BitTorrent client* (*http://www.bittorrent.com/downloads/complete/os/mac*) to the well-done *Transmission client* (*http://transmissionbt.com*) used in the previous hack. Both are good choices, with the official BitTorrent client being a little on the sparse side as features go, and Transmission being a more feature-complete yet still lightweight choice for OS X. That noted, neither client has that Mac feel that OS X users demand.

What would be ideal is a torrent program that looks and acts like a program made specifically for OS X. Such a client exists: Xtorrent 2, which manages to make downloading and uploading *seeds* (completed files) painless, understandable, and controllable. Xtorrent 2 isn't free, but its cost ($25 for the basic version) is minimal considering the functionality and usability the program provides. There's a free trial version available with some features removed, so point your browser to *xtorrent* (*http://www.xtorrent.com*) to get your copy. The trial copy isn't obvious, but when you hit Download XTorrent 2, you'll automatically download the trial version and be presented with a page where you can pick your preferred paid version.

Once downloaded, install Xtorrent in your folder of choice (as always for applications, a good place is the Applications folder). Then fire up Xtorrent and you'll be downloading and seeding files in no time with just a click. Well, after you answer a simple question (see Figure 10-4).

Once you've assured Xtorrent 2 you are authorized to download the files, the program will get busy downloading and seeding the files you desire. But there's more to Xtorrent 2 than just that. In its main window, Xtorrent reveals more than just the file's name and size. You also get information about the *swarm*, which is torrent speak for the number of users transferring the files you're after. This can include any combination of those offering uploads and those downloading the files but, generally, the larger the swarm, the more reliable and faster the download will be.

Xtorrent 2 also allows you to select where your downloads will reside. To adjust this setting, go to Xtorrent→Preferences, and then click the Downloads tab. In Figure 10-5, the destination is an automated folder (see Hack #22) that takes care of seeing the file to its final destination.

Controlling where the files end up is one thing, but depending on your situation, you might also need to control the bandwidth allocated for your torrenting

Figure 10-4.
Xtorrent wants to know if you're authorized to copy the content. Remember only download the stuff you are allowed to!

purposes. Xtorrent 2 (and most clients) offer this control. Take another trip to Xtorrent→Preferences, followed by a click on the Advanced tab. In the Advanced pane, you can set bandwidth limits for both uploads and downloads, change the port used for "listening" for torrents, and disable sharing at certain times of the day. What you'll most likely want to tweak is the bandwidth limits. The default download limit is 100 Kbps, and the default upload speed is 20 Kbps. Depending on the speed of your ISP, you may want to change these settings. For example, if you have a very speedy connection (you're a Google Fiber customer, say), you'll want to raise the limits. If you have a comparatively pokey connection, you'll want to lower the limits.

Share Torrents

Once you've completed a download, you have the full file. Most of us would call the process complete, but in the torrent world (as mentioned earlier), a completed file is called a seed. Since someone generously shared portions of the file and their bandwidth with you, it's considered good etiquette to share the completed file with other users for a time. Xtorrent 2 will take care of the sharing part automatically, so no worries, but if you're determined to be a *leech* (torrent speak for a nonsharing jerk), Xtorrent 2 will allow you to do that, as well. This option is found under Preferences→Sharing.

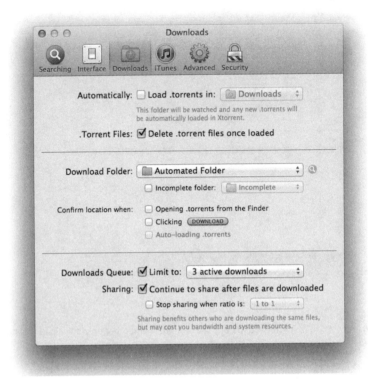

Figure 10-5.
You can set the downloads to show up anywhere you like in Xtorrent's preferences. If you're going to be doing this a lot, you'll want to consider automating the destination folder.

There's a lot more to discover with Xtorrent 2. You can, for example, use the program as a browser or an RSS reader—particularly nice features for those addicted to torrents. You'll discover a huge number of uses beyond torrents after you use Xtorrent 2 for just a little while.

HACK 45 Move Your iTunes Library

You don't have to keep iTunes files where iTunes wants you to. Increase your flexibility by choosing where your iTunes files live.

Maybe you're upgrading to one of Apple's new Macs with a slick little SSD (emphasis on "little"). Or maybe you just buy a *lot* of stuff from iTunes Store. No one's here to judge; I'm just here to help—specifically, to give your iTunes library a little more breathing room.

Not only does iTunes support keeping your library—the actual media files that are taking up all that space—on an external hard drive, Apple also quietly built in a way to make it relatively easy for you to move your growing collection. It goes a little something like this.

First, make sure the new destination for your iTunes library is plugged in, powered, and all caffeinated up for the big move. (I don't actually recommend using caffeine on your hard drive in any way; I have no idea what it'll do to your warranty, so let's not find out today.) Most people who do this use an external hard drive, because hard drive space has never been cheaper and it's still easy to back up with something like Time Machine or *ChronoSync* (*http://www.econtechnologies.com/pages/cs/chrono_overview.html*). But some people use a secondary hard drive inside an iMac (yes, you can do that now) or a Mac Pro.

Speaking of backups, you *did* do a backup of everything before starting all this, right? (If not, see Hack #01.) As the saying goes, it's better to be safe than woefully heartbroken in the off chance something goes wrong while moving years and years of iTunes media.

Next, start iTunes and then click iTunes→Preferences→Advanced. Among the Advanced settings (Figure 10-6) is an option called "Keep iTunes Media folder organized," which is checked by default. If it is, you're in good shape. If it's not, enable it and then click OK, and iTunes will take a little time to do exactly that—tidy up all your files and get them prepared for the move.

Now, in that same Advanced preferences pane, click the Change button and a Change Media Folder Location window will appear. This is where you pick the new home for your iTunes media folder. To do that, click the final destination on your new storage space (Figure 10-7). Then, *if* you want to store other stuff alongside your iTunes library (this step is purely optional), click the New Folder button to create a new folder called something like "iTunes Media," and then click the Create button. Finally, click Open to confirm your new iTunes library location, and then click OK to dismiss the preferences dialog box.

When you click OK, you'll see a dialog box asking if you want iTunes to move and rename the files in your iTunes Media folder to the new location you just specified. This step is a doozy, because it tells iTunes to copy all your media from the increasingly cramped confines of its current studio apartment to the six-bedroom open pastures of the new one. Click Yes and prepare to wait. This step may take some time—anywhere from a few minutes to a few hours, depending on how much of an iTunes-a-holic you are...I mean, how large your library is—so be patient. As long as you have somewhat of a recent Mac, feel free to do other work while iTunes toils away. Just don't restart your Mac or, of course, quit iTunes.

When you've done all your stretches and think you're ready, head to iTunes and choose File→Library→Organize Library. In the dialog box that appears (Figure 10-8), check "Consolidate files," and then click OK to get the iTunes library migration party started.

Figure 10-6.
Make sure iTunes is keeping all your files tidy.

When iTunes is done, its progress window will simply disappear, and you should be all set, *but don't quit iTunes yet*. Open a Finder window, go to your library's *old* location (which is probably in *your Home folder/Music/iTunes*), and drag that folder to the desktop or the Trash—anywhere except its old or new location.

Then, quit iTunes, start it back up, and test a song, movie, or TV show to make sure the move worked. Once you're rocking out with your new library location, feel free to actually trash your old media folder and bask in the glory of getting all that free space back.

Figure 10-7.
Changing the default directory for iTunes Media.

Figure 10-8.
Clicking OK starts the copying. Fortunately, the process is nondestructive—files are only copied, not deleted!

Get Free and Better-Sounding Music for iTunes

Apple has promised a major revamp of iTunes (and it's about time), but here are two timeless tricks that will help you get more out of the current and future incarnations of iTunes.

Envious of friends with days' or years' worth of music in their iTunes library but don't want to infringe on the copyrights of others? Turns out that there are a variety of ways to fill up your library for free! Apple releases free music in the iTunes Store every Tuesday. Typically two or three audio-only tracks and one music video are available for free download (sometimes more than that, and sometimes fewer). How can you grab your goodies? Fire up iTunes and select iTunes Store on the left side of the program's window (Figure 10-9). Once the store loads, in the Quick Links section, click "Free on iTunes."

Figure 10-9.
You'll find "Free on iTunes" on the right side of the iTunes window.

Don't worry—you don't need to hit the iTunes store every Tuesday at 12:01 a.m.; the same songs and video are available for an entire week until they're replaced by a new set. Their purpose is to introduce you to artists and their material—Apple is hoping you'll return to buy more of their selections.

When grabbing the free stuff, don't be choosy; take all the free music available every week. You can delete the songs you dislike, and keep those you enjoy. (Keep in mind that your taste may change over time—music you despised when you were younger can become a favorite in later life.) Once you get the songs from iTunes, you can share them with your other computers and iOS devices just as you would with purchased music.

iTunes isn't the only source of free music—far from it. Amazon.com has thousands of
free MP3s that are available for much longer than a week, and the variety and quality
are actually superior to what's on iTunes. Amazon offers some complete albums, as
well as a dizzying array of individual tracks. Do a web search for "amazon free mp3
downloads" to get started (the specific URL changes often).

Of course, there's a downside to Amazon's free offerings: you need an Amazon account (though you probably already have one). You also have to be good at searching,
using their Cloud Player and/or download manager, and then importing the downloaded selections into iTunes or listening to them from Amazon's cloud.

Those are two good sources for free tunes, but they're bound to leave you wanting
more. Chances are you'll try a quick web search for "free music downloads for itunes,"
and you'll come upon both legal and questionable sources of freebie tracks. Copyright
violations are now serious business for lawyers, which means you need to be careful
about what you obtain for free. Legal is good, and stealing is bad. Unintentionally
downloading viruses and malware can make your digital and analog lives miserable,
too. So be *extremely* careful what you download and from whom.

That doesn't mean that you can't find free tracks out there, it just means that if you
choose to scour the Web for free music, you have to be prepared to invest a bunch of
time and you'll likely have to sit through some excruciating music. For time invested
versus payoff, iTunes is the safest bet: its free offerings are easy to find, a breeze to
download, and there's new stuff every week.

Make Music Sound Better with iTunes' Equalizer

Do your downloaded and imported audio tracks sound crummy on your computer,
regardless of whether you're using its internal speakers, headphones, or external
speakers? In this section, you'll learn to love your iTunes Equalizer.

To open the Equalizer, in iTunes, go to Window→Equalizer. The program's default
equalization (EQ) settings are pretty good for a lot of music. For example, most con-
ventional headphones sound best with the Treble Booster EQ setting (choose it from
the menu at the top of the Equalizer—see Figure 10-10), due to the inherent bass
emphasis of these sorts of headphones. But don't be satisfied—try tweaking the defaults; over time, you'll decide which settings sound best with your equipment and
sonic preferences.

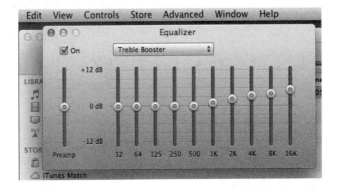

Figure 10-10.
The Treble Booster preset is surprisingly useful for headphones.

If you get frustrated that the built-in EQ settings don't sufficiently improve your listening experience, you can make custom EQs that you can specify for different equipment. You might have one equalizer setup for headphones, say, another for built-in speakers, and yet another for external speakers. To create a new preset, move the sliders up or down in each EQ frequency zone until your headphones (for example) sound as good as possible. Be patient, and listen carefully. When you are pleased with your custom EQ, click on the word "Manual" above the sliders, and then mouse up to Make Preset. Type in your description under New Preset Name (Figure 10-11), click OK, and that custom EQ preset is there forever (or at least until you decide to edit the list and delete it).

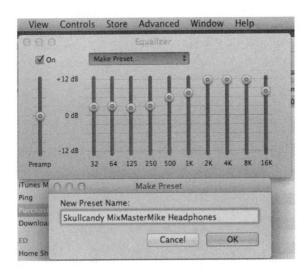

Figure 10-11.
A custom preset for Skullcandy headphones.

You might be wondering why you'd need to resort to creating a custom equalizer setting when Apple includes so many of them (more than 20) with iTunes. Don't be fooled by the apparently obvious names of the EQ presets: some of them will make your music sound horrible, regardless of genre and what you're playing them on. In short order, you may keep a handy checklist of the built-in EQs that are a complete waste of your time.

For example, do small speakers sound best with the Small Speakers EQ applied? Nope—not in my experience. And the Piano EQ works best with certain types of vocal performances, and some instrumental tracks sound best using the Spoken Word setting. You get my drift: experiment and be prepared to dump several of the preset EQs into the dustbin of disappointment.

A few built-in and some custom EQs will likely satisfy most of your listening preferences. My consistent favorites—depending more upon the playback equipment (speakers and such) I'm using than upon the audio source equalization—are Manual, Flat, Acoustic, Jazz, and Treble Booster.

Your ears are unique, and you deserve to hear your music the way you prefer. Regardless of whether you're listening on a Mac, headphones, speakers, or whatever, if you can tell the difference between inferior sound and decent sound, it's worth spending a few minutes with the iTunes Equalizer.

—John "Nemo" Nemerovski

11

Hack Some Hardware

Hardware hacking is the scariest and, for some, the most interesting type of hacking. You've got a Dremel (the high-speed cutting and polishing tool all hackers love), a Mac, and a few spare hours—what could possibly go wrong? The truth is that a lot can go wrong, but when things go right the result is often fantastic. So why not try to beef up that aging laptop? Not enough of a challenge? Then turn it into a tablet computer. And as long as it's in pieces, why not dye it fluorescent green or give it a one-of-a-kind paint job? Hardware hacking is where it is at!

HACK 47 Have Your Mac Automagically Recognize You

What if your Mac knew when you were in the room? It can sense when you're near with the help of some clever scripts and Bluetooth exploits!

In the movies, smart homes automatically greet you when you return after a hard day at work. And while that does sound like a neat trick, until recently it hasn't been very easy to actually accomplish. Fortunately, technology and clever programmers are catching up with the fantasy. With the Mac you already have, your cellphone, and a little scripting, you can be living in a house that automatically does things for you when you arrive; no buttons required.

What's the ingredient that makes this possible? Bluetooth. Although it wasn't designed for this use, it turns out that Bluetooth provides a way for your computer to know when you're home by inferring your presence from the cellphone or other Bluetooth-equipped device you have on your person. And that's good enough to start putting the "smart" in smart homes.

The Hardware You Need

You need a Mac with Bluetooth (which any modern Mac already has) and at least one Bluetooth device, such as an iPhone or iPod Touch (virtually any portable Bluetooth-equipped device will work). No special Bluetooth support is necessary to have your

Mac and iPhone talk, since your Mac doesn't have to actually exchange any information with the device; it only has to be able to detect that the device is within range. I've used the technique described here with an old Nokia phone, a Motorola Bluetooth Headset, and an Apple iPhone. You only need one Bluetooth device, but it needs to be one that you're going to carry around, so the Apple Magic Trackpad is only a good choice if you carry it around in your purse or briefcase.

Get a Grip on Your Bluetooth

Bluetooth is an often-overlooked feature on OS X. Bluetooth just sits there talking to your wireless keyboard and mouse, never doing much to attract your notice except displaying the flashing battery sign to let you know disconnection is imminent. Or maybe you're having Bluetooth connectivity problems. Check your Bluetooth signal strength by heading to System Preferences and choosing Bluetooth. You'll see a list of devices, but all you'll learn is that they're connected. Your Mac knows how strong the signal is but needs to be persuaded to tell you. Option-click the device you're interested in to discover how strong its signal is (Figure 11-1). As with WiFi, numbers closer to zero are better (−10 is much better than −50).

Figure 11-1.
This is a perfectly acceptable signal.

The Software You Need

You need an app that lets you run scripts when it detects the presence of a Bluetooth device. There are a few different apps that can do this, but I use *the Bluetooth Proximity Tasker* (*http://tinyurl.com/c96jlxa*), which is available in the App Store. It's a little clunky to set up, but it does what we need and it's inexpensive ($2 as of this writing).

Mac, Meet Phone

The first step is to formally introduce your Mac and your Bluetooth device (let's assume it's an iPhone) to each other, a process called "pairing." To do this, make sure your device's Bluetooth support is switched on and that it is set to "discoverable" mode. On an iPhone, for example, go to Settings→Bluetooth and turn on Bluetooth. *Don't* close the Settings pane when you're done—it has to be open for your iPhone to be discoverable.

Next, head over to your Mac and follow these steps:

1. Choose System Preferences from the Apple menu, and then click Bluetooth.
2. Make sure that the On and Discoverable checkboxes are turned on. This allows your phone to see that your Mac is available via Bluetooth.
3. Click the + button at the bottom of the Devices list (Figure 11-2); or, if you don't have any devices connected, click the Set Up New Device button. Either way, the Bluetooth Setup Assistant opens.
4. Use the setup assistant to pair the iPhone with your Mac. (Depending on the device, this might involve entering a series of numbers to authorize the connection.)

When you've finished the Setup Assistant, your iPhone will be added to the list of devices in the Bluetooth preference pane.

> Note: It's OK if the status message you see on your phone reads "Not Connected," and if you see a similar status on your Mac. That just means your Mac and iPhone have been formally introduced but aren't exchanging any data. For this hack, no data is sent back and forth—the Mac and phone just need to see each other.

Preparing Bluetooth Proximity Tasker

Next, open the Bluetooth Proximity Tasker app on your Mac. (If you see a dialog box about AppleScript not executing, don't be concerned. This is just Bluetooth Proximity Tasker telling you that it's not going to run any scripts while you're configuring it. This is a good thing, despite the confusing alert.) If you don't automatically see the app's

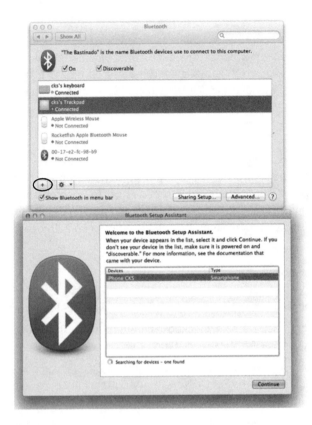

Figure 11-2.
The key is to click the tiny + button (circled) or—if you don't see the + button—the Set Up New Device button. Once your Mac sees your device, follow the onscreen instructions to pair the device.

preferences window, then click the gear icon on the right side of your menu bar and choose Preferences. Next, click the Bluetooth Device button and select your iPhone from the list of devices and then click Select. This tells the app that this is the device you want it to watch for.

Next, tell the app to run an AppleScript when your iPhone is within range of your Mac. To do this, copy and paste a debugged script from AppleScript Editor into Bluetooth Proximity Tasker's In Range AppleScript field. (The next section includes suggestions of the type of scripts to use.)

Bluetooth Proximity Tasker can also execute a script when it *stops* detecting your device, which you configure with the "Out of Range AppleScript" field, but I haven't found this useful for home automation. The reason is that Bluetooth's range is rather limited, so you can't reliably infer that you've left home simply because your device has moved out of range; you might have only gone to the kitchen for another cup of coffee. But if you're simply using the script to trigger the screensaver or something simple like that, the option can be quite useful.

One very nice feature of Bluetooth Proximity Tasker is the Select slider, which lets you set the detection sensitivity. For example, if you want to run the script only when your iPhone is *very* close to your Mac, set the slider towards the right. Or, to run a script when there's no sign of your iPhone at all, set the slider all the way to the left. You'll have to experiment to find the setting that works best for you.

The Delay field defines how often the app checks for the presence of your iPhone. The value you enter here (in seconds) should be appropriate for the actions you've programmed in your AppleScript. For example, if you want your Mac to turn on the room lights as soon as it detects your presence, you'll want to have Bluetooth Proximity Tasker look for your iPhone every minute or so. But if you simply want to announce how many mails you have waiting, then a longer scan interval might be sufficient.

Bluetooth Proximity Tasker is smart enough to only run your script when it notices that your iPhone proximity has changed. That is, it will run the In Range AppleScript code when your iPhone is newly nearby, after having not been detected the last time it checked. Here again is where you'll want to fine-tune the Select slider.

Putting It in Action

The AppleScripts that you use with Bluetooth Proximity Tasker is where all the magic happens, and this is your opportunity to really get creative. You can make your Mac automatically perform anything you can accomplish with AppleScript when you, carrying your iPhone, get within sensing range of your Mac.

If the things you're interested in automating only happen on your Mac, such as automatically checking your personal email account when you come home from work, you don't need anything except the script you want to run. But if you want to control the lights in your home or otherwise reach out beyond your computer, you'll need home-automation equipment and software. Two good software options are *Indigo* (*http://www.perceptiveautomation.com*) or *XTension* (*http://www.shed.com*). In this example I'll use XTension.

My In Range script tells XTension to perform several actions in sequence, some of which use conditions that are tracked for me by XTension. The first thing that happens is that, if the current time is after sunset, a lamp in the entryway turns on. Not only is this welcoming, it provides a visual cue that my Mac has recognized me and has started the script.

Next, the Mac uses text-to-speech to tell me how many phone calls I missed while I was gone. This information is tracked by XTension using *CIDTracker* (*http:// www.afterten.com/products/cidtracker*).

Finally, the Mac announces how many unread email messages I have waiting. It determines this by asking Mail for the contents of a mailbox that only contains messages sent to me by people that I've assigned to a group in Contacts. This is accomplished by a rule that I've defined in Mail.

These are all standard techniques but, as with much of home automation, it's the ability to connect existing pieces in new and convenient ways that creates value and adds convenience.

Now that you know how to trigger actions automatically, the hard part is deciding on the most useful things to have happen. Perhaps you want to have Safari load your favorite websites, or have your appointments read from Calendar. The limit is your imagination, AppleScript ability, and the fun you find in experimenting with different approaches.

—*Gordon Meyer*

HACK 48 Squeeze Some Speed out of an Aging MacBook Pro

It's an age-old question: upgrade that MacBook or spend the dough on a new one? How are your interests best served? This hack helps you decide, and shows you how to install a new hard drive, battery, and RAM modules to give your old machine more zip.

One day you'll pick up your MacBook and wonder what happened to its speed. You'll think, "It's as if an occult hand has reached inside my laptop and slowed my once-speedy MacBook to a crawl." The reason for the perceived slowdown could be many things. You could have too many login items; switch these off in the Users & Groups preference pane. While you're in System Preferences, you should also delete any preference panes you added but no longer use: right-click the obsolete preference pane and select Remove. You might also consider cleaning up your desktop (see Hack #22). If none of that helps—and it might not—create a new user account and see if that restores some of your lost zip.

If none of those tips work, it could be that your Mac *hasn't* slowed down—you could just be comparing it to the latest and greatest MacBook. If that's the case, then it isn't a surprise your MacBook seems slower—it is compared to zippy new machines. The only question left is do you attempt to upgrade it or put that money towards a new machine?

It's a tough decision. First, some caveats: if you're after raw processor speed and power, you'll want to get a new machine, because you can't upgrade the processor on MacBooks. Secondly, if you're jealous of the Retina displays on new MacBook Pros, no amount of upgrading will get you where you want to be, so you should plunk down cash for a new computer.

On the other hand, if you're interested in noticeably improving the performance of your current MacBook, that's something that you might be able to accomplish. In this example we'll be upgrading a 13-inch, mid-2009 MacBook Pro with 2 GBs of RAM and a 160 GB hard drive. The RAM is upgradeable to a maximum of 8 GB. You'll want to check your particular model and your current memory configuration against the maximum RAM at a site like *Everymac.com* (*http://everymac.com*). The larger the difference between your current setup and the maximum allowable configuration, the bigger the performance boost you can get.

Another thing to consider is replacing the hard drive. Traditional hard drives rely on spinning plates and magnets to store data. These are slowly being replaced by faster, less error-prone Solid State Drives (SSDs). Currently, hard drives offer superior storage for the money, but SSD drives use less power and are faster. In this project we'll be replacing the hard drive with an SSD.

That's about all we can really do hardware-wise to improve the performance of the MacBook Pro, but we should also consider replacing the battery. Why? Starting in 2008, Apple shifted from user-replaceable batteries to internal batteries that are supposedly only serviceable by Apple. Since we're going to be opening up the MacBook Pro to make the other changes, why not replace the battery while we are at it? The battery cycle count of the machine I'm using for this hack (that is, the number of times the battery has been charged and discharged) is in the high 700s, so we'll replace it.

Tip: If you wondering whether you should replace your battery, don't just guess— find out for sure! Apple warranties batteries by the number of cycles they've been through and how much charge they hold. For a list of maximum cycles to expect out of your battery (and how to check its cycle count), visit this support page (http://support.apple.com/kb/HT1519). If your battery is nearing the end of its useful life, go ahead and replace it; if not, don't waste your money. If your battery hasn't reached the listed cycle count but is failing, call Apple Support or take your MacBook to an Apple store. [You can find a complete list of technical support numbers for Apple at this support page (http://www.apple.com/support/contact/ phone_contacts.html). In the U.S., the number is 1-800-275-2273.] They might just replace the battery for free!

Preparing for the Hack

Before you get started, you'll need to gather the components you plan on installing. I ordered these items from Amazon, but you could probably find them cheaper elsewhere:

- 8 GB memory (two 4 GB chips), $37.99
- Apple OEM (Original Equipment Manufacturer) battery, $76.40
- Crucial 128 GB SSD Drive, $111.59

In addition to those items, you'll also need tools: a screwdriver that includes tiny Phillips-head bits, as well as an (optional) Torx screwdriver.

Once your parts are on hand or in the mail, it's time to prepare your data for this hack. Preparing your data means backing up. Usually you'd just back up your data, but this time you'll be replacing the *entire* drive, so you might want to consider creating a bootable copy of your hard drive. Time Machine won't do that for you, so look to an app like *Carbon Copy Cloner* (*http://www.bombich.com*), which costs about $40 and is worth the investment. Once your have a copy of Carbon Copy Cloner (or a similar app), clone your drive to suitable media or to its final destination.

Quick Hack: Skip a Step with a Drive Enclosure

In this hack, you'll transfer data from your current drive to some intermediary destination (such as a flash drive), and then from that destination to the drive you'll install later in the hack. That's a lot of data swapping!

You can skip one of the swaps by transferring your data *directly* to the new drive you'll be installing. You can pull that trick off by using a *drive enclosure*. A drive enclosure is everything you need to have an external drive except the drive itself: ports, power, and electronics—the only thing you provide is the actual drive. I used a Rosewill Drive Enclosure ($21.99), but pick a drive enclosure that fits your particular needs. For example, if you're using 3.5-inch SATA drives that you want to connect using FireWire, it's best to get a FireWire drive enclosure for 3.5-inch SATA disks.

Warning: Before you try this on your MacBook, find a take-apart guide for your specific model on a site like iFixit.com (http://ifixit.com). Some models (like the one featured in this hack) are relatively easy to work on, while others (like the new MacBook Retina) are very difficult to modify.

With your data backed up and the new parts on hand, it's time to dive into the warranty-voiding, performance-enhancing part of this hack! It's a good idea to fully drain the battery before you start—you know, use the Mac until it automatically shuts down. (This isn't something we did at Mac Hacks Labs because we didn't realize it would be a good idea until later...) Why bother? Because it's that much less energy you'll have to deal with when messing with your Mac's internals. So either run the battery down or at least shut off your MacBook, and then flip it over. On the bottom, you'll find tiny screws around the edges. Get the appropriate-sized bit (a Phillips-head 00) and remove the screws. You'll note that the screws are different lengths, so devise a scheme so you'll know where the screws belong when you need to put them back in. Once you get the screws out, you'll see something like Figure 11-3.

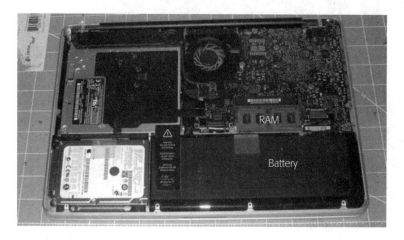

Figure 11-3.
While the case is open, you should take this opportunity to use some canned air to blow the dust out of your Mac.

So where should you start? The hard drive is your best bet. By removing the screws at the top of the drive (these screws are black so you can tell they don't go on the case), a black retention bar was removed and the hard drive popped right out (Figure 11-4).

Gently disconnect the ribbon cables, and then grab a Torx driver to remove the screws from the sides of the hard drive. These screws hold the drive in your Mac. The replacement drive has holes for these screws but no screws, so put the screws in the new drive, attach the cables, and then install the new drive.

In the particular model I worked on, it's much easier to access the RAM with the battery removed, which makes the next step obvious: remove that battery. The battery is held in place by two proprietary Tri Wing screws, but I was able to remove them with a tiny Phillips-head screwdriver. (If you prefer, you can order the proper Tri Wing screwdriver from *iFixit.com* (*http://ifixit.com*) or some other source.) Once the screws are out, carefully remove the battery connector from the main board (be gentle). Then simply lift the battery out of the enclosure (Figure 11-5).

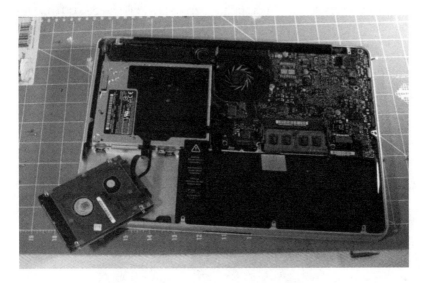

Figure 11-4.
The hard drive comes out very easily on this model, but the ribbons connecting it to the Mac are thin and likely fragile. Use caution and pay attention to how the ribbon cables are connected; you'll want to replicate that setup when you put in the new drive.

Figure 11-5.
The new hard drive is in but the battery is gone. Hopefully the new battery will provide longer run time. Even if it doesn't, it will certainly extend the time until the case needs to be opened again!

With the battery out of the way, you've got much better access to the RAM. Remove the top RAM module first by applying slight upward pressure on it. This causes the module to pop up at about a 45-degree angle; then simply pull it out of the machine. The same method was used to remove the RAM from the second slot. Then put the new RAM into the bottom slot first by inserting it at the same angle at which you removed the old RAM, and then push it flat (Figure 11-6).

Figure 11-6.
Putting the RAM in at an angle. This part was a bit tricky, but I could tell when the angle was correct by the feel of it. Be gentle and don't try to force the modules into place.

Once the RAM modules are installed, it's just a matter of installing the new battery and putting all the screws back where they belong (Figure 11-7). You might notice that there's blue thread-locking material on some of the screws. You could replace this stuff, but you're a hacker—you'll want to get in the case again someday—so ignore it.

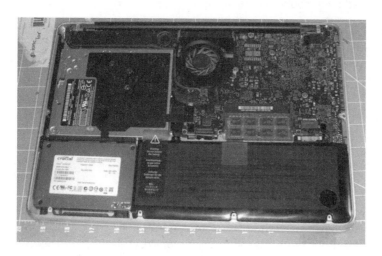

Figure 11-7.
Everything is back in place. The only question that remains is, was it worth it?

Once the MacBook Pro is reassembled, the moment of truth comes: was the roughly $220 investment worth it? If you're not a hacker, you might object that time and effort should be factored into the cost equation but, as the true tinkerer knows, messing with stuff is part of the payoff! Philosophical discussions aside, did the hack pay off? Here are a couple of ways to judge:

- **Battery Life**. Before I cracked open the case, this MacBook Pro would run for about three hours on a full charge depending on what I used it for. After replacing the battery, the MacBook would run for over four hours before shutting down. Not the up-to-seven hours promised when the MacBook was new, but still a good chunk of time. Is the extra hour worth the $75 cost? Well, the battery would need to be replaced at some point, but there's a good chance that by the time the battery had reached the end of its useful life, I'd have bought a newer Mac. So, for me, if I was only replacing the battery, it probably wouldn't be worth it.

- **RAM Performance/Disk Performance**. There are a ton of apps out there for quantifying performance. For the upgraded MacBook, I used Geekbench (*http:// www.primatelabs.com/geekbench*) to generate before and after scores. Before the surgery, the MacBook Pro scored about 2700; after the upgrades, its score bumped up to about 3300. (How informative those numbers are to the average person is a little suspect. Sure, we can compare those numbers and say that the MacBook Pro is 22% faster, but what does that really *mean*?)

With the objective measurements taken and noted, the more important subjective measurements have to be considered. Even if the upgrades technically made the MacBook Pro faster than Deep Blue, that wouldn't matter if the MacBook Pro still *felt* sluggish because everyone would still hate using it.

I decided to try to get a subjective assessment from someone who *didn't* spend half an hour installing the upgrades. Test Subject One—who was unaware that the upgrades had been ordered until the credit card bill arrived—began using the MacBook Pro and asked whether the distinctive O'Reilly sticker had been moved to a new MacBook Pro. When informed that the sticker had not been moved, Subject One asked why the MacBook Pro seemed so much faster. Subject Two just fired up Minecraft and started playing without commenting on either the speed of the computer or his father's kindness (as evidenced by letting him use a MacBook Pro for Minecraft). He was soon grounded.

From further use, it's clear that the MacBook Pro is substantially faster now, but the increase in speed was rapidly adapted to so we didn't really notice it anymore. While the machine is indeed much faster than it was pre-upgrade, it still doesn't match the zippiness of a new MacBook Pro. While the yearnings for a new MacBook Pro remain, the necessity of acquiring one has been staved off (at least until a new O'Reilly sticker can be procured).

Bottom line: the upgrade will likely give us another one to one and a half years out of the MacBook Pro. At a cost of $226, this hack pays off if you get a new laptop every three or four years. But if you wait five years (or longer) between purchases, you'd be better off putting the money towards a new MacBook Pro.

HACK 49 Give Your Polycarbonate Mac a Dye Job

With polycarbonate MacBooks, you get your choice of color—as long as that color happens to be white. It doesn't have to be that way. This hack shows you how to make your MacBook any color of the rainbow.

This project follows in the footsteps of the iBook Rit dye procedure, but with a sandpaper-based twist that takes into account the way MacBooks are constructed. The goal is to create a vibrantly colored MacBook that will stand out in the sea of white and aluminum.

Note: Want color pictures? Want more pictures? Want to email the author of this hack? Visit the online repository (http://braindeadlock.net/macbook-dye-project) for this hack.

Caveats

The MacBook's polycarbonate lid, bottom case, clutch cover, and fan vent cover are all sealed with a strong gloss layer. That means that unlike the iBook others used in earlier, similar hacks, the MacBook's plastic will absorb dye slowly. The display bezel (the plastic around the edges of the screen) is made of a softer plastic, and will absorb the dye very quickly, as will the keys. (The newer black Macbook Pro/unibody line keys are sealed with a gloss layer.)

The only way to remove the gloss layer is with sandpaper. If done improperly, this process can create a coarse surface. But, if properly wet-sanded and grit-stepped (moving from coarser to ever finer-grained sandpaper), it can almost mirror the original finish. Personally, I chose to leave the surface coarse as I don't like gloss. To each their own.

Note: You don't need to remove the gloss layer to dye the plastic, but I've found that the color is absorbed more evenly (and more quickly) when sanded. Also, the Apple logo on my MacBook was painted white, so in order to change its color, I needed to sand off that crappy paint. (Apple lid designers, if you're reading this: dude, come on. Changing the color of the logo was fun. Do you people hate fun or something? C'mon!)

Warnings

- **Not all the plastic on your MacBook is the same**. The display bezel is made of softer plastic than the other plastic parts, and it's also more susceptible to heat. Get its temperature up too high and it'll become deformed, like a Shrinky Dink—and there's no fixing that.

- **Parts are very easy to crack or deform, so take your time disassembling the computer**. Let me be absolutely clear: you can remove *every* part of a MacBook without major force. If you're forcing something, it's likely you've forgotten a screw. Adhesive is used on some parts, which require a *slight* bit of force to remove. The Apple logo is one example. You should use a heatgun to loosen the adhesive and then pop it out. Don't try and force it out—you *will* crack the lid. (I speak from experience.)

- **Just because computers have the same model name does not mean they share parts**. For example, Core Duo MacBooks have completely different motherboard mounts and fan vent struts than Core 2 Duos, which use ZIF low-rise sockets for half of the connectors on their boards. Then 2009 Core 2 Duos changed to a different optical drive connector, and who knows what else. Point is, they're all different, damn it. So get parts specific to your MacBook. *Mactracker* (*http://mactracker.ca/*) is a wonderful resource for this; I can't recommend it enough.

- **You will ruin pans, oven mitts, spoons and anything plastic within a 1 mile radius**. (Okay, maybe not that last one, but hey—shoot for the stars.) Try to keep the destruction to a minimum so your mom/girlfriend/boyfriend/roommate doesn't want to kill you. Also, after you're done with this project, don't reuse any of the supplies you used with food. Rit dye is *toxic* and is meant for clothes, fabrics, and things that don't normally touch your mouth. So keep that in mind.

- **You can't remove the keyboard from the inner top case without a lot of work**. You can take the keys themselves off, but you need to split plastic mold (it doesn't just come apart) in order to remove the keyboard. It's possible, but I went with black accents (from a busted black MacBook) instead of attempting that split. I'd recommend painting that part with the keys and trackpad removed, if possible. If you're more adventurous than me, do it big and post it online so the world can see.

- **The color shown on the dye's label may not match what you'll get**. The first color picked was supposedly a teal dye but was really what I'd call pine green; it still looked awesome, but it wasn't quite what was expected. Rit dye is only a few bucks per package, so it's better to spend a few more dollars and get what you want than to put up with a color you weren't after.

Disclaimer

Just throwing this out there, I accept zero responsibility for your actions based on anything you read here. If you dye half your stove, your cat, your hands, and permanently ruin your computer, it rests on you. ("With great power, comes great responsibility.") Also, the water will be boiling hot, so *be careful and take care*. (Do I need to show you my burn marks/scars? Do as I say, and not as I do.)

Supplies

Now that you've been sufficiently warned, it's time to get to the heart of the project. What's the best place to start when you're doing a project? The supply list, of course!:

- 3 boxes of your favorite Rit Fabric Dye color (the powdered kind; I haven't tested the liquid dye)
- A deep pan
- A cookie sheet roughly the size of that deep pan
- Running water (I recommend a slop sink or shop sink; they're nice and roomy)
- A white MacBook
- Rubber gloves
- A wooden spoon
- Salt
- Sandpaper (120-, 200-, and 400-grit; if you want a smoother finish, get finer grits, too)
- Denatured alcohol or cleaning solvent
- Stove or sustained heat source
- Lots of cookies (to eat in glorious celebration when you are finished!)

Process

The first step, obviously, is to unplug your computer and then take it apart and separate the plastic parts from their metal counterparts. Take care not to leave *any* electronic parts in the dye pieces, or you'll be replacing those parts. I'm not going to detail taking apart the computer here because you might not have the same model I do. Take a look at one of the *take-apart guides* (*http://www.ifixit.com/teardown*) from the wizards at iFixit for instructions specific to your model. Their take-aparts are the absolute best on the Web. Follow them to a T, and you'll be butter.

Now all the glossy plastic pieces need to be sanded down until the gloss layer is completely gone. (The best way to tell when the gloss is gone is when they will no longer glimmer in the light.) If you want a nice smooth finish, start with 120-grit sandpaper, then switch to 200-grit, then 400-grit, and finally 1600-grit; by the end, you should have a very smooth finish. (If you want a *really* smooth finish, you can get superfine sandpaper—up to 4000 grit—at auto parts stores or in the automotive section of your local big-box store.) But I'm not patient enough for that, so I stuck with 120-grit paper all the way through and ended up with a somewhat rough finish but the relative smoothness of the finish is up to you.

Warning: If you use a high speed device like a Dremel to do the sanding you'll likely melt the plastic. The process is best done by hand.

Once the parts are sanded, clean them thoroughly. Denatured alcohol and a paper towel work well, and the alcohol dries quickly.

Next, go get a pair of rubber gloves and put them on *right now*. I don't care if you aren't even contemplating this project—you should be wearing gloves. Trust me.

Then get a pan big enough to hold the largest plastic part (you can't dye the part in stages) that's an inch or so deep. (Make sure the pan is stove safe, like the one in Figure 11-8.) I used a rectangular pan that covered two burners. Fill the pan with water 8 cups of water, and then add two boxes of Rit dye the color of your choice (that's 4 cups of water per dye packet). Add 2 tablespoons of table salt to the water and stir. Place the pan onto your stove, and let the salt dissolve while the pan sits on the heat. As the water starts to boil, place the part(s) you want to dye into the bath. (If you're dyeing the display bezel, keep the heat as low as possible to avoid warping the bezel.) Gently stir the water as you dye the parts, and add water as necessary—it will boil away quite quickly.

Figure 11-8.
The pan used for this project. If you use this kind of pan, you'll probably want to use a gas stove.

It took about 45 minutes for the lid and bottom case of my MacBook to become saturated with the orange dye (Figure 11-9). Darker colors (navy blue, scarlet, black, pine green) may require more time. The display bezel took only 10 minutes to become saturated, as did the clutch cover and display spacers. Check your parts as you go, and flip as necessary. The larger parts require a hotter and longer bath.

Note: Adding too much dye to the bath will cause spotting and inconsistent color distribution, so try to keep "free floating dye" to a minimum. Don't forget to keep stirring your bath throughout the process.

Figure 11-9.
My MacBook lid in the dye bath. The larger parts take more time and require less attention than the smaller parts.

Remove the part from the bath, and clean off excess dye with a paper towel and cold water. Check for even color distribution (Figure 11-10). If it looks good, great! If not, go ahead and throw it back in the bath. The small parts can warp, as I've said, so keep a close eye on them. But the large parts can take a lot of heat/beating/abuse; they're like the Hercules of plastic or something.

Once all the parts are dyed to your satisfaction, you're done! Well, okay, you still have to put your computer back together, but still—you're done with the dying process. After your computer is reassembled and looks awesome, it's time for those cookies I mentioned earlier!

Finished Project

So, originally I had a white MacBook. (I used the white pieces for the lid and bottom case.) I decided that I like the way the black accented the orange, instead of doing full orange. The inside top case is also very difficult to dye, as the keyboard cannot be easily removed, which explains why the entire thing isn't orange: part of it came from a black MacBook that had been killed by too much liquid. The dead machine supplied all the black parts you see and helped the project look even better. And yes, I rock at Halloween.

—*Phil Herlihy*

Figure 11-10.
Here's the dyed and dried lid. It looks fantastic and I'll be the only person rolling with an awesome orange MacBook.

HACK 50   Get that iMac out of the Way

> Need more space on your physical desktop, or want your iMac in a dif-
> ferent place when watching a movie on it? You can easily reposition your
> iMac and get back some desk area with a VESA mount!

Ever since personal computers were first introduced, people have been devising ways to get their computers (or monitors) out of the way when they weren't using them. It makes a lot of sense: you could save space, have a little more control over your setup, and so forth. But, unfortunately, it also wasn't very practical. People had way too much stuff plugged into their machines to hang them on a wall or put them on an articulating arm. A typical iMac user, for example, might have a printer, a keyboard a mouse, a Time Machine drive, and a network cable. But all those things can be connected wire- lessly now, so the only cord you have to connect to your iMac is a power cable. Only one cable hooked to your iMac makes adding a VESA mount to your machine a much more enticing idea. (VESA is short for Video Electronics Standards Association; they're the group that came up with the standards for mounting flatscreen monitors and TVs.)

Before you start, you'll need to collect a few items. Most importantly, you need a VESA mount (which you can get at a variety of places; I bought mine from Amazon), the VESA mount adapter that Apple makes (which works with 100 mm VESA mounts and is available from *Apple (http://apple.com)* for $39), and whatever you want to mount your iMac *to*. This hack uses an articulated arm, but if you prefer, you could mount your iMac flush to a wall. The important thing when choosing what you'll mount your iMac to is ensuring that the mount has 100 mm mounting holes—you don't want to have to drill those holes yourself. You also want to make sure the VESA mount can handle the weight of your iMac. The newest iMacs are very light at about 12 pounds, but mid-2010, 27-inch iMacs clocked in at a little over 30 pounds, so keep an eye on the limits of the hardware you're using.

In my case, I had a dual-monitor setup that was deemed to be overkill (though not by me), so another computer was procured so the "extra" monitor now sits next to a Mac Mini. The absence of a second monitor opens up some desktop possibilities. More room for drawing, more room for projects, and so forth—*if* we could get the iMac out of the way. "Before" shots are essential for this kind of project, so Figure 11-11 shows the starting point.

Figure 11-11.
A beloved setup consisting of a TV, an iMac, and a second monitor.

Removing the iMac's Stand

The first step toward articulated-arm nirvana is removing the iMac's stand. If you take a look at the back of an iMac, you'll notice that there doesn't appear to be an intuitive way to pull the stand off (and just grabbing it and yanking is not a good idea). Turns out the secret to removing the iMac's stand is in the VESA Mount Adapter box you got from Apple (Figure 11-12). Open it to get started.

In the box, you'll find some hex wrenches and a Torx driver, plus a weird flimsy plastic card. You'll need the card and the Torx driver to remove the stand. Put something soft

Figure 11-12.
The VESA Mount Adapter from Apple has all the tools you need (you won't even have to head to the garage to grab a Phillips-head screwdriver).

down on a table (such as a blanket) and then gently set the iMac on it screen-side down (Figure 11-13). Make sure the stand extends over the edge of the table you're using, because the edge of the stand will be in front of the iMac when it's removed. Once your iMac is face down, cram the flexible plastic card in the top of the slot where the stand goes in the iMac at a 45-degree angle as shown in Figure 11-13.

When inserted properly, the card will trip a latch and the iMac stand will move towards the ground, exposing the attaching screws (Figure 11-14, left). (It was helpful to apply very gentle pressure downward on the iMac stand so that the stand would move when the latch was engaged.) Once you see the screws, remove them with the Apple-supplied Torx driver. You'll reuse these, so don't let them roll off the work area and into the AC vent or anything.

Installing the Adapter

With the stand removed, you can now install the VESA adapter. Grab the installation kit and place the flange (the piece with eight screw holes) on the piece sticking out that the stand was attached to. The flange is machined so that, while the mount point sticks out at an angle, the flange sits flat on the back of the iMac. Make sure the tiny hole in the middle of the flange is pointing towards the top of your iMac (Figure 11-15).

The next step is to add the actual VESA adapter. Place it on your iMac with the text towards the bottom of the iMac (in Figure 11-16, the top of the iMac is the edge closest to the camera). You'll only have one screw small enough to fit in the middle hole on the VESA adapter; that's the center screw. You have to make it a lot tighter than you

Figure 11-13.
The iMac face down on a table pad (wouldn't want any scratches on the screen). Note the RAM-installation instructions on the bottom of the stand, which will come in handy if you ever need to change out the RAM on your iMac. Once the iMac is comfortable, use the card included in the VESA kit to expose the screws that hold the stand on. (Don't worry: you don't need an overly hirsute arm to pull this part off.)

probably expect, so torque that thing down until it's flush with the VESA mount. If you're not comfortable applying that much force, tighten it down until you feel comfortable.

Once the center screw is in, you can add the side screws. The VESA adapter is designed so that it will be perfectly square no matter how bad a job you do installing it, so this part can get a bit tricky. If you can't simply spin the side screws into place, get a flashlight and peer sideways into the screw holes to check that they're properly aligned with the adapter (the holes have to line up pretty precisely). If the hole looks too high, you need to tighten the center screw some more. Otherwise, turn the VESA adapter until everything is lined up, spin the screws in with your fingers, and then tighten them with the included hex wrench. Congrats—you've installed the VESA adapter!

Installing the Articulated VESA Mount

The following steps will vary depending on the exact VESA mount you've decided to use. I used an Ergotron (Motto: "Ergotron—the most ergonomic Transformer of them all!") MX Desk Mount LCD Arm (Figure 11-17). My hope was that, since Ergotron obviously didn't spend any money coming up with a decent name, all their resources went into a quality product.

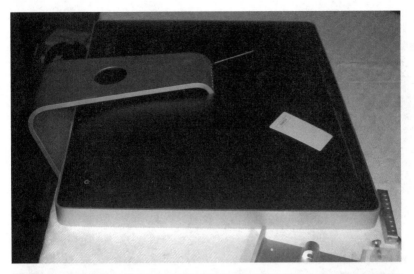

Figure 11-14.
Top: the iMac stand rotated enough to expose the screws holding it to the iMac.Bottom: the stand removed from the iMac. Don't lose those screws!

Figure 11-15.
The flange in the proper position. Screw the screws back in and you're ready for the next step.

Middle Screw   Side Screw

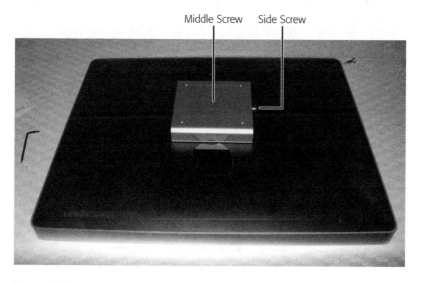

Figure 11-16.
Install the middle screw first—you can't install the others until this one is in properly.

Figure 11-17.
The articulating arm I used. It looks nice, but since it will be behind the iMac few will see it.

With this arm, you have two installation options. One is to mount it on the side of the surface you're attaching the iMac to. The result is nondestructive, but the hardware will stick out about a quarter of an inch from the surface—a substantial distance if it's a desk that sits against a wall. The other option is to install the device through a hole in the desk. The hand-built desk I use already has inexpertly cut slots to thread cords though (Figure 11-18, top), so I went with the second option.

Like the Apple VESA adapter, the arm comes with hardware for installation. *Unlike* the Apple-supplied stuff, the Ergotron hardware is kinda confusing (Figure 11-18, bottom). That is to be expected with multiple mounting options.

Installing the arm was straightforward (Figure 11-19). After I did that, I attached my chosen mounting option to the bottom of the arm with the included screws.

After you tighten the arm down (crawling under the desk is the worst part of this experiment), you're ready to attach the iMac. Before you do that, test the screws that came with your VESA mount to make sure they fit in the holes in the Apple VESA adapter. They should spin in easily. (If they don't, a trip to the hardware store may be in order. If that fails, a call to the manufacturer may be in your future)

Once you've decided everything is in order, get someone to help while you attach the iMac to the stand. Voilà—you're done and your iMac is now much more movable (see Figure 11-20)!

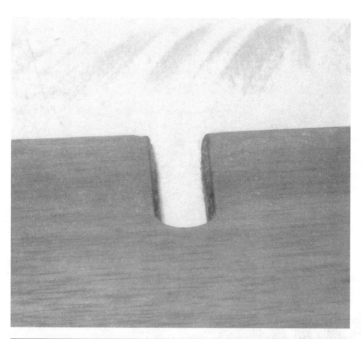

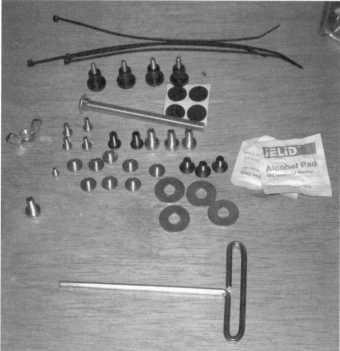

Figure 11-18.
Top: The pre-cut slot in the desk. If your desk doesn't have one, it might be time to break out the power tools. Bottom: the Ergotron kit. (The alcohol pads are supposedly included so you can clean off oils and grease left over from the manufacturing process, but I suspect their real purpose is first aid.)

Figure 11-19.
The arm is in place, but the stand hasn't been tightened down.

Figure 11-20.
Top: iMac all the way against the wall—more room! Bottom: iMac all the way forward for up-close work.

Have an extra Wii Remote lying about? Don't let it collect dust—use it to run your Mac!

In Hack #50, you learned how to mount an iMac to a VESA mount. A moveable iMac turns out to be great for a lot of different reasons but, as you'd expect, there are unintended consequences. Getting the iMac out of the way was nice for drawing and desk-space considerations, and it also made it nice to watch movies on from a distance. But having to use a mouse or a trackpad while you're watching a movie just screams paste-eater, so you need alternative.

There are a few different ways to communicate with your Mac, but anything involving a cable won't work for this situation. That leaves spoken commands (which I've tried and have found to be less than ideal), control it via WiFi (certainly possible), and controlling it with a Bluetooth device. The idea of controlling your Mac with a Bluetooth device isn't far-fetched at all—you already do it if you use a wireless keyboard, trackpad, or mouse.

The Apple-supplied kit is straight out—keyboards, trackballs, and mice are designed to sit flat and be used in close proximity to the computer, and the Apple Remote...ugh. What would be ideal is something that could be used farther away from the iMac.

Note: You can use your wireless keyboard or trackpad farther away from the computer if you're determined to do so. At Mac Hack Labs, we were able to use a trackpad 48 feet away from an iMac and then ran out of basement.

What controller uses Bluetooth, is specifically designed for pointing at the screen, and just happens to be available to fathers who don't mind stealing from their sons? You guessed it: a Wiimote! With a name that cute, you might be tempted to jettison the idea, but don't—it works surprisingly well. Let's get your Mac working with your re-purposed Bluetooth controller.

Before trying to make the Wiimote work with your Mac, it's a good idea to see if it already does. Open the back of the Wiimote and push the orange button. Choose "Set up Bluetooth Device" from your Mac's menu bar, and you'll see an entry called Joystick; select that option and your Mac will attempt to pair with your Wiimote. Since this hack doesn't end here, you can probably guess what happens (Figure 11-21).

Figure 11-21.
Don't be discouraged by the "The pairing attempt was unsuccessful" message on this screen. This step lets you know that your Mac can get the Bluetooth signal that the Wiimote is sending out. Don't think of it as a failure, think of it as a promising sign!

After your Mac tells you that the Wiimote refused to pair with your computer, you need a way to trick the Wiimote into thinking it's okay to pair with your Mac. At this point, you could write a program to do just that, but happily you don't need to go to all that effort: someone has already gone to the trouble and written DarwiinRemote. Point your browser to *this page (http://darkcooger.net/DarwiinRemote-OSX-10.8.dmg)* to download the program.

> *Warning: If you're using Mountain Lion, be sure to get the version 10.8 of Darwiin-Remote. Mountain Lion doesn't work with earlier versions of DarwiinRemote, so if you install one of those versions instead, you'll just end up frustrated.*

Once you download the *.dmg* file, double-click it and fire it up. You'll be told to pair the Wiimote with your Mac by pushing the 1 and 2 buttons simultaneously (just like you do with the Wii). Once the pairing is made, you're off to the races (Figure 11-22).

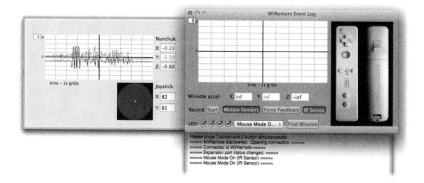

Figure 11-22.
DarwiinRemote in action. You can use the program to monitor the joystick, the accelerometer in the nunchuck, and even the balance board if you wish.

Once everything is running, you've got some choices to make. In this case, the point was to use the Wiimote as a mouse, so use DarwiinRemote's drop-down menu to choose "Mouse Mode On (Motion)." Congratulations—you now have a horrible mouse! (Well, at least when I tested it, it was horrible). It's a great time to remember that Command-Q quits a program, because if you try to mouse to DarwiinRemote's menu to quit, you'll have to fight the Wiimote to get there.

This is a pretty big problem, but recall that you set the mouse (technically, the Wiimote) to Motion mode. This means the Wiimote is relying solely on its built-in accelerometer. But the Wiimote was designed to use the accelerometer *and* infrared sensors. This is no problem if you have a Wiimote sensor bar lying around. Just hook it to the Wii, power it up, and then place the sensor bar in front of your Mac. In DarwiinRemote, change "Mouse Mode On (Motion)" to "Mouse Mode On (IR)" and you'll be able to use your Wiimote as a mouse!

While adding the sensor bar solves that problem, it's still not really a workable solution. You have to have a Wii near your computer, you have to keep the Wii plugged in, and the fact that this solution involves a cord violates the spirit of Hack #50. What we need is a wire-free way to power the sensor bar. The sensor bar works on 5 volts, but it's just 10 infrared lights, so its power tolerances aren't super tight. The loose tolerances allow a few methods to attack the problem. If you look very closely at the plug end of the sensor bar cable, you'll see two contacts (Figure 11-23).

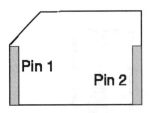

Figure 11-23.
For the Wii sensor bar, pin 1 is ground, and pin 2 is 5 V. The outer shield is not used. It also might be the simplest pin out in history.

With a lot of patience and some luck, you can cram a couple of wires onto the contacts, hook those up to a battery (I used a 9-volt battery), and power the sensor bar in a non-destructive manner. Or, if you don't mind destroying the sensor-bar cable, you can attach it to a USB plug and use power from your Mac to power it. Alternatively, you can buy a 9-volt connector and wire it in to the sensor-bar cable. In the future, the current configuration will be changed out for the USB-powered option, but until the current 9-volt battery runs out, the super-ugly hacked-together version will work (why waste a battery?).

Once you've got control of your Wiimote and everything is working as you expect, it's time to make some changes so things work even better! Select DarwiinRemote→Preferences, and you'll be greeted by a page with multiple panes (Figure 11-24). These panes let you assign keys, create a new profile by clicking the Add button, and even manually calibrate your Wiimote "mouse."

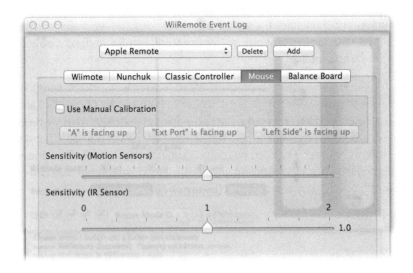

Figure 11-24.
The Mouse tab is where you calibrate your Wiimote. You can control just about every aspect of the Wiimote by using the various tabs shown here.

When everything is set up the way you want it, you can put your mouse away and control your Mac from up to 16 feet away using the Wiimote. (Your Mac will likely receive the Wiimote's signal from a greater distance, but 16 feet was the max distance used in the design of the Wiimote, so beyond that you're kind of taking your chances. Plus, unless you make the cursor really big or are part eagle, you won't be able to see what you're doing anyway.)

HACK 52 Turn Your MacBook into a Tablet

> Wishing for something as portable as an iPad with the power of a MacBook? You can get just that with some bold hacking and ingenious modding. (This device even runs Flash!)

The era before the iPad/iPhone and tablet boom was a time when people were longing for a tablet Mac. A lot of people, and some companies, created tabletized Macs before the iPad showed up. Those projects helped to fill a gap in a Apple's offerings—after all, Apple hadn't released anything truly handheld oriented since the Newton MessagePad. (In honor of that device, I call this project the MessagePad.) Every year, there were rumors of the next iTablet. And at the time, it was fairly difficult (though far from impossible) to procure OS X/9–compatible touch overlays for cheap.

This project was on my list for ages. And now I've finally finished it! There certainly is a giant continuum of portable, touch-oriented devices that have existed over the years, and where this one fits in, I'm not sure. But if these features seem compelling and you have the budget, give this hack a shot:

- Resistive 13-inch touchscreen (as opposed to a capacitive one; you'll learn the difference in a sec)
- User-facing iSight camera
- Rear-facing iSight camera with colored flash (optional)
- Teensy 2.0 USB development board
- 32 GB SSD
- Sleep switch
- mDVI port
- USB 2.0 port
- FireWire port
- Gigabit Ethernet port
- Line in
- Built-in speakers

That's a nice feature set, but it comes at a price: this tablet is heftier than an iPad. On the other hand, you can do everything on it that you can do with a Mac.

Warning: This project entails doing a lot of (nearly) irreversible things to your expensive computer. Undoing these changes would require replacing a nice pile of parts. Know this going in.

Know Your Model Before You Begin

As mentioned in Hack #49, it's important to remember that just because computers have the same model name *doesn't* mean they share parts. For example, core Duo MacBooks have a completely different motherboard mount and fan vent strut than other MacBook models. And 2009 Core 2 Duos changed the optical drive connector, and who knows what else. The point is, they're all different, so be sure to get parts specific to your Apple order number or design year. *Mactracker (http://www.mactracker.ca)* is a wonderful resource for this.

Absolution of the Author

While this project is nowhere near as dangerous as my Macbook Dye Project (see Hack #49), it's still dangerous. Working with Dremels, sharp cutting tools, drills, routers, and other equipment can be very hazardous. I don't cover all of the safety steps here, but goggles, dust masks, gloves, clamps, and an apron help *a lot*. Remember: *caution and planning are the best defenses against accidents*. These things can hurt you and/or people around you. I'm not responsible if you drill through your favorite desk, your pinky toe, your cat, your laptop, your new TV, or anything else that may happen based on what you read here. You can also ruin your laptop, if you're not careful (which is more important than that life and limb stuff, right? Who needs limbs?). Be more careful than I was and you'll be fine! In other words: do as I say, and not as I do.

If none of that scared you, then you are an enterprising individual and you should high-five yourself because you've got what it takes to tackle this project. Let's get started!

Supplies

It's best to gather all the supplies before you begin. You *could* acquire them as you progress, but that would slow you down quite a bit. Most of these items are easy to find, and I've included links for the more difficult ones:

- Pre-unibody white MacBook (I used the 2007 MacBook 3,1 – Core 2 Duo, GMA X1300)

- 13.3-inch 16:9 eGalax Touch Overlay (or use the overlay of your choice; it's wise to keep the same aspect ratio)
- Normally open push-button switch
- Normally open SPST toggle switch
- iMac G5/Intel iSight board
- "Thin" USB hub (Try to find a hub that supports high-power devices; these usually have nice-sized capacitors in them)
- 8 GB flash drive
- 22 AWG multistrand wire
- 28 AWG single-strand wire
- Spare set of MacBook lid magnets (or any flat neodymium magnet that will fit)
- Electrical tape
- Gorilla Glue
- Any Dremel with cutting, buffing, and smoothing discs
- *Sugru self-setting rubber (http://www.sugru.com)*
- Cake (to eat in celebration when you're done!)

If you decide to include the optional rear-facing flash, you'll also need:

- *ShiftBrite module (http://tinyurl.com/shiftbrite).* I used a 1.0 module, but I'm sure a 2.0 module would work just fine.
- *Teensy 2.0 USB development board (http://www.pjrc.com/teensy)*

Caveats

- **Once you start cutting into your MacBook's lid, there's no going back**. Measure everything roughly 4,000 times before you make your cuts. (One exception: there's some tolerance for error on the viewport for the LCD, so don't let it bother you if it's slightly off. Just do your absolute best to make it straight, and the Sugru will do the rest. Don't worry: this advice will make sense later.) The point is, measure a million times, cut once.
- **The touchscreen isn't a perfect fit**. With the touchscreen overlay I used there's a ~25 px cutoff on the bottom of the screen. I've tried to mitigate this using forced resolutions in OS X, but the LCD's firmware is programmed to crop to available area, so my efforts have been fruitless. That said, if you position the overlay so the blackout area is on the bottom, there's very little loss of screen real estate. Take your time and do your research, and you might be able to find a better option.
- **The touchscreen has a couple major drawbacks**. The touchscreen I used for this project is *resistive*, whereas the touchscreens you're likely most used to

(iPhones, iPads, etc.) are *capacitive*. Resistive touchscreens can only accept input from a single point of touch at a time (so no multitouch), they're affected by heat, they can't be bent or crushed without breaking, and they have low resolution. So take your expectations for the overlay and take them down a couple of notches. It's relatively difficult to do precision work with this kind of screen (so kiss those dreams of running Photoshop, or using this as a serious drawing tablet, goodbye), but it's well suited for day-to-day work and gaming (Plants versus Zombies is awesome on here, for example).

• **Don't try and use the Bluetooth's USB port directly**. This port and the Bluetooth board itself are both 3.3 V, so it won't properly power any of the hubs or devices commonly available.

Procedure

First off, remove your Macbook's display and optical drive. I'm not going to detail taking apart the computer here—I'll leave that to the mages at *iFixit* (*http://www.ifixit.com/teardown*). Their take-apart guides are the absolute best anywhere. Identify the Mac you're using, follow the appropriate guide, and you'll never lose your way.

Warning: Parts are very easy to crack or deform, so take time disassembling the computer. You can disassemble every part on the computer without major force. If you're forcing something, it's likely you've forgotten a screw. Adhesive is used to secure some parts, such as the Apple logo, which requires a slight bit of force to remove. You should use a heatgun to loosen the adhesive and pop it out. Don't try and force it out or you will crack the lid (I speak from experience).

Set the bottom case, battery, and their assorted counterparts aside for now, and focus on the display. The basic idea is to turn the LCD around in the lid and use the lid as our new display bezel. To get started, remove all the guts from the display housing, but leave the lid magnets alone, and save the sleep magnet for another project or your fridge. Once you've got the LCD out with its mounting frame, remove the mounting frame from the LCD by unscrewing the handful of small screws around the edge. Then remove the iSight camera from its aluminum frame, but leave its plastic bezel attached. Finally, remove the hinges from the lid (where we're going, we don't *need* hinges). The lid should now be (mostly) empty.

Place the frame back into the lid, but don't screw it in. Use the frame as your guide for marking where you have to make the cuts in the lid. The goal is to turn the LCD around and reattach it to its normal frame, giving it a nice stable mount, and relieving us of some tedious fabrication work. Once you've made the markings where to cut, triple-check that it looks right (see Figure 11-25). If so, cut the lid where you marked. Then check fitment of the LCD in the new hole. (Using the frame as the cutting guide will actually leave a small border of dead LCD space. Later on, we'll use the Sugru to fill this gap and add stability to the touch overlay.)

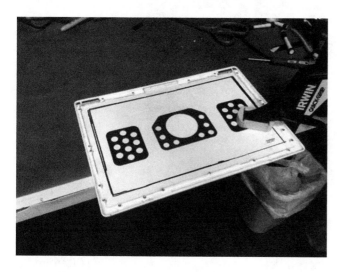

Figure 11-25.
The former lid of the MacBook marked, clamped, and ready for cutting. This will be the bezel for the MacBook MessagePad so you'll be looking at it a lot.

Next, choose the orientation of your touch overlay, and figure out where the ribbon cable will have to surface. Then use your Dremel to remove any plastic standoffs that may be in the way of where the ribbon will go. Make sure you smooth it out, as those ribbons are very fragile. You may have to make a small notch in the LCD mounting frame to allow the ribbon to pass through. Once that's done, attach your LCD to its original mounting frame in the reverse direction, so it faces the new hole in the lid. There are a couple ways of doing this. You can drill holes in the LCD's mounting frame (because none of the original holes will match up) and then use the LCD's original screws to reattach it, or you can Gorilla Glue it to the frame in the reverse direction. I chose the latter, but I recommend the former (another "Do as I say, not as I do" moment).

Now, while the glue is drying (or you're reveling in your frame-drilling prowess), use your smoothing wheel to thin out the plastic around the inside of your new *bezelid*. (Awesome word, yeah? Bezel+lid.) The touch overlay cannot be smooshed between the bezel and the LCD, and presently there isn't enough clearance to fit it in there. So shave 1 mm or so off of that bezelid around the overlay, and then you should be good to go. If in doubt, test your overlay and LCD in place, once the glue is dry. If the touch seems to be wonky or sticking to one side, there's likely to be a crease. Test and test again (Figure 11-26).

Figure 11-26.
Testing the touchscreen overlay to make sure it will function properly when everything is assembled. Don't rush this step or you'll regret it later.

Once there seems to be enough clearance, tape your overlay to your LCD+frame. (I ran tape around the edges, and added a strip over the "dead" area on the bottom of the LCD to protect it.) Make sure the overlay is stable and in the right position on your LCD. (This is where the overlay's shortcomings become apparent; it's too short vertically to fill in.) Next, mount the LCD inside the bezelid with the taped-on overlay. From the front of the bezelid, you can see the electrical tape boarder now. These are the areas where you should apply your Sugru (it can be white or whatever color you want) to create a nice soft border, and you can taper the border so that you can reach the very edges of the LCD to touch. It's a hard thing to describe, but just use your best judgment. Sugru is a lot like Play-Doh, only it hardens into a permanent rubber-like form. It will firmly hold the touch overlay in place inside the bezelid, and be nice and soft on the user's fingers.

Now, test your overlay again. Looking good? Try the 25 pt Calibration inside the eGalax Touch menu. Better? Awesome. The hard part is almost done, so give yourself a second to be proud of your work. Now let's mount the user-facing iSight camera. The iSight can't fit in its previous position due to the framing change. So, instead, we'll use the part of the frame where the hinges were previously mounted as this area has ample space. Use your Dremel to smooth out a surface dead center of the "bottom" of the bezelid. Then find a drill bit the size of the iSight lens and drill dead center. This is going to take a little trial and error. Next, remove the plastic bezel from the iSight. The lens can float freely attached to its PCB, or be disconnected; the microphone will stay attached to the bezel. Align the bezel in the smoothed area with the hole you drilled for the lens, and then glue it in place. When it's dry, pop in the iSight (Figure 11-27) and you're good to go! You should probably tack down the iSight PCB with some tape, screws, or glue. Exactly how to secure your iSight PCB is a decision that I'll leave up to you.

Figure 11-27.
Securing the iSight. You can skip this step, but you'll lose all the cool functionality of the iSight. Plus, you paid for it when you bought your MacBook!

One last part for the new top case, and then you're done! Take your spare set of lid (neodymium) magnets and glue them in place in the two magnet-less corners of the lid. Try to align them against the other two magnets mounted in the bezelid's frame. (We're going to use these later to attach the top case to the bottom case.) Magnets make it easier to do maintenance in the future, but also provide a strong bond for carrying around. The aluminum iMacs, for example, are held together by magnets. Kinda neat, huh?

Top case—*done!* Time for some cake! But not too much—don't want to go into a sugar coma (yet). Now, set your awesome new top case/bezelid/thingy aside.

Bottom case time. This is a good opportunity to take off your heat sink, replace your thermal grease, and clean out your fans. Once that's done, remove the logic board from the bottom case and place it on a soft surface (foam works well) until you're ready to do your soldering. At this point, I attached my power button and sleep toggle to the solid metal area in the fan vent, near the Bluetooth board. It's notable because air can't pass through it, so use your Dremel or drill to cut holes in this area the right size for the switches you chose. Then screw your button and switch in, and fill in any gaps with Sugru. Take care not to bend the metal strut that's built into the bottom case. After cutting this, make sure to thoroughly clean the bottom case, as this cut produces aluminum dust, which is very bad for the logic board and electronic components.

We won't be re-using the optical drive, and chances are yours doesn't work anymore anyway. (They've got a shelf life of 2 years in these machines.) If you're looking to save weight and don't care about the rear-facing camera, 8 GB recovery drive, or Teensy, you can skip the hub installation, tie your touch-driver board into your Trackpad/

Keyboard USB port, route the power and sleep buttons, and you're done! But, that way isn't anywhere near as much fun.

Now, by far the hardest part of this is soldering onto the trackpad USB connector. That's where we'll pull signals for the power button and the USB hub to host our other add-on devices. Use a fine soldering tip, watch a bunch of how-to soldering YouTube videos, and take your time. To pull this off, you'll need a diagram of *the pinout* (*http://cyrozap.com/2010/08/18/macbook-core-duo-logic-board-keyboard-connector-pinout/*). The power button is active when it's pulled LOW to ground. So, whenever you ground that pin, the computer will boot. Attach the power-signal wire to one side of your power button, and then attach the other side of the button to a grounded area. USB ground works just fine. Test!

The other four pins listed are an internal USB port used by the MacBook's trackpad and keyboard. We're going to take that and attach it to a hub to add some devices. Solder your hub onto those pins and place it into your empty optical drive bay. Use small wires so you can route them in the lanes on the logic board, and double-check the pins to be sure they're matched properly (Figure 11-28). Once that's done, boot it up and test. Hub works? Rock on. (An alternative method for this part is to use one of the external USB ports. I won't detail that process here, but those pins are a lot easier to solder onto.)

Figure 11-28.
The successfully soldered wires. This step isn't strictly necessary but it does make the final product much better in day-to-day usage.

Next, strip your 8 GB flash drive of its casing, wrap it in tape or heatshrink, and then attach it to the hub. Then glue the hub down in the corner of your empty optical drive bay so it's out of the way. Take this time to tape your touchscreen controller to the bottom of the LCD panel. Keep it out of the way, shorten the USB cable that attaches to the hub to the shortest length possible without making it ballshard to connect when you're reattaching the top case.

Now it's time to install your rear-facing camera! For this part, I used an iSight from a 17" Intel iMac. You can use an iSight from any 15" or 17" iMac G5, or 17" or 20" white Intel iMac, or just about any iSight camera—or even just a USB webcam like *Macam* (*http://webcam-osx.sourceforge.net*) where the pinout is available. Since almost all iSights are just USB, it's fairly easy to ascertain the pinout.

Grab your iSight and pop out the clips for the plastic bezel holding the lens. Gently detach the lens from the bezel (it may be glued on; I've encountered some that were and some that weren't). Again, go slowly—the lens and ribbon can be damaged very easily. Next, cut the bezel using snips so it can be turned down at a 90 degree angle instead of forward. Drill a hole in your optical bay roughly the size of the glass lens protector (this piece doesn't help with image modulation, it just protects the lens from debris/dust), and then pop the bezel/lens protector in. Check your orientation and then glue the bezel in place. Since the glass is a cube rather than a sphere, there may be some space in between the two. If so, use a little Sugru and neaten it up. I also used a couple of foam pads to lift up the board to the right height; use your best judgment to determine that. Once everything is dry, attach the board!

Now, it's time to wire it up. I know it's tempting to plug that iSight into an iLink (FireWire) cable and fire it up, but *don't do it*. The board is not actually FireWire; despite its connector, it's *USB*. Check the wire colors if you don't believe me! You can actually just snip off that end, since we're not going to use it. Get a male USB A end, and solder it onto the iSight, matching the wire colors (Figure 11-29). Done! For sanity, you should boot up your system and plug your iSight in to double-check that the port works. If everything's good, tack your lens to the plastic bezel, tack the board down, and then clean up those wires!

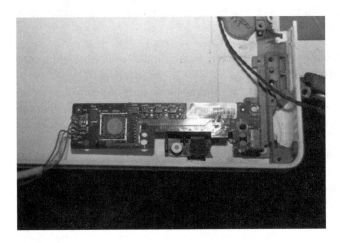

Figure 11-29.
The iSight in place and wired up to a USB cable.

> *Tip: I seal all of my solder connections with hot glue, just to prevent shorts and give the wires some strain relief. I use a full-size hub to make components and wires easy to change, but it does occupy a significantly larger amount of space. You could do better by removing all of the USB female A ports and just soldering directly to the hub PCB.*

Now, I'm sure you're thinking "Where are we putting the inverter?" I'm getting to that. I moved my inverter to the empty optical drive bay with the rest of the components. It's a four-wire connection, and can be extended without knowing the pinout. Cut a single wire at a time, and attach it to your extension. Seal the connections with heatshrink tubing. IDE/floppy ribbon cables are the perfect size for these extensions, and are quite easy to deal with. (40-pin and 80-pin cables don't work very well.)

Next, we need to make sure the top case has four magnetic objects to attach itself to when we close the case. I took a water-damaged scrap top case that I had and popped off the two metal alloy pads that the lid uses to grip the bottom case. I then glued them in their respective places on the bottom case. That covers the lower area. For the top...I used razor blades with tape over the blades. I don't recommend that method. Any rectangular piece of metal (preferably *not* sharp) will work, but not all alloys are magnetic! Glue them in place in the corners of the fan strut. Done! (See Figure 11-30.)

We're in the home stretch here. Solder two wires onto the pins of the sleep switch as shown in Figure 11-31. Then run these two wires to your toggle switch. Now, when the switch is in the on position, the system will think the lid is closed and go into sleep mode. Open the switch, and the computer wakes up.

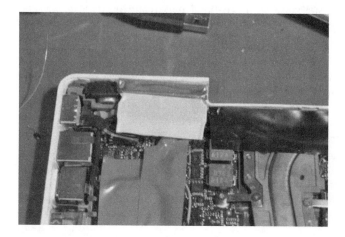

Figure 11-30.
Razor blades taped in place to act as catches for the case.

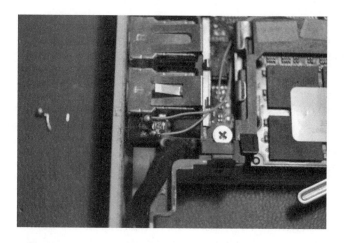

Figure 11-31.
The switch used to sleep and wake the MessagePad.

I used Sugru to seal the optical drive slot and smooth out the side of the case, as well as seal the areas where the hinges previously were. You can also protect the bottom of the user-facing iSight with a bit of Sugru. It really works wonders.

Finally, install your SSD (see Hack #48), RAM cover, and battery. Then attach all of the cables for your top case, route the cables so they aren't stressed when the bezelid is shut. Let the magnets hold the two pieces together and...you're done! Boot it up. Revel in the glory and wonders of your own Mac OS X tablet.

After all that, it's time to install some software that'll make using this thing easier (and possible). You'll want a copy of *MacFlip* (*http://tinyurl.com/b5wpoko*), a free, accelerometer-based screen-orientation app made for the Axiotron Modbook. You may also want to install *smcFanControl* (*http://www.macupdate.com/app/mac/ 23049/smcfancontrol*), which lets you tweak the speed of the device's fans so they vary based on power state.

To enable the onscreen keyboard, head to System Preferences→Language & Text, click the Input Sources button, and then check the box next to Keyboard & Character Viewer. Once that's done, you'll see a keyboard-like icon in the menu bar. Click that icon and, in the drop-down menu, select Show Keyboard Viewer. Voilà—an onscreen keyboard will appear!

Now you're *all done!* Hug pandas. Eat cake and initiate a sugar coma.

The MessagePad in Use

This device isn't perfect, but it's pretty cool. Here are some things I've learned from using it:

- Pecking at the onscreen keyboard is a bit of a bother. As mentioned earlier, the touch overlay doesn't support multitouch, so you can't use modifier keys.
- The tablet's battery life is about 4 hours of active use. Later generations have better sleep-power consumption, and should be able to sleep for long periods of time. The generation I used does not, but can sleep for a week or so before depleting its battery.
- The system is surprisingly light, and definitely comfortable to hold. It's large, but nice. I enjoy using it.
- Tap-to-click is an absolute must; double-clicking on things is tiresome using the touchscreen.
- The LCD should be protected under a layer of lexan. Without that, pressing on the overlay means pressing on the screen's glass, which is very bad for the screen. This configuration works, but could be much better with some protection. It could even be made waterproof with a significant amount of work.
- Speakers don't quite reflect sound towards the user without the lid. When placed on a surface, though, it's very loud.
- The device gets moderately warm, but nothing uncomfortable.
- MacFlip can't do vertical screen orientation (it just scrambles everything). It will also bury the menu bar in the dead zone if it's flipped the opposite direction.
- A higher quality overlay would make this even more awesome.

—Phil Herlihy

Index

We'd like to hear your suggestions for improving our indexes. Send email to index@oreilly.com.

X

About the Author

Chris Seibold is an engineer, writer, and cartoonist residing in Knoxville, Tennessee. As an engineer, he has tackled such diverse processes as powder coating and hot dog casing manufacture. As a writer, he has focused on computing and written for a variety of online and traditional media, including serving as Senior Contributing Editor for the Apple Matters website and contributing hacks to *iPod and iTunes Hacks*, with a talent for making the complex accessible to the interested but harried user. As a cartoonist, he has produced both cartoon strips and editorials. Chris also managed to spend some time producing radio shows relating to sports. As soon as he hits television, the trifecta will be complete. Chris lives with his wife, young son, and what is quite possibly the world's dimmest canine. He has a degree in Physics from the University of Tennessee but has yet to find work involving frictionless inclined planes.

Colophon

The cover font is Adobe ITC Garamond. The text font is Benton Sans; the heading font is Benton Sans; and the code font is Dalton Maag's Ubuntu Mono.

Have it your way.

O'Reilly eBooks

- Lifetime access to the book when you buy through oreilly.com
- Provided in up to four DRM-free file formats, for use on the devices of your choice: PDF, .epub, Kindle-compatible .mobi, and Android .apk
- Fully searchable, with copy-and-paste and print functionality
- Alerts when files are updated with corrections and additions

oreilly.com/ebooks/

Safari Books Online

- Access the contents and quickly search over 7000 books on technology, business, and certification guides
- Learn from expert video tutorials, and explore thousands of hours of video on technology and design topics
- Download whole books or chapters in PDF format, at no extra cost, to print or read on the go
- Get early access to books as they're being written
- Interact directly with authors of upcoming books
- Save up to 35% on O'Reilly print books

See the complete Safari Library at safari.oreilly.com

O'REILLY®

Get even more for your money.

Join the O'Reilly Community, and register the O'Reilly books you own. It's free, and you'll get:

- $4.99 ebook upgrade offer
- 40% upgrade offer on O'Reilly print books
- Membership discounts on books and events
- Free lifetime updates to ebooks and videos
- Multiple ebook formats, DRM FREE
- Participation in the O'Reilly community
- Newsletters
- Account management
- 100% Satisfaction Guarantee

Signing up is easy:

1. Go to: oreilly.com/go/register
2. Create an O'Reilly login.
3. Provide your address.
4. Register your books.

Note: English-language books only

To order books online:

oreilly.com/store

For questions about products or an order:

orders@oreilly.com

To sign up to get topic-specific email announcements and/or news about upcoming books, conferences, special offers, and new technologies:

elists@oreilly.com

For technical questions about book content:

booktech@oreilly.com

To submit new book proposals to our editors:

proposals@oreilly.com

O'Reilly books are available in multiple DRM-free ebook formats. For more information:

oreilly.com/ebooks

O'REILLY®

Spreading the knowledge of innovators   oreilly.com

©2010 O'Reilly Media, Inc. O'Reilly logo is a registered trademark of O'Reilly Media, Inc. 00000